ILLUSTRATIONS by David Rees

DISPATCHES FROM THE DUMB SEASON

ILLUSTRATIONS by David Rees

THE NEW PRESS

NEW YORK
LONDON

Requests for permission to reproduce selections from this book
should be mailed to: Permissions Department, The New Press, 38 Greene Street,
New York, NY 10013

Published in the United States by The New Press, New York, 2005
Distributed by W. W. Norton & Company, Inc., New York

LIBRARY OF CONGRESS CATALOGING-IN-PUBLICATION DATA

Taibbi, Matt.
    Spanking the donkey : dispatches from the dumb season / Matt Taibbi.
       p. cm.
    ISBN 1-56584-891-8
       1. Presidents—United States—Election—2004.   2. Political campaigns—United States.
   3. United States—Politics and government—2001-   4. Deception—Political aspects—United
   States.   5. Taibbi, Matt.   6. Journalists—United States—Biography.   I. Title.

E905.T35 2005
324.973'0931—dc22

                                                                            2005041486

    The New Press was established in 1990 as a not-for-profit alternative to the large, commercial
publishing houses currently dominating the book publishing industry. The New Press operates in
the public interest rather than for private gain, and is committed to publishing, in innovative ways,
works of educational, cultural, and community value that are often deemed insufficiently profitable.

www.thenewpress.com

Composition by Westchester Book Group

Printed in the United States of America

2   4   6   8   10   9   7   5   3   1

Contents

NOTES AND ACKNOWLEDGMENTS

A few notes about the structure of this book. It was originally intended to be a straight campaign trail diary, focused mainly on the Democrats. For a variety of reasons, some of them financial and some involving a series of near nervous breakdowns I had along the way, it didn't work out as planned. Some of this has been published before; some hasn't. Some of the pieces, in particular the ones I wrote for *Rolling Stone,* contain a lot of material that never made it into print. Overall there are long campaign trail pieces, some reporting on the anti-war movement, and in between are columns from the *New York Press* that fill out the chronological period between the beginning of the war and the grim ending of Bush reassuming his seat in the Oval Office.

I must thank particularly my editor at The New Press, Colin Robinson, who put up with a whole range of shameful behaviors on my part in order to get me to fulfill my obligation to finish the book. I think I tried to beg out of the book on about six different occasions, but Colin, being British, has an ability to make one feel like an ass in a way that sounds like encouragement, which was probably what was needed under the circumstances.

I would also like to thank the editors of the *New York Press,* my good friends Jeff Koyen and Alex Zaitchik. I would like to thank also all the rest of the staff at the *Press*—Lionel, Sarah, Kate Crane, Steven Psyllos, the designer formerly known as Nick Bilton, and everybody else there. The *Press* is a great place to work.

Paul Fallon, the publisher of the *Beast,* is a friend whom I wish I could thank in some other, more meaningful way. I hope Paul runs for Congress again and I hope he wins in a landslide and subsequently finds a way to embezzle enormous sums of money from the Ways and Means committee. Thanks also to John Curr and to Jeanne Noel-Mahoney of the Buffalo office of the NYCLU for letting me wander their offices with impunity. When John is arrested by the FBI under some obscure provision of the Patriot Act, I promise to write something nice about him around the time of his execution.

Thank you also to Will Dana at *Rolling Stone* for helping me through several difficult assignments, and also to Katrina vanden Heuvel at the *Nation,* whose husband knows less about basketball than he thinks he does.

On a more personal note I would like to thank some friends and relatives as well who helped me during two very difficult years of my life. Thank you to my mother and father, to Kevin McElwee, to Preston and Jessica for helping with the *Beast,* and to Masha, to whom I keep this promise too late.

INTRODUCTION

No country in the world is harder to write about than the United States. It might be easier for a foreigner. If you look back in history there are any number of foreign writers who came to this country and got it exactly right, and who still managed to find a way to be sympathetic about the place, even as they scathingly described the people who actually lived here.

As a Slavophile who grew up reading Russian books, I can think just off-hand of about a dozen such writers who escaped to America from the dreary hell of the old Eastern bloc, ripped the natives of their new home to shreds, but still managed to write about the country affectionately. Just think about *Lolita*, where every character Humbert Humbert encountered was a philistine buffoon, except that the love object of the book was a beautiful American girl, and the scenery was an awesome paradise of majestic mountains and deserts and quirky resort hotels.

Or there was one of my favorites, Sergei Dovlatov, who came here late in life with his family after a life of poverty, prison, and troubles in the Soviet Union, and described America as a haven of peaceful absurdity, a place where there was perhaps less to write about but more ease in living. Or there was Joe Brodsky, or the vicious Pole Leopold Tyrmand . . . Solzhenitsyn mellowed for a brief period of time when he was here—reverting to fervent anti-Americanism only when he returned to Russia late in life and went on one of those dreary anti-Western rampages that old Slavic mystics seeking to carry the mantle of Dostoyevsky do when they start worrying painfully at the end of their days about their patriotic legacy in the old country.

It is often easier to be generous about one's adopted country than about one's home. When one sees the grotesque abroad, it's easy to see the humor in all those visible warts, to pass it all off as the amusing shortcomings not of Your Own Kind, but of mankind in general—a more abstract personage.

I don't mean to compare myself to any of those Russians, but I went through a similar process when I lived abroad and worked as a journalist in Russia for ten years. In that time I saw, over and over again, examples of the very worst kinds of behavior human beings can demonstrate toward one another. In many cases I managed actually to participate in these scenes, just to get closer to them, to experience them for myself—and I came away still feeling tremendous affection for the place.

In one instance, myself and a friend with whom I traveled quite a bit, a professional clown named Alexei Dindikin, walked into the Sanaksarsky Orthodox monastery in Mordovia and took jobs as migrant laborers at a construction site. This was the kind of setting that might perhaps have been common around the world 500 years ago but in modern times, and particularly in the Western world, has to be a rarity; it is a place where the Orthodox brothers keep in crude barracks a stable of indentured servants, mostly drunks and addicts and criminals, who perform slave labor in hideous conditions in exchange for room and board.

We had to turn in our passports at the door, making it theoretically impossible (until we confessed to being journalists) for us to leave, and submit to a series of draconian living restrictions: we were not allowed to read anything "worldly," and could be severely punished for so much as looking at a newspaper. Only the Bible was allowed. There was no drinking of any kind, and anyone who wanted to have a conversation with a female of any age or have a drink of vodka had to sneak off the grounds at night and steal into the neighboring village, which was still a peasant village in the truest sense—a place where actual paper money had not been seen in years and all trade was done by barter. Work during the daytime was a relentless hell of hauling and laying brick in searing heat amidst swarms of mosquitoes so thick that we had to wear bandannas to keep from breathing them in.

Alexei and the other workers and I had only two pleasures on the job. One was the ration of five "Prima" cigarettes we were given per workday; we were allowed five-minute breaks during each day to smoke these. The second was food, three square meals a day in the monastery cafeteria. Some of the workers were adept smugglers and managed during the day to pinch food from the cafeteria so that we could have snacks in the middle of the workday.

Because the work was so hard I didn't particularly enjoy that experience, but in observing it I felt untroubled by the outrage and disgust and shame I might have felt if I had been Russian. Instead the chief emotions I felt were sympathy and fascination. I was a witness to something terrible, but I was not an accomplice to it. What happened in Russia was not, ultimately, my problem, not so long as I could leave.

Which is what I did, in the spring of 2002, when I decided to see if there was a way I could feel the same way about my own country. I had left America as a twenty-one-year-old. When I came back, I was thirty-two, and mentally probably much younger than that. I had no job, no money, and I knew almost nothing about the place where I was born. My last significant experiences in the States had been in college in New York, when by far the most important thing I'd had to worry about was how to keep my bank balance above $250 and at the same time maintain a long-distance relationship with a girl who went to school "far away" in Massachusetts.

It wasn't long after I'd returned and founded a Buffalo newspaper called *The Beast* that I noticed I was having a problem working in the States. No longer personally disconnected from the subject, I found that everything I tried to write about was corrupted with a sense of disgust, self-loathing, disappointment, and shame. There was simply no possibility of covering American politics from the point of view of my own constituency, which was the worst and most loathsome of all: I was an upper-class white child of privilege, brought up in the liberal Northeast, for whom any outrage about the direction of American politics

and culture was by definition entirely intellectual in nature and mostly disingenuous. Even *I* didn't care about my problems, and I certainly didn't want to expend valuable time caring about the problems of other people like me.

There was therefore an element of preposterousness in my shaking my
fist at Fate here at home, a preposterousness that had been missing in all
those years that I had been simply telling the stories of hard-luck Russians.
Here I was not an impartial observer, but a walking, breathing element of the
whole complicated scenario, a compromised player by birth with a definite
role in what was clearly a very confusing, inscrutable, and seemingly preda-
tory commercial society—one that was gearing up for war and an important
election just as I came home.

There being an enormous market for coverage of it, I soon found myself
assigned by various publications to cover the American presidential election.
And that's when I really began to have problems.

I found out fairly quickly that the emotions I felt coming home—disgust, self-
loathing, disappointment, revulsion—were not specific to my own predicament as a returning expatriate. Except for a brief moment at the outset of
2003, when a half-million people or so descended upon Washington to
protest the war, what I mostly encountered traveling around the country was
a kind of low-grade cynicism and grumbling resignation about the Gigantic
Bummer the presidential election was about to provide for them. America, I
discovered, is a country that feels badly about itself, and when it is motivated
to participate in politics, it does so mainly out of hatred and contempt for the
guy on the other side, not inspiration or idealism.

This is as true of the Democrats, who overwhelmingly were more motivated to get involved with the election by their hatred of George Bush than
by enthusiasm for their candidates, as it is for the Republicans, who (as I
found out when I went undercover to work with them) were driven to get involved primarily by a fear that godless liberals were planning on comman-
deering their churches to bugger each other there in Muslim headdresses.
Within this paradigm there was an obvious danger for any journalist trying to

cover the situation, which was to choose one of the two sides and wave that flag for them in print.

From where I stood this relentless emphasis on these two particular takes on the election—that the Democrats are traitors, or the Republicans are Nazis—well, it was suspicious to me that they both got so much play in the media. It was equally suspicious to me that there was so little discussion of the possibility that there was something systemically wrong with the entire process, that this "fierce contest" between two political antagonists might actually be a red herring obscuring the fact that the entire political season was a farce and a con game—aimed at distracting the population from an enormous propaganda campaign designed to advertise the impossibility of change, and the inevitable triumph of a certain statistical range of the Same Old Thing.

But this idea was not easy to get at. It was an amalgam of one hundred thousand different aspects of our society that conspire to make us who we are—a nation that is mostly afraid of weirdly trivial embarrassments (looking bad, not having a flat stomach, not having enough money, not knowing how to pick up girls in bars, having cheap furniture) and has been conditioned over time not to dream of Big Things. Instead, it dreams of little things: having a little more, looking a little better, feeling a little less fat and hopeless, having a slightly less outrageous occupant in the White House.

To suddenly be thrust into the middle of the primary season and have to digest all of these things, and then later make sense of them succinctly enough to explain the tragedy of a stuffed suit like John Kerry winning the Democratic nomination—this is not easy. Covering the American presidential race requires the detailing of a long backstory that shows an America deadened by television, decades of unquestioning submission to the whims of corporate employers, the relentless media vilification of past protest movements, the brutal campaigns of advertisers who make ordinary people ashamed of their inadequacies (and therefore more willing to accept the endorsements of the glamorized stronger set), the continual and unchallenged circulation of such falsehoods as "electability" and the need for "tough" pro-military leaders, and so on.

Before the campaigns even begin, the whole process is corrupted by a broad range of bogus unspoken assumptions that the vast majority of Americans accept unquestioningly as facts. Accepting these assumptions, the population tends to buy the election process and the way it is presented to them as something rational and even dramatic in its own way, and not as the cynical parade of appalling frauds that it really is.

One of the great dilemmas of people who I think looked at this election intelligently and with the best interests of the country at heart was the problem of George W. Bush. In 2000, when Ralph Nader actually did fairly well, there was a serious debate in the progressive community about whether or not it really made sense to choose sides between two major parties that at the time seemed almost completely identical in their ideological outlook.

But the presidency of Bush, who proved to be a monster advancing his surprisingly perverse undead agenda with unusual enthusiasm, tempered that kind of thinking this time around. The fact that one of the two parties was *significantly worse* than the other added to the illusion, happily perpetrated by the mainstream media, that something was "really at stake" in this election. Therefore much of the election process was covered at face value, and huge numbers of people who might have been persuaded to think otherwise focused entirely on the bugbear in the White House and convinced themselves that the correct politics in this season was to expend all their energy in unseating him.

That they failed at this was disappointing, of course, but what was lost on most people was the degree to which the belief in the fraudulent electoral system was reaffirmed. This was symbolized most pointedly, I think, in the number of commercial advertisers that used "election" themes as selling campaigns (everyone from Snickers to Jack Daniels to Barbie to both Miller and Budweiser, and a dozen or so others). People were engrossed and engaged by the "drama" of this election, to the degree that Madison Avenue could confidently sell products using the election theme. That Bush won was one outcome, but the other one was that the presidential election won back its cachet—and this, to me, was the much bigger result.

In the bubble of the presidential campaign, where almost every person was fake and every quote was contrived, I was never able to find that same method I used in Russia. I was never able to find that area of sympathy to organize my thoughts around, not even deep within myself, as an American who was involved.

I think now that this is a problem that is not peculiar to my professional difficulties but extends to America in general. We are a country that has a large majority that on some level knows something is terribly wrong, but can't find any positive idea that it can follow and build upon. We are having problems finding that thing we love about our country, and about ourselves, so that we know to fight for it and protect it. When we march, we're marching *against,* not for. We don't have the faintest idea what we would want, even if we thought what we wanted was possible, which we most certainly don't.

On the other hand we know that sitting on top of us is a gigantic commercial and media machine that never leaves us alone for a minute, arrogantly claims the power to define our identities as members of demographics, and insists that we make our choices within the narrow parameters it lays out for us. It sells to us an America that is static and everlasting in its ways and whose rules will only ever change slightly, if at all, and one of its greatest amusements is the public humiliation of anyone who makes the mistake of asserting otherwise.

Like many Americans, I felt lost under the weight of that antagonist when I came home. I felt helpless and overwhelmed and small, and less of a man than I had felt living in Russia, where there was more dignity and acceptance in the life of an anonymous individual. I didn't know what to think about this problem, what to say about it, and I certainly didn't know how to approach covering its crushing headline act, the presidential election.

I still don't. In two years of this election season I did not see much that suggested to me that a great groundswell of change is on the way. But I do believe there is a strategy to pursue in the meantime, and that is to refuse to be lied to. That is something that is possible, even in the short term.

The presidential election, as presented by the media, is a great tour de force of lies, and if we get better at disbelieving them, there is a possibility that the liberating truth that we are all looking for will emerge on its own. Much of what is in this book is about those lies, how to identify them, and how properly to disbelieve them.

They are lies about polls, lies about the way politicians are labeled, lies about the concerns of the electorate, lies about the health of the electoral system, lies of word choice in campaign articles, lies of emphasis, lies hidden in the quantity of filed material, lies about the impartiality of the reporters who cover the campaigns, lies about the viability of third-party options, lies about the efficacy of lesser evilness, lies that make wars, lies that close factories, lies told by media companies that are no more American than Kim Jong-il, the Saudi royals, or S.P.E.C.T.R.E.

This election of George Bush was a defeat for America, but the bigger defeat was that the population spent two years allowing itself to be lied to. For two years we allowed this idiotic farce of an election to insult our dignity as human beings. We should all feel sick about it. I do. I feel sick enough to spend the next two years puking my guts out. But maybe if we learned to swallow fewer lies, we'll feel less sick the next time. I think it is not unrealistic, at least, to hope for that.

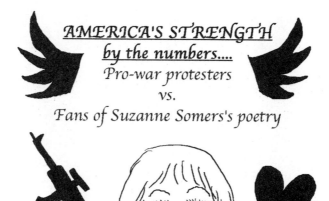

**AMERICA'S STRENGTH
by the numbers....
Pro-war protesters
vs.
Fans of Suzanne Somers's poetry**

YOU WAIT UNTIL 10:30,

YOU LIBERAL BASTARD

1

IRAQT-UP!
At the D.C. Rallies, a Few Hundred
Thousand Go Missing

Originally published in The Beast, *this piece about the February 2003 anti-war rally in Washington is included here to show one side of the beginning of the campaign season—when there was an enormous amount of idealistic political energy organized against the war. By the end of the campaign, this energy would be mostly gone—replaced with a more confused show of support for a candidate who had supported the war, John Kerry.*

Washington, D.C., Saturday, January 17, 2003—It is cold as a bitch out here. Journalism of any kind, in fact, is practically impossible. Less than ten minutes after arriving here at this small tree-lined park in the shadow of the Washington monument, I had to ask *Beast* publisher Paul Fallon for an extra pair of gloves to put on over the thin leather ones I was wearing. If you've ever tried to take notes on a legal pad in below-freezing temperatures while wearing two pairs of gloves at the same time, you can understand the obstacles I've faced.

It's been a difficult morning. We had come out early that morning for the first—and most disturbing by far—of the weekend's Iraq-related protests. The

February 1, 2003, *The Beast*.

main event, the anti-war protest at the mall sponsored by International A.N.S.W.E.R. (Act Now to Stop War and End Racism), was due to start at 11 A.M. This pre-event, scheduled for 9 A.M., was the day's journalistic appetizer, a freak show too tantalizing for any responsible press organ to ignore. It was the prowar demonstration, run by one of the most amazingly named organizations in the history of American activism.

MOVE-OUT stood for Marines and Other Veterans Engaging Outrageous Un-American Traitors.

The MOVE-OUT protest was like a caricature of a left-wing paranoid's idea of a staged CIA diversion. It had all the elements of a low-budget piece of fake political theater: a suspiciously high level of press participation (according to our careful count, there were eighty "protesters" and forty journalists), a pile of carefully rationed "protest" placards with high production values (a nicely airbrushed painting of George Bush in a muscle-bound Uncle Sam pose), a near-total absence of local protesters, and, last but not least, a single well-dressed, smiling, traitorous black person representing the "cause" (Kevin Martin, head of the "African-American Republican Leadership Council"). This thing was about as spontaneous as the applause for Comrade Stalin at the Fifth Party Congress. Offered the chance, I would have bet serious money that at least half of the protesters were secretaries and janitors from the NSA offices.

My hands were numb because I had kept them out of my pockets for long stretches in a frantic attempt to record for posterity the amazing rhetoric of the MOVE-OUT speakers. Some of the speeches were of a type not seen since Bluto rallied the troops in *Animal House*. Only this wasn't slapstick comedy; this was real. Martin gave a typical speech: "Our troops have always been there for us," he said, "from the time of World War I, when our soldiers beat back the fascists in France. . . ."

I turned to Paul. "France?" I said. "Fascists? What the fuck is he talking about?"

Paul shrugged. "Forget it," he said. "He's on a roll."

•   •   •

Paul and I had come down here from Buffalo to take part in the A.N.S.W.E.R. anti-war rally, and I have to admit that my expectations were low. Like most young Americans, I've been trained to think of protests and demonstrations as something shameful and vaguely embarrassing—something one outgrows, like Journey albums, or those hour-long showers you took when you were eleven and twelve.

It's not hard to see why people my age (in their early thirties and younger) think that way. Our parents were all part of a scrupulously documented protest generation that they subsequently renounced. Oliver Stone aside, the movies and documentaries the people from our parents' generation made about the 1960s inevitably describe a generation that was maybe well-meaning in a bluntly stupid kind of way, but on the whole extremely indulgent, narcissistic, and naive, a bunch of rich jerks flinging their braless chests and stinky beards in the direction of their parents' grim, sexually repressed, business-driven world.

Our parents are ashamed that they left behind all those movies of them burning their bras and eating acid at Monterey. They're ashamed because they ultimately became everything they were against back then: cynical, greedy careerists. That's why they created this atmosphere that celebrates the uncompromising protest of Mohandas Gandhi on the faraway Asian continent as brave and principled, but teaches us that protest in our own country is just something that's nice to try when you're young, before you get a real job. To be socially conscious today, the older generation tells us, all we have to do is watch *Silkwood* a few times, and recycle. All the really hard work here, after all, was already done in the 1960s.

I admit to being influenced by all of this. My previous experiences with protests have all tended to confirm the worst stereotypes about modern activism. In anti-globalization, pro-environment, and anti–Kosovo War rallies I saw almost exclusively well-off people of my age and class dressed down and plainly living out some revolting Oliver Stone–inspired 1960s fantasy (the most damning evidence of which, incidentally, is the tendency of these protesters to run to the cameras and start mugging in John-and-Yoko poses as soon as TV crews arrive). More than once I've come across protesters who barely even knew what they were protesting; the important thing, obviously, was the protest itself, the poetic act of participating.

But the most glaring problem with all of these protests I've seen is this sense that no one involved in them actually hoped to accomplish anything. At so many of the protests of our generation, you can sense a sort of willingness to comply with the wishes of our parents—protest, sure, but only do it for the "experience," as something to do. Turn it into a sort of street theater, a way to meet girls. Whatever you do, don't make it matter. In a glib, permissive age where dissent, protest, certain forms of civil disobedience, and even the occasional arrest are superficially acceptable and even encouraged, the only real taboo when it comes to having political convictions today is meaning it. And in thirty-two years I haven't seen anyone break that taboo on any real scale.

Washington would be a little different. Not that it mattered. In order to even hear what happened there, you had to be there. Our illustrious national press corps saw to that.

At the MOVE-OUT protest in the morning I had gotten into an argument with some of the mainstream reporters covering the event. Not that that was surprising. A blatantly staged media event like the MOVE-OUT demonstration is the kind of thing that any journalist with even a sliver of a conscience left is bound to be extremely defensive about having attended.

After all, one would be hard-pressed to think of any circumstance not involving a progovernment counterdemonstration in which forty journalists from major news organizations would attend a 9 A.M. weekend rally involving eighty illiterate morons. To use the Russian expression, crayfish will whistle in the mountains before eighty environmentalists in a park on a Saturday morning draw so much as a college radio intern, much less forty of the country's heaviest press hitters. The mere presence of so much press at the MOVE-OUT demonstration was monstrous.

So when I arrived at the scene I thought it would be amusing to count the total number of journalists, as opposed to actual protesters. And wouldncha know it, some members of the working press were offended by the exercise.

"You shouldn't be doing that now," a bearded Reuters hack told me, after suffering the indignity of being counted. "It's too early. The bulk of the crowd won't show up until later. Like around ten-thirty."

"Well," I said. "The *Washington Post* said this thing was supposed to start at nine. It's now nine-thirty."

"The *Post* was wrong," the Reuters man snapped. "If you want to be honest, you'll do this later."

"Let me get this straight," I said. "You're actually worried that I'm going to undercount these yahoos?"

"I'm saying," he said, "that if you want to be fair, you'll count when the crowd really shows up."

Next to the Reuters man stood a young blonde woman in black horn-rimmed glasses who identified herself as a reporter for the *New York Times*. She didn't offer her name, but another reporter there later told me that she was an assistant to *Times* reporter Lynette Clemetson. She'd been listening to my exchange with the Reuters man and decided to chime in.

"And the important thing isn't the numbers," she said. "This demonstration has more Vietnam veterans."

I shook my head, stunned. "Are you kidding?" I said. "The other demonstration will have a hell of a lot more vets than this one, I'm sure of that."

She frowned. "No," she said. "That one's going to be mostly college students. Kids."

"Maybe so," I said. "But just in terms of sheer numbers . . . I mean, even half a percent of 100,000 is going to be ten times more vets than we're seeing here. There are about fifty people here, for Christ's sake."

"No," she said, not convinced. "No, this one will have more."

A third personage, a scrawny redneck protester in a baseball cap and a Gore-Tex face guard, was listening in. "That's the slimiest journalism I've ever seen," he said, jumping in. "You're in here and you're going to count us before we're even here. You wait until ten-thirty, then you'll see how many of us there will be. You're yellow journalism scum."

"Settle down, Beavis," I said.

"You wait until ten-thirty, you liberal bastard," he said.

I shrugged and walked away. An hour later, after suffering through numerous historically confused speeches about our victories over fascists in France and our spectacular, as-yet-unrecognized military successes in Vietnam, I counted all over. The final tally, again, was eighty protesters and forty journalists, and that included the five-man Guardian Angel security entourage that followed speaker Curtis Sliwa. I sought out a Gore-Tex face in the crowd.

"Hey, Chester," I said. "Eighty to forty. Nice turnout."

"Fuck you," he hissed. "We represent the real America."

"You know," I said, "I once went to a Suzanne Somers book signing. There were like three hundred people there. It was a book of poetry."

"Fuck you," he repeated.

A few yards away, a mealy-faced young man in a blue button-down shirt named Eric DuVall was quietly taking notes. An intern under Washington-based reporter Jerry Zremski, he was the representative of the *Buffalo News*. We would later spot him in the crowd at the main demonstration. Like me, he was observing the crowds. Only his conclusions would be a little different from mine.

Right from the start, there were two things about the A.N.S.W.E.R. demonstration that were startling. The first was its staggering size. I'd read about the last demonstration in November and had tended to believe the conservative estimates of the crowd size, not believing that more than a very small number of people like me would be sufficiently motivated to go anywhere to protest the inevitable. But the crowd at Washington last weekend was truly gargantuan.

Police admitted to the *Washington Post* that it was the largest anti-war rally since the Vietnam era, and that it was much larger than the October rally. I personally could not see the end of the crowd. It took a good half-hour to make my way to the front of the crowd, and from a speaker platform up on the press podium I was able to get a look at the gathering as it stretched back along the Mall. Even from an elevated position, I couldn't see the end.

Later on, when the crowd filed out to march to the Navy Yard, it proved impossible to determine how far the line of people stretched. The length of the march was several miles, and, again according to the *Washington Post,* the crowd was still entering the beginning of the route at the Mall when the first marchers at the front reached the Navy Yard.

From where I sat, there was no question that there were at least 200,000 people present, and probably closer to 300,000. The extraordinary turnout was the chief topic of conversation along the march: time after time, I spotted marchers turning to look back, shaking their heads at the trailing crowd, and saying, "Holy shit!" Walking in a gathering this size, you get a sense of its building kinetic energy and potential destructive power: a chain-link fence near the Mall that obstructed a group of shortcut seekers, for instance, simply blew away like dandelion fuzz once the crowd decided to walk through it. This was far different than the feeling one gets exiting an NBA game, for instance.

Back to the size later. The second thing that was striking about this crowd was that, despite the fact that it was composed largely of middle- to upper-middle-class whites, there was no name politician from either major party there to address it. Given that a Pew survey taken this week showed that a majority of Americans (52 percent) felt that President Bush had not yet made a convincing case that war was necessary, one would have thought that at least some opportunistic politician from the Democratic Party would have decided to attach his or her name to the anti-war effort. But the only politician of any stature at the event was the Reverend Al Sharpton, a doomed candidate for president with too much political baggage to really be an effective champion for anything.

Put two and two together and what you get is the amazing realization that this crowd, perhaps the largest to gather in Washington in the last thirty years, has no political representation whatsoever in today's America. Almost certainly representing a vastly larger number of people in the general population, the anti-war crowd has simply been excluded from the process.

The eighty nitwits at the MOVE-OUT event could reasonably claim one sympathetic U.S. senator per demonstrator: the 200,000+ at the A.N.S.W.E.R.

event couldn't claim even one. The only real clout it could claim was its own physical presence at that particular moment.

All of which makes sense, because from the very beginning, the character of this war has been that of a giant end-run around common sense, around international law, around political reality, even around basic human logic. When you've spent half a year getting your head around the idea that a terrorist attack by Islamic fundamentalists somehow necessitates the immediate invasion of an unrelated secular dictatorship, or that opposing an offensive war is somehow evidence that one "hates America" and is a traitor, it isn't hard to see how 250,000 people in this country these days can actually, in real terms, be numerically fewer than 80.

Nonetheless, it seemed like everyone in the march, myself included, was shocked to find themselves in the middle of so many other like-minded people. It was clearly a group that was not used to being in the majority and was intoxicated by the experience.

"No way did we expect this many people," said Nick Salter, eighteen, who was with a large group from Cherry Creek High School in Colorado. "But we felt like we had to come out here. It's now or never for our generation."

"It was a sense of obligation," said Chris Kezzara, twenty-three, a bartender from Detroit. "But I came by myself. I wasn't expecting so many people."

"Shit, of course not," said Lee Turner, a social worker from Brooklyn, when asked if he expected so many people. "But it doesn't matter. We'll wake up tomorrow and find out from the newspapers that there were only 15,000 of us or something."

That didn't seem likely. During the march I was convinced that the only possible angle the media could take on this protest was one that met the sheer size of it head-on. There were all sorts of peripheral stories about the protest to cover: the uncertain future of the protest leadership (the reported affiliation of A.N.S.W.E.R. with the Workers' World Party was an uncomfortable undercurrent that ran through the entire event), the fact that the protests were taking place on Martin Luther King Day, the protests in the light of waning international support for the war (the line the *Washington Post* in fact ended up taking). But the only story any observant journalist could really take out of this event was the fact that it was (a) massive and (b) extremely diverse, an exponentially larger and broader crowd than had attended even the last A.N.S.W.E.R. rally a few months ago. If the snapshot the media got from Seattle was a gang of hippies standing in front of a row of broken store windows, the picture from this one should rightly have been seven lonely College Republicans cringing behind a "Hippies Go Home" banner high up on a balcony as tens of thousands of obvious nonhippies screamed for them to come down to the street level for an ass-whipping.

"Get down here, you cocksuckers!" shouted a huge black kid with corn-rows. The Republicans said nothing and just grinned.

"Hang on," I said. "It's a trap. No one really dresses like that."

Indeed, one of the "protesting" Republicans was wearing a circa-1977 argyle V-neck sweater.

"Yeah," he said. "Whatever. Let's get them down here anyway."

About a half-mile down the road, the remnants of the MOVE-OUT crowd (about seven people) were huddled behind a row of policemen, shouting through a megaphone at the waves of bemused protesters.

"We are the majority!" one of them was saying. "We are the majority! We are America!"

At the time, that sounded like a joke. Then I got up the next morning and checked the newspapers.

According to the vast majority of American newspapers and news services, 30,000 was a solid estimate for the size of the Saturday crowd. Each of the news outlets used a different rhetorical means to avoid a true description of the crowd size that day.

Fox News was among the most disingenuous. On Saturday evening, the news crawl was telling viewers that "at least 30,000 gather in DC to protest military action in Iraq: a smaller group demonstrated in support of action."

Well, "at least 30,000" is not technically incorrect, of course. There were "at least 5" there as well. But we all know what Fox was saying.

The Associated Press reported "tens of thousands" of protesters, but also quoted a police spokesman as saying that a "permit had been issued for 30,000 protesters." That 30,000 figure would be roundly circulated in the headlines of AP-subscribing papers around the country.

The *New York Times,* which caught flak for undercounting the last A.N.S.W.E.R. protest as well as an anti-war protest in London, did not even speculate on the crowd size, remaining content with the designation "thousands" in the headline ("Thousands in D.C. Protest Iraq Plans").

Reuters, whose reporter had worried so much that I might undercount the MOVE-OUT demonstrators, contented itself with the wording "thousands marched on Washington and San Francisco," and noted that while organizers claimed 500,000 protesters, there were no official figures.

Crowd-counting is a tricky business. It used to be the province of the National Park Service, but it has stopped counting crowds since Louis Farrakhan sued them for allegedly undercounting the Million Man March. It is therefore somewhat understandable that officials might be reluctant to release an estimate. But there is caution in reporting, and then there's common sense. If there were just 30,000 people at that rally, I'm a Chinese jet pilot. Any reporter with two eyes could have seen that this was a matter of hundreds of thousands of people, not tens of thousands. And yet all of this careful language was used to leave the impression of a smallish rally, half the size of a good college football crowd, balanced out by an only somewhat smaller rally in support of the war. If ever there was a case of the media simply lying outright to the public, this was it.

On the day after the protests, I tried to track down representatives of the offending news agencies and demand an explanation. In each case the best answer I could get was "No comment." D.C. Fox News reporter Molly Hennenberg laughed in my face when I cornered her on the street and asked how her station could possibly have counted 30,000 people at the previous day's rally.

"Gosh, I'm sorry," she said, flicking a piece of lint off her glowing white winter coat. "I wasn't on yesterday. I just can't comment."

"Well," I said, "doesn't it bother you that they got it so wrong? I mean, you saw the crowds yesterday."

She smiled again, almost as if to say, "Oh, this is so cute!" Then she said, "Look, I have to go on the air. I really have nothing to say. I'm sorry."

Worse still was the *Buffalo News*. Its headline presented the unequivocal pronouncement: "30,000 in DC Protest War Plans." The spill headline read: "Protests: Polls indicate mixed feelings on Iraq war; veterans rally for Bush."

That wasn't the worst part. The actual article claimed:

"Protests stretched from San Francisco to Hong Kong to Moscow, but the Washington march was by far the largest, though it was much smaller than a similar event in October. That protest drew 100,000; police said Saturday's rally drew 30,000."

The *BN* was the only news organ in the country that concluded that the Saturday rally was smaller than the October rally. Even the *Washington Post* quoted Metropolitan Police Chief Charles H. Ramsey as saying that the rally was not only "bigger than October's," but also that it was "one of the biggest ones we've had, certainly in recent times." Not even Fox News sunk as low as our hometown paper. When I caught up with A.N.S.W.E.R. chief Brian Becker the next day, and told him what the *Buffalo News* had reported, he was flabbergasted.

"They said what?" he asked.

"They said it was smaller than October," I said.

"And it wasn't a wire story? It was their own reporters?"

"Yup," I said.

"Jesus Christ," he said, kneading his forehead.

The *Buffalo News* report was doubly irritating for me because I'd actually seen one of their reporters, Eric, twice during the day, and even met him. After I told him I was with the *Beast,* he was polite and even seemed friendly. A cursory examination seemed to show that this was a human being in full control of his faculties. How he could possibly have gone home after a day of watching these events and filed that bullshit story was beyond me. The fact that he'd shaken my hand left me feeling raped. After I returned to Buffalo, I decided to call him.

"Eric," I said. "Matt Taibbi from the *Beast.* We met this weekend."

"Oh," he said. "Hi."

"I was wondering how you guys came up with that 30,000 figure. It seemed like there were a lot more people than that there."

"Well," he said. "That wasn't me. That was [lead reporter Jerry Zremski]. I think he got it from a wire report."

"Okay," I said. "Why would he need a wire report, if you were there?"

"I don't know," he said. "But if Jerry got it from a reliable source, then I'm cool with that."

Jesus, I thought. This kid is barely out of college, and he's already completely full of shit.

"Wait a minute," I said. "You were there. Do you think there were 30,000 people there?"

He paused. "I couldn't give you a figure," he said.

"Why not?" I said. "You can't say if there were more or less than 30,000 people there? You don't have your own opinion?"

"I didn't have a good view," he said.

Jesus Christ. A good view?

Sunday, the second day of the protests, was a disaster. The main crowd was all gone and only a group of student protesters remained. Their goal was to march to the White House and engage in "civil disobedience." And that's exactly what happened. After a brief standoff when the police abruptly canceled the permit to march in front of the White House, the group ran around a corner, outflanking the police, and parked itself in front of the White House gates. Once there, a small group of teenage camera-mugging assholes jumped the fence and then kneeled on the ground with ear-to-ear grins as they waited to be subdued by the cops. When the police sighed and cuffed them, the crowd chanted, "This is what a police state looks like."

Minutes later, the worst of the worst happened. A group of ebullient and clearly overweight teen granola types parked in front of a gang of mounted cops and, bursting with self-satisfied smiles, sang out the dreaded "Give Peace a Chance." When the TV cameras showed up, they started the song over and flashed peace signs at the cameras. They looked like they'd just gotten through to the next round of *American Idol*. You'd never guess, from looking at them, that a war was about to start. They didn't even look like they were worried about midterms, much less war.

The sixteen smiling dickwads arrested that day were given major airplay all around the country. Thanks to the wires, the TV networks, and even small-time flunkies like Eric DuVall, they were made the official face of the anti-war movement. It's that easy to hide a few hundred thousand people in this country.

PEACE BEGINS
WITH PEACEFUL
PRESS CONFERENCES

2

SPRING/SUMMER 2003

Cleaning the Pool

The White House Press Corps Politely Grabs Its Ankles

After watching George W. Bush's press conference last Thursday night, I'm more convinced than ever: The entire White House press corps should be herded into a cargo plane, flown to an altitude of 30,000 feet, and pushed out, kicking and screaming, over the North Atlantic.

Any remaining staff at the Washington bureaus should be rounded up for summary justice. The Russians used bakery trucks, big gray panel trucks marked *Bread* on the sides; victims would be rounded up in the middle of the night and taken for one last ride through the darkened streets.

The war would almost be worth it just to see Wolf Blitzer pounding away at the inside of a Pepperidge Farm truck, tearfully confessing and vowing to "take it all back."

The Bush press conference to me was like a mini-Alamo for American journalism, a final announcement that the press no longer performs anything

---

March 11, 2003, *New York Press*.

akin to a real function. Particularly revolting was the spectacle of the cream of the national press corps submitting politely to the indignity of obviously preapproved questions, with Bush not even bothering to conceal that the affair was scripted.

Abandoning the time-honored pretense of spontaneity, Bush chose the order of questioners not by scanning the room and picking out raised hands, but by looking down and reading from a predetermined list. Reporters, nonetheless, raised their hands in between questions—as though hoping to suddenly catch the president's attention.

In other words, not only were reporters going out of their way to make sure their softballs were preapproved, but they also even went so far as to *act* on Bush's behalf, raising their hands and jockeying in their seats in order to better give the appearance of a spontaneous news conference.

Even Bush couldn't ignore the absurdity of it all. In a remarkable exchange that somehow managed to avoid being commented upon in news accounts the next day, Bush chided CNN political correspondent John King when the latter overacted his part, too enthusiastically waving his hand when it apparently was, according to the script, his turn anyway.

KING: Mr. President.
BUSH: We'll be there in a minute. King, John King. This is a scripted. . . .

A ripple of nervous laughter shot through the East Room. Moments later, the camera angle of the conference shifted to a side shot, revealing a ring of potted plants around the presidential podium. It would be hard to imagine an image that more perfectly describes American political journalism today: George Bush, surrounded by a row of potted plants, in turn surrounded by the White House press corps.

Newspapers the next day ignored the scripted-question issue completely. (King himself, incidentally, left it out of his CNN.com report.) Of the major news services and dailies, only one—the *Washington Post*—even parenthetically addressed the issue. Far down in Dana Millbank and Mike Allen's conference summary, the paper euphemistically commented:

"The president followed a script of names in choosing which reporters could ask him a question, and he received *generally friendly questioning.*" [Emphasis mine] "Generally friendly questioning" is an understatement if there ever was one. Take this offering by April Ryan of the American Urban Radio Networks:

"Mr. President, as the nation is at odds over war, with many organizations like the Congressional Black Caucus pushing for continued diplomacy through the UN, how is your faith guiding you?"

Great. In Bush's first press conference since his decision to support a rollback of affirmative action, the first black reporter to get a crack at him—and this is what she comes up with? The journalistic equivalent of "Mr. President, you look great today. What's your secret?"

Newspapers across North America scrambled to roll the highlight tape of Bush knocking Ryan's question out of the park. The *Boston Globe:* "As Bush stood calmly at the presidential lectern, tears welled in his eyes when he was asked how his faith was guiding him. . . ." The *Globe and Mail:* "With tears welling in his eyes, Mr. Bush said he prayed daily that war can be averted. . . ."

Even worse were the qualitative assessments in the major dailies of Bush's performance. As I watched the conference, I was sure I was witnessing, live, a historic political catastrophe. In his best moments Bush was deranged and uncommunicative, and in his worst moments, which were most of the press conference, he was swaying side to side like a punch-drunk fighter, at times slurring his words and seemingly clinging for dear life to the verbal oases of phrases like "total disarmament," "regime change," and "mass destruction."

He repeatedly declined to answer direct questions. At one point, when a reporter twice asked if Bush could consider the war a success if Saddam Hussein were not captured or killed, Bush answered: "Uh, we will be changing the regime of Iraq, for the good of the Iraqi people."

Yet the closest thing to a negative characterization of Bush's performance in the major outlets was in David Sanger and Felicity Barringer's *New York Times* report, which called Bush "sedate": "Mr. Bush, sounding sedate at a rare prime-time news conference, portrayed himself as the protector of the country. . . ."

Apparently even this absurdly oblique description, which ran on the *Times* website hours after the press conference, was too much for the paper's editors. Here is how that passage read by the time the papers hit the streets the next morning:

"Mr. Bush, at a rare prime-time press conference, portrayed himself as the protector of the country. . . ."

Meanwhile, those aspects of Bush's performance that the White House was clearly anxious to call attention to were reported enthusiastically. It was obvious that Bush had been coached to dispense with two of his favorite public speaking tricks—his perma-smirk and his finger-waving cowboy one-liners. Bush's somber new "war is hell" act was much commented upon, without irony, in the postmortems.

Appearing on *Hardball* after the press conference, *Newsweek*'s Howard Fineman (one of the worst monsters of the business) gushed when asked if the Bush we'd just seen was really a "cowboy":

"If he's a cowboy he's the reluctant warrior, he's Shane . . . because he has to, to protect his family."

Newsweek thinks Bush is Shane?

This was just Bush's eighth press conference since taking office, and each one of them has been a travesty. In his first presser, on February 22, 2001, a month after his controversial inauguration, he was not asked a single question about the election, Al Gore, or the Supreme Court. On the other hand, he was asked five questions about Bill Clinton's pardons.

Reporters argue that they have no choice. They'll say they can't protest or boycott the staged format, because they risk being stripped of their seats in the press pool. For the same reason, they say they can't write anything too negative. They can't write, for instance, "President Bush, looking like a demented retard on the eve of war. . . ." That leaves them with the sole option of "working within the system" and, as they like to say, "trying to take our shots when we can."

But the White House press corps' idea of "taking a shot" is David Sanger asking Bush what he thinks of British Foreign Minister Jack Straw saying that regime change was not necessarily a war goal. And then meekly sitting his ass back down when Bush ignores the question.

They can't write what they think, and can't ask real questions. What the hell *are* they doing there? If the answer is "their jobs," it's about time we started wondering what that means.

On Board

In the New World Order, All I Want Is a Job

I should be man enough to admit it. I've had a change of heart. After the events of last week, I realize I was all wrong, all along. About everything. I understand it all now.

Watching that amazing scene of the Saddam statue being toppled, I understood finally not only what this was all about, but also who *I* was and what my part had been. And I wasn't ashamed the way one is of a crime, but ashamed the way one is of having made some ridiculous and embarrassing mistake of inexperience, like showing up for your first day of college thinking you look suave in clothes that people stopped wearing three years ago. We just didn't get it.

With all this hand-wringing about the war, we were acting like the shrieking chick in every horror movie ever made, freaking out and always running stupidly upstairs away from the vampire, straight to the room from which there is no escape. We can't even run in a straight line without knocking over furniture and tripping and falling and giving the slow-moving monster time to gain; meanwhile, he's moving effortlessly. He *floats* up the stairs, arms folded calmly in front of him, while we fall down five times on the way up.

April 15, 2003, *New York Press.*

We lock ourselves in a room, turn around, blink, and he's there in an instant—he has some other way of moving, one not known to us. And we want to scream, but nothing comes out as he leans over and depresses his hot fangs into our neck, never guessing that. . . .

It feels *good*. Yes, that's what I thought as I watched the statue scene unfold. I could almost feel the blood mixing in my neck, and it was a warm obliterating rush like straight dope. I'm an American. America rules the world. It feels good. No more need to be ashamed now; it was useless to resist. More to the point, there's no more need to deny it: I want in. I want to be part of this awesome, destructive revolutionary power.

Sign me up. Tehran. Pyongyang. Moscow. We Americans must get used to all kinds of climates. I'm white and I went to college—that ought to give me some kind of status. A member of the torturing class. Good enough at the very least for administrative duty, somewhere at the far edges of the empire.

Morning on a beautiful spring day on the shores of the Black Sea. I am deputy mayor of a little town near what used to be Yalta. Perfect for me— mountains, beaches, Slavic with an Asian minority, and plenty of disposable people. I am walking through town en route to the outdoor cafe where I always have my breakfast. I'm dressed in my civilian uniform—crisp khaki all over with glowing green alligator cowboy boots and a kind of wide-brimmed outback hat bedecked with gold cord and four-foot ostrich feathers. Afraid of what it might mean, no one on the street makes eye contact with me. Across the street, an old *babushka* carries an armful of bread loaves, her eyes fixed on the ground.

"Hey," I shout, in English. "You. How much for a loaf of bread?"

She stops, then struggles to get out the words. "Mmm . . ." she says. "Meester mayor. Twenty cents for breat!"

I strike her hard across the face with the back of my hand and she goes flying. "Bitch!" I scream. "Not for me it isn't! For me it's *free*!"

I bend down to snatch a loaf off the ground and quickly lift up my head to look around. Just as I expected: everybody pretends not to watch. I walk on, spurs jingling.

Ah, this is the good life. I have everything I want here. Days of leisure, and nights. . . . Yes, how to describe the nights? This used to be a resort town, and I entertain a lot of visitors. I often get journalists on vacation here from tours at the front. They wear uniforms too, now, sharp suits emblazoned with skulls. The other night, Aaron Brown and his crew were here, and we stayed up all night at the Turtle Club, snorting coke with strippers. I had Aaron all wrong; he's a great guy with a great sense of humor. And he's a *professional*. At the end of the night I offered to take him out of town to the country, where we could get ourselves a couple of farmer children, but he said no, he couldn't, he had to get back to his suite and file.

My house is a palace. Gravel driveway with two Lincolns in it; full-size basketball court with Plexiglas backboards in back; pillars and servants' entrances. I eat sitting in a high-backed, jade-encrusted chair at the head of a long table fifty feet away from my wife at the other end. We haven't spoken in nine months. It's ecstasy. I spend most of my time in my quarters, either writing letters in the computer room (I have a personal correspondence with star NFL safety Brian Dawkins) or lounging on the plush leather furniture of my basement den, eating peanut butter and honey sandwiches and jerking off to old videos of *Gidget* that I watch on the giant, high-resolution digital television that stretches across a whole wall like a huge bay window.

Sometimes I carry a sword and go walking through the villages. There is a girl in Podelkino who is genuinely in love with me; she dreams that I will give her an American child. Perhaps I will. I'll make this my own personal Little Rock, a faraway princedom full of children bearing the leader's face. But I can always have favorites, my Podelkino girl.

There are problems, of course. The mountains are full of rebels and I am, naturally, their prize target. It's kind of a game I play with them. When I first got here, I was afraid. Now I know they wouldn't dare. Sometimes I go riding on a horse, alone, right through their territory as F-16s break overhead. . . . Just trot right into a hovel, pull out a young girl, slice her up like a lobster. And stand there. I dare you, you fuckers. I fucking *dare* you.

Back at the cafe. Rolls, coffee, a fruit plate. A boy has brought me my mail.

There is a package. I open it. Finally: my Kontainment Kubby SP-90 Deluxe
Livestock Sorting Stick, special delivery from Grand Rapids, Michigan. The
top-of-the-line cattle prod. Three long feet of pure juice. Cost me $99.95 of
my own money. I wonder if it works.

"Waiter!" I shout. "Waiter!"

The polite young man with the parted hair whishes forward, carrying a
tray of water glasses. "*Da, Meester Mayor?*"

I zap him. He shrieks and tosses the tray straight up in the air, water and
glasses flying behind him like shrapnel. Screams in the restaurant, panic, then
sudden quiet. Like a beach at night after the tide. He picks himself up off the
floor, wipes his trembling hands on his apron, then smiles, relieved he didn't
spill anything on me.

"Very good, sir," he says, nodding. "Ha, ha, very good!"

Applause and breakfast. When I'm done, I lean back in my chair with a
glass of prune juice, throw on the Discman headphones. My favorite album,
then and now: *Doggystyle.* Perfect for the moment. *E Pluribus Unum,* baby.
Send me anywhere you want.

Wired, Tapped

Four Against Six Just for the Treatment—Easy!

DOC. #4562-BNVV03 NYFBI
SAC Anderson, G., rep.
Surveillance of writer/journalist Matt Taibbi. Transcript of intercepted tele-
phone conversation with entertainment attorney Aaron Weintraub, 4-16-03
Time: 4:37
Initial: GA
IC: AM
OG: W
Activity Recorded: 3792-14
Taibbi, observed awake and pacing back and forth in his lighted apartment all
night, calls Weintraub at 4:37 A.M.; the phone answers on the nineteenth ring.

April 22, 2003, *New York Press.*

TAIBBI: Aaron! It's (unintelligible), you hairy fucking (inaudible)!

WEINTRAUB: Uh . . . Jesus. Matt?

TAIBBI: Of course it (inaud.), fucking (unint.), ha, ha!

WEINTRAUB: What's that noise? Is that the national anthem?

TAIBBI: (shouting) Hell, yeah, dog! I'll turn it down! (Noise diminishes.) You know, if you really listen to the anthem, it's really a beautiful song!

WEINTRAUB: Do you know what time it is? It's like five in the morning!

TAIBBI: More like four-thirty. What, are you asleep?

WEINTRAUB: (sighing) You know, I should have known. Masha called me yesterday from her office. She's worried about you.

TAIBBI: Worried about me? Why?

WEINTRAUB: She says that ever since the war ended, all you do is pace around the apartment all day, blow coke, listen to Britney Spears, and move toy tanks and ships around on some huge map you bought.

TAIBBI: (laughing) Yeah, I guess that's true!

WEINTRAUB: And she says you've been reading the Bible.

TAIBBI: Yeah! Fucking *sad* book!

WEINTRAUB: (sighs) This hasn't been going on the whole two weeks, has it?

TAIBBI: No . . . I mean, yes! I mean, who cares? Aaron, listen, I've got this ingenious idea! This one is going to make us high six figures. Are you listening?

WEINTRAUB: It's not another screenplay, is it? Because you never even started the last—

TAIBBI: Aaron, wait, listen, this is one hundred times better than that one. Hang on. (Makes prolonged snorting sound.) Aaaah . . . Okay, get this. Feature movie called *Who Wants to Be Next!* It's got action, airplanes, tits, the whole thing! It can't miss!

WEINTRAUB: Okay. Who's in it?

TAIBBI: Who's in it, Aaron? America's in it, that's who. Okay, listen up. Opening scene. Some shithole suburb in some place like Tennessee. Or maybe Indiana. Whatever! Ordinary house, garage, Dodge Caravan, concrete everywhere—you know, idyllic. Two adolescent kids, the boy's into sports, the girl's all gothed-out and listens to Marilyn Manson, sibling rivalry, but they love each other underneath it all—you know, we're diverse, but we get along! Dad does something security-related for the government that's intellectual, he saves whales for the fire department or something. Mom's that fucking bitch from *The Truman Show* . . .

WEINTRAUB: Uh . . . Laura Linney?

TAIBBI: Right, exactly, Laura Linney! Anyway, they're home one night, ordinary night. Dad's writing a book about Mount Rushmore, mom's working out on the home gym, she's got that serious working-woman look on, you know (wincing) "Just . . . another . . . mile!" Jimmy's picking on little Tess because she's got a new necklet with a peace sign on it, he keeps punching her on the shoulder. And then suddenly a gang of Syrian terrorists bursts into the house, all laughing like pirates, and immediately starts tying up the kids and wrecking shit.

WEINTRAUB: Who are we rooting for at this point?

TAIBBI: The family, Aaron, definitely the family! We're with them all the way!

WEINTRAUB: And why are terrorists bursting into some random house in the Ohio suburbs?

TAIBBI: Indiana. . . . Because they're terrorists, Aaron, that's why! That's what they do. Anyway, Mom and Dad come rushing in and they're freaking because the kids are all tied up and crying. And Mom's like, "Steven! Why don't you do something! Get a gun!" And Dad's like, "Lisa, you know I don't believe in them!" And Linney throws her hands up in the air—how useless her husband is! And meanwhile two of the terrorists are checking out little Tess. One of them grabs the necklet and says to the other in Arabic—you can see the subtitles: "Ha, ha, look at this!" And the other one's like, "Peace! The fools!" And right then and there they chop off the kids' heads with a big scimitar, and the one guy palms the peace necklet and they go running out the back door, laughing and carrying the heads . . .

WEINTRAUB: Wait—what did they come in there for in the first pl—

TAIBBI: . . . and as they leave there are arterial blood spurts from the kids' necks and they get all over Mom, who just can't stop screaming, and Dad is all silent because he knows at that moment that she's going to divorce him. There should be a kind of swaying close-up of his face for that shot, his grave, conflicted face should come in and out of focus, you know, like Soderbergh in *Traffic*. . . .

WEINTRAUB: Who is he?

TAIBBI: Who's who?

WEINTRAUB: Dad. Who is he?

TAIBBI: Oh, I don't know. An everyman type with vague countercultural credentials . . . Jay Mohr.

WEINTRAUB: How about David Spade?

TAIBBI: Yeah, he'd work, I guess. And he'd do it, too. The fucker.

WEINTRAUB: He sure would.

TAIBBI: Whatever. (Pauses, snorts.) All right! Cut to the Oval Office. Jennifer Garner is president! She's having an encrypted videophone conversation with our secret European agent, who's, uh, Stellen Skarsgård, and he's telling her that the EU is behind all the terrorism and that they're using coded messages in ordinary Yahoo chat rooms to give terrorists coordinates they can use to put scrofula and bubonic plague and AIDS in our reservoirs. So Garner turns to Chief of Staff Don Cheadle and he's like, "We're going to have to intercept those messages." And she'll be like, "But that's a violation of civil liberties! It's unconstitutional!" And Cheadle's like, "It's the only way." And the next thing you see is Garner having her Kennedy–Cuban-Missile grappling-with-a-decision scene, walking alone through the residence at night. She's in skimpy lingerie and you can see her mound clear through her panties, but it's not like it's pornography because, uh, there are all these flags and portraits everywhere.

WEINTRAUB: Matt—

TAIBBI: Meanwhile, Allen Iverson is organizing all the good rappers to weed out the terrorist-sympathizing rappers who include DMX and whose songs are also on the soundtrack, which is produced by Sony. Then from there it's pretty obvious. . . . We invade, and Dad from Indiana is now a killing machine in the Marines. . . .

WEINTRAUB: Is Dad a *perfect* killing machine? Or just a killing machine?

TAIBBI: Shit, right, I'm sorry. Dad's a *perfect* killing machine. Makes bombs with decks of playing cards and shit.

WEINTRAUB: Okay.

TAIBBI: Right. Anyway, in the end he's bayoneting over and over the Syrian who killed his kids, saying, "I got you, you son of a bitch, I got you!" And then he kneels down and sees that peace necklet around the guy's neck and that's the poetic last shot, a close-up of the peace sign. . . . All the enemies killed . . . and . . . and . . . wait, that's . . . that's stupid.

WEINTRAUB: Matt.

TAIBBI: Oh, God. I think I'm coming down.

WEINTRAUB: You should get some sleep.

TAIBBI: God, Aaron, I'm sorry, I'll let you go. . . . Jesus, how depressing.

WEINTRAUB: It's okay.

TAIBBI: You don't have any downers, do you?

WEINTRAUB: Um . . . I think I've got some Xanax.

TAIBBI: How about a Vicodin? You have any of those left?

WEINTRAUB: Okay, yeah, I'm not going to lie, I've got a few of those left.

TAIBBI: Can I have one?

WEINTRAUB: All right. Come on over.

TAIBBI: I'll be there in fifteen minutes. Shit, Aaron, I'm sorry, I don't know what I was thinking.

WEINTRAUB: It's okay. We've all been there. And hey, remember, you've got that rewrite work for Canal Plus.

TAIBBI: (cheerily) Yeah. The cheese documentary. Thank God.

May Day, May Day
The Soviet United States Holds Its First Annual Holiday Parade

The Soviet Government is the only Government in the world which is unhesitatingly championing the unity and independence, freedom and sovereignty of Turkey and Persia, Afghanistan and China. . . . The oppressed masses sympathize with the Soviet Union because they regard it as their ally in the cause of emancipation from imperialism.

—J. V. Stalin, *Concerning the International Situation,* 1953

We are committed to freedom in Afghanistan, in Iraq, and in a peaceful Palestine. The advance of freedom is the surest strategy to undermine the appeal of terror in the world.

—George W. Bush, last week

Welcome to the U.S.S.A.—the United Soviet States of America. The Winter Palace was officially stormed last week, on the deck of the U.S.S. *Abraham Lincoln.* The proletariat finally has its dictatorship.

I had not planned on watching George Bush's "Top Gun" speech last Thursday night. I didn't think that I could handle it. My mental health has not been so good lately. I hadn't watched television since the second week of the war, because I was beginning to experience painful headaches and hallucinations.

A change in diet and a month away from TV eased the symptoms, but when I broke my vows last week—to watch the NFL draft—they came back in a hurry. Less than an hour into the ESPN broadcast, I was deep into a nightmarish fantasy in which I imagined I was watching NFL coaches select the next Jews for the oven. I'd watch Paul Tagliabue ascend to the podium, and I'd hear: "With the fourth selection in the draft, the New York Jets select . . . Moishe Kimmelman." Cheers, scattered boos, etc.; spindly Polish banker holding up his new red-and-white pajamas for the sporting press. . . .

So I went off TV again. My nights were still strange. Last Tuesday I spent eight dollars in quarters while quietly eating dinner (a Blimpie tuna-fish sub) in a private viewing booth of a porn parlor on Forty-second Street. Four simultaneous screens of grunting, fucking, and sucking: more calming than television. Then, last Thursday night, I tried to go to a National Day of Prayer service at the Calvary Baptist Church on Fifty-seventh Street (it had been recommended by one of the many evangelical news groups I subscribe to), and somehow instead ended up, by means of some frightening unconscious accident, at *The Ellen Degeneres Show* at the Beacon Theater.

Clearly, I needed some rest. So I went home—and made the mistake of turning on the television. A half-hour later, I was watching a shot of George Bush waving goodbye to a throng of adoring sailors dissolve into a black screen, leading to the chilling voiceover that I did *not* imagine: "We now return to *Friends,* already in progress."

It was at that moment that my headaches went away, and I realized that I had woken up in the Soviet Union.

It has become fashionable on the left and in Western Europe to compare the Bush administration to the Nazis. The comparison is not without some superficial merit. In both cases the government is run by a small gang of snickering, stupid thugs whose vision of paradise is full of explosions and beautifully designed prisons. Toss in the desert fatigues motif and the "self-defense" invasion tactic, and there does seem to be a good case.

But it's way off. It's wishful thinking. The Reich only lasted twelve years. The Soviets reigned for seventy-five. They were better at it than the Nazis, and we're better at it than the Russians. Ask anyone who's lived in a communist country, and he'll tell you: modern America is déjà-vu all over again. And if ever there was a Soviet spectacle, it was Bush's speech last week.

Think about it. Huge weapons on display, in foreground and background. The leader who has never fought dressed in full military regalia. Crowds of adoring soldiers and "shock worker" types dressed in colorful costumes, carefully arranged for the cameras. A terrible, excruciatingly dull speech, twenty minutes of incoherent, redundant patriotism (Bush used the words *free* or *freedom* nineteen times in an 1,800-word speech) and chimpanzoid chest-pounding.

On *May Day*.

That was Red Square every year for about seventy straight years. And now it is a most natural fit in our society.

The genius of the Soviet system—and now the genius of ours—was that it appealed not to the hatreds and passions of its people, but to other, more dependable qualities: laziness, banality, drunkenness, cowardice. It gave you a piece of sausage and a bottle of vodka and asked only that you take a few minutes to cheer some pictures of tanks rolling into Prague. Its leaders (with the exception of Stalin) were a succession of Bush-like plodders who were dumber than your chimney-sweep uncle and could barely speak their own language. For vacations it sent you to Bulgaria or Sevastopol because anywhere that was *really* abroad was "not safe." And when you were in Bulgaria, you were thrilled to find that just across the street from your hotel, they had the same "Cafeteria #6" that you had back in Magadan or Vologda or whatever dank hole you came from.

It's no wonder that McDonald's is such a hit in modern Russia.

The genius of the Soviet system was that it was *deep*. It was pervasive; its essence ran through the entire society, and after a while did not need to be imposed from above. The drunken slob collapsed in a Siberian train station was the same person as the ruler of the country. As if through one mouth it spent seventy years babbling voluminously in every direction about nothing, while behind the scenes it quietly lived off slave labor and human flesh. It worshipped talentless celebrities and genuinely preferred its atrocious, flavorless food to the great cuisines of the outside world.

Jennifer Lopez and Tom Clancy would have been perfect fits in the Soviet Union; they would have worn medals in public and ridden the trains for free. The mechanism is a little different here—but the monolithic, irresistible instinct toward mediocrity is the same.

So is the fawning sentimentality, and the preposterous fake idealism. In Soviet times, a man who was afraid to speak frankly on any topic in front of his own children and whose neighbor had disappeared two days before was capable of shedding real tears over the plight of the American Negro, a popular Soviet cause for decades. You see the same thing here in the States: no job, no health insurance, fucked for life by the credit bureaus, but swelling with pride over the sight of an Iraqi child with a candy bar.

Modern observers look back at the early Soviet days and wonder how it is that people could possibly have believed those fantastic tales they read about in the state papers—the lurid descriptions of fascist terrorists and wreckers who conspired to poison reservoirs and turn up rails and put broken glass in sausage in the most faraway, seemingly irrelevant places in Siberia and the far north. The answer probably is that they wanted to believe them. Because that was what was in their hearts. It wasn't a lie that was being put over on them. It *came* from them.

Few sane people survived those early years to pass on genes to the next generation. The ones who did remained in careful hiding for decades while they waited for the beast to rot from within.

That may be our only hope in the States, because the problem isn't removing George Bush. It's the rest of it. This whole thing, all around us, is a package deal. From war all the way back to *Friends,* already in progress.

Heads of Industry

A Maverick Mogul Takes On—and Takes Out—the Big Guys

Wall Street Journal
Page A1
By Steve Liesman
June 6, 2023

Things looked so different twenty years ago.

The year is 2003, the month is June, and Matt Taibbi—a little-known columnist for a doomed New York weekly called *New York Press*—is upset. The Federal Communications Commission (FCC) has handed down a historic 3–2 decision that paves the way for what the upstart reporter perceives to be the monopolization of nearly all the country's media.

The FCC decision eased old restrictions that prevented major corporations from owning television stations and daily newspapers in the same markets. It also raised the limit of maximum household access by television broadcasters to 45 percent, making it possible for large media conglomerates to dream of a day when control over public information would be confined to just a few powerful insiders.

To Taibbi, a self-described "typical alternative media malcontent," the decision spells the beginning of the end of what was to be a spectacularly mediocre career.

Little does he realize that the decision has set into motion a series of events that would land him, twenty years later, in control of a single television station that would make a mockery of the old Nielsen ratings system, frequently attracting the attention of up to 97 percent of America's viewing households.

According to Taibbi, the story of the Guillotine Channel begins just one week after the FCC decision. He was attending a Nets-Spurs NBA final

June 10, 2003, *New York Press.*

match-up with NBC reporter Mike Taibbi—the man he believed at the time to be his father.

"It was in the second quarter, and I knew something was wrong, because Mike's head really wasn't in the game," Taibbi, now fifty-three, recalls. "I was on my way to get some nachos when he told me to sit back down. 'Matt,' he said, 'I have something to tell you. I'm not your real father.'

"I was stunned. I looked at him, and I was like, 'What?' And he said, 'Look, I'm sorry. And the truth is, I don't even *like* basketball.' Then he shook his head, got up, and just left me there. That was the longest game I'd ever seen."

Taibbi shakes his head. "I don't even remember who won."

Soon after, following a lengthy investigation of adoption records, Taibbi made the explosive discovery that his birth father was none other than Fox Chairman Rupert Murdoch. His mother? Imelda Marcos. According to Taibbi, the two had dabbled in Satanism together in the late 1960s, resulting in a secret pregnancy and a hushed-up birth.

Following the revelation, the younger Taibbi suffered a complete nervous breakdown and remained institutionalized for much of the next six years, drifting in and out of catatonia and fugue states while physicians struggled for a cure.

The rest, as they say, is history. Taibbi eventually gained the strength he needed to confront Murdoch, and—to the surprise of everyone—he was ultimately accepted into the Murdoch family. The media giant grew close to his estranged son in his final years of failing health, when the latter tended to Murdoch.

"We played this game called 'Hide the oxygen,'" recalls Taibbi. "Dad would give me this plaintive look from his bed, and that would be my signal to rip off his mask and hide the tank. Then I'd hide somewhere in the penthouse and wait for him to find the buzzer to call the butler. When it was all over, I'd hug him. It was wonderful."

In his last days, Murdoch changed the succession of his company fortune, thrusting the older Taibbi ahead of the previously anointed heir, Lachlan

Murdoch. In 2013, Taibbi assumed full control of News Corp, which then reached some 68 percent of American households.

The shake-up sent shock waves through the industry. Advertisers responded diffidently to Taibbi's Nero-esque early programming decisions, which, as most citizens will recall, included the use of his news networks to promote a failed presidential bid by a police horse as well as the reality show, *Survivor: AIDS*. In response, industry insiders quickly circled the wagons, pressuring banks to call in News Corp loans and influence Washington to recall News Corp satellite licenses. The word was out in the boardrooms of America: Taibbi had to go.

It was then that Taibbi hit upon the masterstroke of his career, engineering an escape from his predicament that would leave him the most powerful man in America for a generation to come.

He negotiated an unusual buyout with his competitors: in exchange for his complete interests in News Corp, Taibbi asked for an apparent pittance.

"I asked for a single cable channel with a permanent license, one million dollars, a staff of ten, and an old Buick Electra," he recalls, grinning. "Plus a little paperwork."

The "paperwork" was a buyout contract to be signed by each and every one of the employees of News Corp, General Electric, Viacom, Disney, Time/Warner, Paramount, and the New York Times Company. Buried in the contract was a small clause that made each employee pledge "full and enthusiastic" cooperation in any future reality programming Taibbi might launch.

"He had every single media employee in the country crowd into an airplane hangar in St. Louis to sign the contract," recalls FAIR founder and media critic Jeff Cohen. "It took weeks."

With the signatures collected, Taibbi launched the Guillotine Channel. For the premiere, Taibbi assigned ten crack Russian mobster employees to arrest Fox News chief Roger Ailes, drive him to the TGC studios in Burbank, and, using a restored eighteenth-century French guillotine, chop off his head on live television. The privilege of releasing the rope was awarded to a Hispanic single mother in Los Angeles, whose application was chosen via a televised lottery. Due to the buyout contract, the entire arrangement was completely legal.

The channel was an overnight success. Advance response for the second televised event was so enormous that Taibbi arranged to have the beheading of aging talk-show legend Bill O'Reilly aired on a pay-per-view basis. Some 165 million Americans paid $119 to watch the historic broadcast, which featured uproarious live commentary by prisoners at the supermax prison facility in Wallens Ridge, Virginia.

Subsequent programming innovations increased ratings still further. "I'm not sure who came up with the idea of dressing up the victims in French aristocratic costumes, but that was clearly a key element of our early success," Taibbi says now.

"The sight of Michael Eisner wearing that wig and that pancake makeup, being dragged to the stage in a silver brocade waistcoat. . . . That was clearly a landmark moment in the history of American television. I usually let the viewers do the work, but for that one, I got to apply the mole."

Today, the Guillotine Channel is by far the most popular network on television, and plans are underway to launch a series of spin-off channels, including Guillotine 2 and Guillotine Family. In the last quarter, profits of TGC corporation were estimated at $4 billion a day.

Industry insiders are quick to note the irony of its success.

"The argument for deregulation twenty years ago was that, regardless of access, the networks still had to attract viewers," says Ari Glomberg of the American Enterprise Institute. "The idea was that the preferences of the viewing public would act as the natural check on the power of the media companies, *instead* of government regulation."

Glomberg laughs. "The companies never foresaw that their behavior would make America hate them so much that something like Guillotine could come along and wipe them out with a single frequency. It turns out the market really does work."

Elongate Thy Foe

In Search of the 50,000-Word Enemy

I've decided to apply for a civilian job at the Pentagon. I want to be the guy that comes up with each day's description of the counterinsurgent Iraqi enemy for press releases.

Whoever they have now is good, no question about it. I've been a fan of his work since the first week of May. Under his tutelage, the average length in print of the described Iraqi enemy has jumped from about four or five words in May ("pro-Saddam Baath Party holdouts"), to about ten to fifteen words in June ("Forces loyal to the regime of the deposed dictator Saddam Hussein"), to the current twenty to twenty-five words (see below).

I believe I can do better. I am certain that, put in charge of the program, I can get the description up to 200 words by September, and more than 1,000 by the New Year. In fact, I can envision a time when the capsule description of the Iraqi enemy can be stretched to the length of a Henry James novel. Once we do that, the might of the United States can no longer be questioned.

The evolution of the description of the post-victory Iraqi enemy has been messy, marked by fits and starts and dead ends. I've actually been saving print descriptions of the enemy like baseball cards, organizing them according to length. As of July 3, I have almost a complete set in the range of one to twenty-seven words. Looking back on the list now, it's pretty clear why some advanced to become part of the evolutionary picture, while others went the way of the dinosaurs. Here's a quick review of some of the major players in the market:

"Loyalists" (one word): In the aftermath of the first real wave of anti-U.S. attacks, about a month after we declared victory, a few scattered newspapers began experimenting with this one-word characterization, figuring that readers were educated enough by then to know what they were talking about. Previously, the attackers had mostly been "Saddam Hussein loyalists," "Baath Party

---

July 8, 2003, *New York Press.*

loyalists," "pro-Saddam loyalists," etc. My favorite "loyalist" tab to date, incidentally, is "die-hard loyalists of Saddam Hussein" (Newark *Star-Ledger*), which
actually recalls another promising favorite, "Saddam-regime die-hards" (American Forces Press Service).

It made a kind of sense that we could drop all of the modifiers and just call
the bad guys "loyalists," but when the papers tried that a month or so ago, it
somehow came out sounding too Belfast, too Generalissimo Francisco Franco,
and it was quickly dropped. I haven't seen "loyalist" standing alone for weeks.

Two other one-word candidates for the job have yet to play themselves
out fully: *terrorists* and *Iraqis*. I'm actually not sure why the Pentagon didn't
go with *terrorists* from the start. That's what I would have done. If I were in
charge, all of Iraq would be filled with terrorists: terrorists demonstrating in
the square in Fajullah, terrorists demanding water and electricity, "terrorist
elementary schools," "terrorist libraries," "terrorist swimming pools." Had
we gone with that from the start, we could have just shot anything that
moved and never had to worry. But this insistence on dividing Iraq up into
good Iraqis and bad loyalist Iraqis has hopelessly complicated the picture.

Iraqis is a possibility the Arab press is dangerously close to exploring. Already many Arab news services describe the attackers as mere *Iraqi fighters*
(this designation has also appeared on Reuters). Needless to say, that will
never work as a long-term solution here in the United States. Not only is it
seditious, but it's also boring. There are better possibilities to explore:

**"Baath Party activists loyal to the deposed Iraqi dictator Saddam Hus-
sein"** (eleven words): This was actually a very early designation by the wacky
folks at the *Sunday Telegraph,* but it foreshadowed later developments. It was
innovative on several fronts: it told a story (about Saddam being deposed), it
was pleasingly long, and it made a value judgment about the motives of the
attackers, calling them "activists." The whole idea of the anti-U.S. attackers as
"activists" was echoed later on by numerous papers that pointed a finger at
"remnants of the Baath Party movement," a description that draped Saddam
Hussein bureaucrats in the garb of Berkeley Free-Speechers or marchers on
Selma.

Needless to say, the whole movement/activist idea never stuck, although the concept of "remnants" definitely has. *Remnants,* for me, recalls body parts, bits of feet and fingers left after the blast, and this is exactly why this word works so well in this context. *Remnants* reminds readers that the enemy is part of an extinguished whole, which is why *remnants* continues to figure in the mix of most descriptions even today.

"Iraqis who remain loyal to Saddam Hussein and Islamic militants from other countries eager to kill Americans" (seventeen words): From Knight-Ridder services a few weeks back. I like this one not just because of the addition of imported Islamic fighters (there were hints of this even early on), but also because those militants were not just militants, but militants *eager to kill Americans.* Not angry or desperate enough to kill, but actually *eager* to kill, like a bunch of little bearded, drooling Draculas clawing at the gates.

"Remnants of Saddam Hussein's Baath Party, anti-American Islamic fighters coming into Iraq and common criminals" (fifteen words): This was from CNN a few weeks ago. The addition of "and common criminals" was a major advance in the genre, "criminals" presumably being code for "everybody else." The foundation for a Balzacian gallery of human types has been laid; from here it's not hard to see a future in which we find ourselves fighting a narrative tale of the whole developing human race in all its imperfections. All that's missing is a plot to hang it on, and the president himself took the first steps in that direction just last week:

"Former Baath Party and security officials who will stop at nothing to regain their power and their privilege enjoyed under the deposed Hussein dictatorship" (twenty-four words): A hybrid of a Bush quote and the reporting of the American Forces Press Service. By now, with the beginnings of a plot and three main suspects (loyalists, foreign terrorists, and criminals) to draw from, we can easily take this Bush formula and expand the description to fifty or sixty words. Here's how I might do it:

"The attacks were carried out by former Baath Party officials who will stop at nothing to regain their power and their privilege enjoyed under the deposed Hussein dictatorship, anti-American Islamic militants who are coming in from other countries and are eager to kill Americans, and common criminals seeking to sabotage Iraq's transformation to democracy."

This is still too tight for my tastes. I still see a lot of room to move here:

"Once again stopping at nothing to regain the power and privilege they enjoyed under the deposed Hussein dictatorship, former Baath Party officials joined the sufferers of Aarskog syndrome, foreign terrorists who are coming in from other countries and are eager to kill Americans, a brilliant scientist who underwent a dramatic change in character after falling into an acid bath in an accident that left one half of his face disfigured for life, common criminals seeking to undermine Iraq's transformation to democracy, a curious man in a bowler hat who speaks only in short beeps, and the rapper Ol' Dirty Bastard in plotting a series of attacks against American forces currently maintaining order in the free Iraqi state."

That's just one possibility. Believe me, this thing has legs. All I want is a chance. Mr. Rumsfeld, I'm waiting by the phone.

3

DEAN-A-PALOOZA
A Front-runner Takes to the Skies

Coffee.
Cinnamon rolls.
Be a fan of breakfast again.
    —slogan for Holiday Inn Express. The commercial shows a crowd of
    crisply dressed businesspeople cheering ecstatically as a hotel worker
                carries a plate of cinnamon rolls to a buffet table.

Chicago, Illinois—forget about Texas, where we've just flown in from; this is, hands-down, the hottest political event I've ever attended. The penultimate stop on Howard Dean's "Sleepless Summer" tour is a rally held on the roof of a convention center where, a few floors below, the Communications Workers of America are holding their annual conference.

It is boiling up here. I have no idea what the actual temperature is, but the effect of the sun on the concrete rooftop is incredible. I'm reminded of something I read in a history textbook once about Ivan the Terrible herding prisoners of war from his conquest of Pskov into Red Square, and roasting

A version of this piece appeared in the October 6, 2003, *The Nation*.

them alive on a giant frying pan. Like all the events on the tour, this one is massively attended, mostly by what appear to be twenty- and thirtysomething college graduates. The thousands of bodies all crammed together on the roof create a double-sizzling effect. On the cobalt-blue dress shirts of those few in attendance not dressed in white Dean T-shirts (the Steve Jobs–ish denim-colored dress shirt and khaki pants are a characteristic costume of the Dean supporter), you can actually watch the sweat stains expanding by the second.

Far to the front, the candidate, also dressed in blue, is beginning his speech. "We're going to have some fun at the president's expense here today . . .," he begins, setting off a ripple of applause.

Get rid of George Bush. Be a fan of breakfast again.

I frown and scribble in my notebook: "Chicago. 5."

This is the tenth time I have heard Dean's speech in the last three days, and I've developed a code system to describe it. Dean's stump speech has fifteen or sixteen interchangeable parts that vary slightly from venue to venue, but contain the same punchlines each time. After the third time I heard the govenor speak, I broke the speech down and numbered each of the parts, memorizing the numbers so that I could record each speech simply by writing down the numbers in sequence. My notes for Portland, Oregon, for instance, read, "PORTLAND: 4-5-1-6-3-7-8-9-10-11-15-12-13." The abbreviated Town Hall address the next morning, on the other hand, reads, "SPOKANE: 7-9-2-6-3-10."

There isn't space enough to set down the entire code here, but here are some examples. 7 is the Iraq section, one of Dean's favorites and one of the most closely scrutinized parts of his address; it begins with the candidate showing "toughness" by explaining why he was in favor of the first Gulf War and the invasion of Afghanistan ("They killed 3,000 of our people and I felt it was a matter of national security"), then moves on to emphasize in martial tones that, as commander-in-chief, President Dean *would not hesitate* to send troops abroad to defend our country. 7 then ends in an applause line: "But I would *never* send our sons and daughters to die overseas without telling the truth about why we were going!"

1, usually the opener of the Dean speech, is about balancing the budget and concludes with a small rhetorical flourish: "If you want to balance the budget, you'd better elect a Democrat, because Republicans don't know how to handle money!" [Applause.]

9 outlines a theory of nonconfrontational foreign policy, which contains the line "We won the Cold War and didn't fire a shot," and elicits cheers with a call for a return to "high moral purpose" in our international behavior.

10 is the bit some of the reporters refer to as "The List." It's about health insurance and it finishes by asking why, if we're the most powerful nation in the world, we can't do what "the British and the French and the Germans and the Japanese and the Italians and the Irish and the Israelis and the Canadians" have done, that is, insure their citizens. The applause in *10* usually kicks in somewhere around the Italians, and if it gets loud enough the candidate will sometimes skip the last phrase: "Even the Costa Ricans!"

(The latter phenomenon first came to my attention at the first stop on the tour, in Falls Church, Virginia: when the crowd wiped Dean out in the middle of the Canadians, *American Prospect* reporter Garance Franke-Ruta tapped me on the shoulder and said, "Hey, he forgot Costa Rica!")

When Dean in Chicago moved from *5* to *3* ("This president has run up a $3 trillion deficit . . ."), I split the roof and ducked into the air-conditioned lobby. There was a credit-card-operated Starbucks vending machine there that quickly robbed me of two bucks when I tried to get a bottle of water. In the language of this campaign, I apparently lacked "connectedness" with the machine. Hungover and in a foul mood after an extraordinary night in San Antonio involving some Dean staffers (more on that later), I punched the machine with my fist.

"Bitch!" I screamed. "Give me my fucking money!"

Just then I noticed that someone was watching me. A bookish-looking girl in her mid-twenties was successfully pulling a soda out of the neighboring

credit-card-activated Pepsi machine. She was carrying a notebook and looking at me sympathetically. "Are you okay?" she said. "Do you want me to get
you one from this machine?"

I unclenched my fist and tried to smile. "No," I said. "That's okay. Thanks,
though."

She smiled. "That's okay," she said, then stuck out her hand. "I'm Olivia.
Are you covering this?"

I then noticed that she was looking at my name tag. It identified me as
Press, but the name was wrong. In one of the additional humiliations of that
morning, the Dean campaign had failed to supply me with a credential for
the CWA convention. Every one of the other forty or so journalists on the
trip got a personalized press nameplate, including reporters from such publications as *Modern Physician* and the *Memphis Flyer;* only the *New York Press* had
been overlooked. As a result, I had had to take a substitute tag from a Dean
staffer named David Horwich, and that's whose name was pinned to my
chest. It was a totally accidental thing, but it was adding to my karmic problems. I shook her hand.

"David Horwich," I said.

"Olivia Cobiskey. Nice to meet you," she said. She explained that she was
a freelancer who covered politics for some Middle Eastern newspapers; she
had lived in Israel, had some contacts over there, was just starting out in the
business. She asked me who I wrote for.

I looked around, then looked back at her. *"Guns and Ammo,"* I said quietly.
Why not? The governor had a good rating from the NRA.

"Really?" she said.

"Yeah," I said. "The governor's actually on our next cover. He did this
spread where he's . . . shooting a pig with a bazooka."

"That doesn't sound like Howard Dean," she said, frowning.

"You don't know the governor," I said. "When we were doing the shoot, we
kept proposing things that he could shoot with the bazooka. We were like,
'How about a straw target? How about a mannequin?' And he was like, 'How
about a pig?' "

"And you were like—a pig it is?"

"Exactly," I said. "I mean, he didn't even hesitate."

"Wow," she said, laughing.

Ten seconds later the pig story was in the past and she was commenting that *Guns and Ammo* must pay very well. "All of those trade magazines . . .," she said. "That's great work if you can get it."

"Yeah," I said. "And the sports mags are great, too."

She shook her head. "Maybe I should go into sports," she said.

"It can't hurt," I said. "You might as well try."

We went back outside to catch the speech. While Dean in the background pushed through *12* and *13*—"Blah blah blah *John Ashcroft!*" [hooting and boos], "blah blah blah *send him back to Crawford, Texas!*" [cheers and raucous applause]—we exchanged contact numbers. I told her to look me up if she was ever in New York. She said she would, then disappeared into the crowd.

I went back to taking notes on the speech. A few minutes later, Governor Howard Dean dealt me a very big surprise.

The previous day, we'd flown in the morning from Spokane to Austin, Texas, where the governor was scheduled to make a brief appearance at a fundraiser before hopping on a bus to a rally in San Antonio.

An old friend of mine, Kevin McElwee, who now lives in Dallas, had arranged to drive down to meet me at the Austin event, then drive me to San Antonio. When I arrived with the rest of the Sleepless Summer contingent at the site of the fundraiser (a restaurant on the outskirts of town called the Ruta Maya), Kevin was already there waiting for me.

"Hey," he said. "The cops were just here. They just rustled out a squatter across the street with shotguns."

I looked to where he was pointing. Right behind the two Sleepless Summer buses were a pair of squad cars with flashing lights. About fifty yards away I could see a crude canvas roof spread out over a pair of trees. There was an African style tent city not seventy yards from the site of the governor's fundraiser.

I mentioned to one of the reporters that there were cops with shotguns sweeping a group of squatters across the street. He nodded, then quickly disappeared into the Ruta Maya, looking bored.

Traveling with a huge pack of nationally respected journalists is a very funny thing. At least two or three times during the course of the trip, something objectively amazing but irrelevant to the immediate assignment of the Sleepless Summer tour would happen right under the noses of twenty or thirty reporters, and they not only wouldn't budge—they wouldn't even see it.

Sometimes the commotion would even have something to do with Dean, and they still wouldn't move. The best example of that had been the previous afternoon on the tarmac of the airport in Portland, Oregon. We had just finished watching an enormous Dean rally at Portland State University—about 5,000 people turned out, an enormous number for a candidate at this stage of the election process—and we were now in line, waiting to get into the campaign plane, nauseatingly dubbed the Grassroots Express by the Dean staffers.

(The plane inside was decorated with plastic tufts of grass. "At least it's better than John Edwards," cracked Craig Gilbert of the *Milwaukee Journal-Sentinel*. "His bus in Iowa is called the Real Solutions Express.")

Due to post-9/11 security issues, the process of boarding the charter plane required a lengthy TSA-mandated search procedure, which itself is interesting because George Bush apparently has a waiver of these procedures for his campaign trips, allowing him to save time and travel to more stops per day.

But that's another story. The issue in this case is that the wait on the hot tarmac was a real pain in the ass, and most of the reporters, when they were in line, had little on their minds other than getting the whole thing over with as quickly as possible and getting into the plane to wolf down their campaign-provided bag lunches.

I was at the back of the line in Portland when I noticed the candidate standing off by himself in front of the nose of the plane. Against a background of a blue sky, he was standing before campaign staff photographer John Pettite and making a series of grotesque contortions—pointing variously at the camera and off to the side, making a rapid-fire series of painful-looking grins, puffing out his chest. It took me about two seconds to realize where I'd seen this act before. Howard Dean was selling me a tape deck in Queens!

"I don't want to sell you anything," I said. "I'm just CRAAA-ZEEE!"

All the reporters in the back of the line whipped around and stared at me in plain disapproval. Only Sandeep Kaushnik of the Seattle paper called the *Stranger* laughed. He and I talked it over for a minute and decided to go see what the governor was doing.

It turned out that Dean was having photos taken for the cover of a book he has coming out soon. Pettite later told me that campaign finance rules prohibited Dean from having the picture taken at an actual campaign event like the Portland rally. "That would be a use of campaign money for a private venture," Pettite explained. "We had to do it after one of the events."

The sight of the governor up close in midpose is an image I won't likely forget soon. Without any prompting from Pettite, he was feverishly muttering snippets from his stump speech in the middle of the Crazy Eddie gesturing. "We're going to have some fun at the president's expense today . . . heh heh. . . . We're going to take America back. . . ."

Pettite snapped away. The governor looked deranged. It didn't seem to bother him that Sandeep and I were standing there, taking notes. By the time we got back to the line, most of the reporters were on the plane.

Anyway, in Austin the reporters were apparently not interested in the squatter fracas. Kevin and I crossed the street and found a burned-out homeless couple, covered in scabs and dirt and with about four teeth apiece, sitting anxiously on a pair of ancient lawn chairs. They had a small pup tent that was covered in duct-tape patches, and the man—sunburned and with a scraggly beard and glasses—was playing glumly with a hyperactive pit bull puppy.

"Nice dog," I said, walking up.

"Thanks," the man said. "His name's Scooby."

"Doobie?" I said.

"*Scooby,*" the woman said. "Like Scooby-Doo. 'Cept he's Scooby Wicker."

We introduced ourselves. John and Cynthia Wicker were originally from Michigan and had come down to Austin to look for work. Somewhere in there was an epic tale of a traveling booze-case marriage, but we didn't have time to hear it.

"What happened?" I asked, pointing to a trio of shotgun-wielding cops in the distance.

"That guy over there—in that tent—he hit me with a hatchet," Cynthia said, pointing.

"Warn't a hatchet," interrupted John. "It was a big ole stick."

"Whatever," she said. "A big ole stick. That guy is crazy. He's always coming over here and bothering us. At night, you know, he's always stabbing holes in our tent with a knife. You can see the patches."

I could.

There were three groups of tents. I pointed in the direction of the cops. "He lives over there?" I asked.

"He lives in this one"—she pointed to a giant, relatively luxurious tent behind me—"*and* over there. He's moved over there lately because there're some elderly people he can take advantage of."

"Takes their stuff," assented John.

The cops, meanwhile, were walking over from the old people's tents toward the big luxury tent. Trailing behind them was a surprisingly clean-cut-looking man in jeans and a blue polo shirt, and he was in handcuffs.

"He claims he works for the CIA," John said. "Also said he was in the marines and fought in the Gulf War. He's always telling some kind of story."

"He buries his weapons," Cynthia said. "His knife—he's got it buried." She stood up and called out to the police. "You've got to DIG!" she screamed. "He keeps that stuff BURIED!"

"No work down here at all," John muttered. "It's all taken by Mexicans. Ain't no unions down here except the electrician's union."

"And you're not an electrician, so that sucks," I said.

"Nah," he said. "If I was, I'd join, but I'm not."

"Who called the police?" I said.

"Well, we did. We had to. I mean, he was getting really violent," Cynthia said. "But they're not here to kick us off. The owner of the property said we have two more months to stay on."

Meanwhile the police were drifting in our direction. As they did, the suspect started walking, crablike and sideways but still in handcuffs, back in the direction of the old people's tent.

"Officers!" he called out. "I'm just walking behind you here, this way! Just so you know!"

"Okay," said the one female cop, who still had her shotgun drawn.

"Well, I'll let you go," I said. "You see, there's a guy running for president here, he's giving a speech right across the street there."

"No shit," said John.

"Yeah," I said. "Well, good luck."

"Thanks," they said.

On the way out, Kevin and I nodded to the cops. "Officers," I said.

They nodded. Behind me I heard the puppy yipping at the cops. Back at the event, Dean was already speaking. I didn't go inside, but the speech was being broadcast on a loudspeaker outside the restaurant. When we got there, he was just settling into 4.

"We need *jobs* in America. We've got to build roads and infrastructure, and invest in renewable energy," he was saying. "And we've got to bring broadband Internet communications to even the most remote parts of America, so that those communities can share in the economic development of this country."

I raced back across the street, where the cops were finishing up with the Wickers.

"Forget something?" John said.

"Nah," I said. "I was just listening to this guy's speech. He was saying that we need to bring broadband Internet communications to the country, so that there would be more jobs. I was just wondering if you thought that was a good idea."

"Jeez, I don't know," John said. "I guess it would be nice. I think they got that—what is it?"

"Broadband Internet communications," I said.

"Well, I don't know," John said. He turned to Cynthia. "Do they have that at the Salvation Army center?"

"No," she said. "They don't have anything. All they got is this job training counselor who don't do shit. You apply for all these jobs, and they don't even take your messages. Now there's a place you ought to do a story on. We stayed there like three months."

"It was four," John said.

"It's like jail," she said. "Lockdown at seven o'clock. Full of black people, all dealing drugs left and right. The guy who runs the place, he once had this restaurant deliver all this fancy food there, and then he took it right out the back, loaded it up, and took it home. Probably ate it all himself."

"There's a place you ought to do a story on," John agreed.

" 'Course, it's nice that he wants to do that, this guy," Cynthia said, pointing in Dean's direction. "But it'll never come to anything. We're moving back to Michigan anyway."

"Going to go back and work in the fields. I got an uncle," John said.

"Well, I've got to get back," I said.

"Thanks for coming by. Thanks for listening," Cynthia said. "And tell that guy there's peoples living in a tent over here."

"Will do," I said.

"I'm voting for Bush anyway," John said. "At least he's *doing* something."

It is probably already possible to speak of the existence of a "Howard Dean problem" in liberal America. The outlines of the problem are as follows: vast numbers of people, horrified by George Bush and desperate for a positive change, have geared up this election season to throw their weight behind anything resembling a human being. Along comes Howard Dean, a well-spoken, obviously intelligent man who opposes the war in Iraq before it is politically expedient to do so, bluntly calls George Bush by all the names he deserves, and quickly builds an impressive insurgent candidacy, largely on his own, through the strength of a remarkable Internet version of a word-of-mouth campaign. To many, the choice seems obvious.

But thirsty people can have faulty vision, and when your eyes have burned you enough times, you begin to fear the mirage more than the thirst. And therein, for Howard Dean, lies the problem.

In the past six months the very success of Dean's campaign has become, for some, an indictment against him. Anything this popular has to be phony. Iconoclasts of all stripes have lined up to attack him, including voices of the left like Alexander Cockburn and Norman Solomon. On the liberal side, critics have pointed to his refusal to support cuts in military spending, some seeming inconsistencies in his campaign finance positions, his support of the death penalty in some cases, and his refusal to energetically disavow the corporate economy.

These criticisms have provoked a discussion over just how much may be overlooked in the effort to unseat George Bush. This debate—the Howard Dean problem—has gathered such redundant steam in recent months that one now sees on the Internet articles with such extraordinary titles as "A Case Against the Case Against the Case for Howard Dean."

Six months ago, when I first started investigating the Democratic candidates for 2004, Dean seemed to me the only one whom I would trust not to steal my silverware. Now I'm not so sure—but that might not be Dean's fault. As I found out on the Sleepless Summer tour, no candidate with "momentum" looks good up close; and the realities of modern campaigning make it hard to spot a mirage, even at close range.

The first axiom of campaign journalism, one that should be memorized by any reporter who tries it, goes as follows: *Substance is impossible.*

Dean's supporters almost universally declare that they were attracted to the campaign because the governor is "different," "not the same old thing," and "not a typical politician." Literally dozens of people I talked to along the way had the same feeling about him, ranging from teenage students (Maggie

Desmond, seventeen, of Waukesha, Wisconsin; she was with the "Waukesha H.S. Liberals Club") to lawyers (Judie Rettelle, a volunteer manning the press entrance at the Fall Church event) to smart young filmmakers (Faith Radle, thirty-one, of San Antonio, who produced a cool indie film called *Speeder Kills*). Even Cecil Andrus, the amiable and charming former governor of Idaho, insisted that Dean was a different kind of political creature.

"I just don't go for those stereotypical politicians, the kind in the Senate," he told me, on the tarmac in Boise. "You know, with the. . . ." He made a gesture.

"With the hairdos?" I asked.

Andrus, who's bald, laughed. "Well, if they've got hair at all, they're suspect," he said.

But it was hard not to notice that all of the people surrounding Dean were veterans of the same-old, same-old Democrats that willed into being the Ralph Nader phenomenon. Dean campaign manager Joe Trippi is a longtime Democratic political consultant who has worked on the campaigns of Edward Kennedy, Walter Mondale, Gary Hart, and even current Dean opponent Richard Gephardt. (In the latter campaign, Trippi was one of a group of "killer" consultants, along with people like David Doak, Bill Carrick, and Robert Shrum, whose attack-dog political strategizing was immortalized in Richard Ben Cramer's book on the 1988 campaign, *What It Takes.*) Trip coordinator Matt Vogel worked for Gore, as did Kelly McMahon, Dana Singer, Aram Kailer, and numerous other Dean operatives appearing at one time or another on the Sleepless Summer tour.

Patricia Enright, Dean's bubbly communications director, is a veteran of the Clinton White House, where she once held the title of public affairs chief. It took about eight minutes into the trip for every reporter on board to start referring to Enright as "Trish." In her early thirties, Trish reminded me of one of those bawdy girls you knew in college who could handle herself in a game of quarters. Her signature move on the tour was to bend over laughing mid-conversation and rest her head—*Oh, God, that's so funny!*—on your shoulder. By Seattle, the fourth stop on the trip, there were Trish-prints on the shoulders of pretty much every reporter on the plane. I didn't get mine, though, until San Antonio, when a group of reporters and staffers went out for drinks on the sanitized, overpriced Riverwalk restaurant strip after Dean's late-night rally.

I was already in a Irish bar called Durty Nelly's, drinking with Kevin, when Trish, Vogel, and *New York Times* reporter Jodi Wilgoren came in. We all stood next to each other, but the three of them were carrying on some kind of wonky conversation on their own, and we didn't butt in. But after about ten minutes I noticed that a beered-up post-frat-boy type was accosting Trish, blasting her with Rush-Limbaughisms about liberals and how we didn't understand that it was America's right to dominate the world. "That's your PROBLEM," he kept saying, accenting the "PROB" with index finger thrust to within a few inches of the Dean staffer's forehead.

Enright was being polite, but the guy just wouldn't go away. Vogel, a mealy young ex–investment banker who appears to sleep in a blue blazer and tie, was standing back and trying not to get involved. "Liberals" do not fight in bars.

I leaned over and nodded at the guy. "Hey, Chet," I said. "Why so loud?"

"Who are you calling Chet?" he said. "I'm Greg."

"Whatever," I said.

"You on the campaign, too?" he asked.

"No," I said. "I'm a reporter."

He snorted. "What do journalists make, about fifty grand?"

I *wished*. "That's about right," I said.

"I make one-twenty. I'm a food-service manager," he said, pounding his chest.

"Good for you," I said. "Your lover must be proud."

Before I knew it, he was standing in between Kevin and me, and a full-scale, drawn-out drunken shouting match was underway.

"You liberals just don't *get it*," he was saying. "Look at what we do for people around the world. Look at Nigeria. You think those people would be living the way they are if we weren't there? They don't know how good they have it."

I frowned. Nigeria? What the fuck was he talking about? "What, working waist-deep in a chemical swamp for Shell Oil, for a dollar a week or whatever?" I said.

"You see, that's just what I'm talking about!" he said. "They're lucky to have Shell Oil there!"

This went on and on for about an hour. I tried about a dozen times to wrap it up, at one point unsuccessfully insisting for twenty minutes that I wasn't waiting with bated breath for Hillary Clinton to run for president.

I leaned over to Trish and Vogel. "Hey, I can't get rid of this guy," I said.

Trish did the shoulder thing. "Sorry, hon!" she said, and quickly went back to Vogel-Wilgoren. You could have calculated the circulation of the *New York Press* very accurately just by measuring the speed with which she threw off shoulder-anchor. Cut loose, I drifted back to Ditto-head.

But a few minutes later, our friend, who said he was down from Dallas on a business trip, suggested that he might call his friend, a coke dealer, and get "a couple of eightballs" so that we could really argue it out. I'm not the biggest coke fan, but the suggestion definitely changed the tenor of the conversation.

"Just let me call my guy," he said, dialing his cell phone. "This shit is *pure*. Trust me. We'll all get along real good after that."

"Well," I said. "You know the old joke about coke. A Jew is in a stall doing lines with Hitler, and he's saying, 'You know, you had some really *good ideas* back there.'"

"Exactly," he said. He nodded in the direction of Trish, who was leaving with Vogel and Wilgoren. "You know her?"

"Not really," I said.

"Man, I'd fuck her," he said. "I really would. I'd fuck her."

"I probably would, too," I said. "But the paper I work for isn't big enough."

He looked back at his phone. "My boy should be calling back any minute," he said.

We waited around for what seemed like an eternity, during which time Greg violently shook both of our hands about a dozen times. Finally I got pissed. "Where's your boy?" I said.

"Shit," he said. "He'll call soon. I *promise!*"

Election season, it appears, is fully of empty promises. "We're out of here," I said finally.

"Wait," he said. "I've got a bunch of valiums up at the Marriott . . . let's go back up there."

That would be a great way to go, I thought: dead from a suicide cocktail in a San Antonio Marriott, an expletive and Hillary Clinton's name on my lips. Feeling the onset of a bad mood, I declined and went back to my own hotel, where Kevin and I spent a half-hour watching the enormous four-inch fanged insect *Hemiptera belostomatidae* swim back and forth with the speed of a human child across the hotel pool, until we finally passed out.

A few hours later, I joined up with the campaign again, and headed off to Chicago. I fell asleep quickly on the plane, but was woken up soon after, as I had been several times on the trip, by the sight of the remarkable Wilgoren climbing over my seat.

Wilgoren is about five-foot-three, built like Joe Klecko, and the very picture of a pushy, glibly shoptalking, print news machine. The *New York Times* ought to be very proud of her. In every situation, she pushed her way to the front, barking questions and comments in all directions and generally planting the *NYT* flag in the middle of anything that smelled like news. At least twice on the trip I had been roused from a sound horizontal sleep across three airplane seats to see her climbing over me. Each time she sat atop the seat in front of me, leaving her gigantic ass to dangle over the edge, directly in my face. Each of these instances was a signal to me that Howard Dean was making his daily plunge into the press section, an event the *NYT* naturally had to have the best seats in the house for.

Much has been made of Dean's alleged brusqueness and discomfort with the press. He has been called "angry" and "shrill" in his media portraits, and it is a generally accepted legend that Dean and reporters simply do not like each other. This was, in fact, a central thesis of Jonathan Alter's *Newsweek* cover story. Among other things, Alter wrote: "Dean is no favorite of working reporters, who generally like their candidates funny and solicitous." Alter added pithily: "As do voters."

No one on the plane saw this. In fact, many of the reporters on the Sleepless Summer tour commented upon the absence of the "angry, shrill" Dean of legend. "I don't know where they got that from," said Jackson Baker of the *Memphis Flyer*, one of the true nice guys on the place. "I just don't see it."

Neither did I. From where I sat, Dean appeared friendly, composed, and at ease with the press, often keeping his cool and his wits in extraordinary circumstances. The very geography of the 737 made the daily plunges difficult logistical tasks. In order to be fair and give all the reporters equal access, Dean couldn't just stand at the front of the press section and hold forth; he had to begin at the front of the aisle and gradually, bit by bit, make his way to the back, bringing all the press with him. He'd keep his head on a swivel, answering questions in rapid-fire succession ("Yes, I speak a little Spanish. . . . The difference between civil unions and gay marriage, that's where the religious question comes in. . . . We're going to run a national campaign right from the outset. . . ."), while at floor level, his feet would be continually moving here a step, there a half-step forward. It was a subtle act to maintain.

In some cases Dean's attempts to reach out to the press were rendered torturous by the realities of air travel. In one instance, in a scene that would be endlessly crowed over by reporters afterward, the captain of the Grassroots Express, Dave Gates, commanded his passengers to return to their seats in anticipation of turbulence. Dean shot a look back toward his seat at the front of the plane, but he was too slow: in an instant, the enormously tall, gangly, and curly-headed *Rolling Stone* reporter John Colapinto swept in and cleared a seat in the middle of the row next to Dean.

I remember this very clearly because the jean jacket Colapinto took off the seat he ended up tossing behind his back, and it landed in my lap. Dean, not wanting to be impolite, slid into the seat. Colapinto then jumped into the aisle seat, sandwiching the candidate between himself and *Modern Physician* reporter Liz Beckley.

Dean was now in a serious pickle. Apart from the two reporters on either side, he was faced with half-standing, tape-recorder-wielding *Journal-Sentinel* reporter Gilbert in the row in front of him, while the *Flyer*'s Baker was behind him, holding a tape recorder over his head. Next to Baker, also behind Dean, was one of the candidate's media handlers, Courtney O'Donnell (whom one married reporter, who shall remain nameless, described as having "the best rack of any spokesperson of this or any campaign"), quietly supervising the situation.

Each of the reporters quickly began firing questions at them, each question irrelevant to the previous one. Gilbert was asking about campaign strategy, Beckley about health insurance, and no matter how Dean answered any of these questions, Colapinto would interrupt to grill the candidate on his rock 'n' roll preferences. "Who are your top five bands?" he asked.

"Uh, well, there's Buffalo Springfield . . ." Dean began.

"How are you going to pay for your health insurance plan?" Beckley asked.

"Well . . ." Dean began.

"What about guitarists?" Colapinto asked. "Which guitarists do you like?"

"Well, there's Clapton . . ." Dean said.

By now I was watching the scene very closely. Dean clearly had realized that in the position he was in, it would be impossible to make eye contact with each of the surrounding reporters as he fended off their questions. He therefore decided to keep his eyes focused directly on the in-the-upright-position tray table in front of him. It was a remarkable scene, a candidate for the presidency, staring desperately at a tray table, muttering out a seemingly random series of phrases: "I was one of those who was disappointed when Dylan went electric. . . . We can't take on the insurers just yet because they will kill any initiative. . . . I think voters in the South will respond to the message. . . ."

After this performance, Colapinto, the poor bastard, became a figure of much amusement in the press pool. At a bar in San Antonio the night after that scene, some of the reporters and Dean staffers deliriously relived the incident.

"Duh, what guitarists do you like?" mimicked Gilbert, sipping a massive frozen margarita.

"That guy looked like a fucking freak," said another reporter, who then placed a pair of looped fingers over his eyes to represent Colapinto's black octagonal glasses. He laughed. "What do you think of Clapton? What do you think of Clapton?"

Trish Enright, also bearing a margarita, jumped in. "The first thing that I thought of when I saw him was the *Where Is Waldo* cartoon," she said. "Seriously, as soon as I saw him, I was like, 'Where is Waldo? *There* is Waldo!'"

Jesus, I thought. I'd better be careful what I ask Dean.

Not that I got much of a chance. For those of us who didn't get private one-on-one interviews with the governor—which was most of us (I even made a request on behalf of the weeklies for a group interview, to no avail)—the only way to actually reach the candidate was to fight through the feeding frenzy in the daily plunges and hope against hope to keep his attention long enough to get something substantive out of him. But I learned pretty quickly that in that group of journalists, this was the longest of long shots.

Though he'd seemed sane at first, I'd recently become somewhat suspicious of Dean since entering the trip, but not for the usual reasons. Some other journalists whose opinions I generally respect, or at least can read without puking, have blasted Dean for being a phony and a Trojan Horse liberal, but from where I sat the most troubling thing about Dean, if you watch him enough, is that he's never teaching me anything in his speeches, just stating positions on issues I'm already familiar with.

I think I speak for a lot of people when I say that one of the reasons I've become so disenchanted with the Democratic Party is that it never addresses the issues that are actually important to me: the grotesque commercialism of our society, the preeminence of corporate culture and values and the lack of political opposition to corporate activity, the lack of career options in our economy that aren't either openly meaningless or grossly demeaning to the human spirit. . . . Like a lot of people, I'm desperate for a leader to help me make sense of these things, to explain to me the causes of these problems, and to tell me how to act and what to do to change things for the better. But mainstream politics offers me no such person.

What it offers instead is a series of positions of varying reasonableness on the same narrow issues that have been sold to voters as the sum total of "politics" for the last twenty or thirty or forty years: tax policy, balanced budgets, educational spending. None of the proposals are ever fundamental changes, since our politics always assumes that the American system—the same system that brought us thirty million people watching video coverage of Al Roker's gastric stapling—is the best system there is and cannot be improved. The candidates therefore become buffoons straight out of Voltaire: crusaders for change, campaigning on a platform of minor improvements to this best of all possible worlds.

Dean does not venture beyond these parameters. Whether this is merely because he is a cautious politician, or whether it is because he simply has nothing to say beyond his stated positions, seemed to me the chief question surrounding his candidacy. It is not an easy one to answer, either, and particularly not on the Grassroots Express, as I was to find out.

On my third day on the plane, I finally figured out the dynamics of the plunge and managed to fight past Wilgoren to get right in the governor's face, lunging over a seat to thrust a tape recorder in his face.

"Governor!" I said. "You talk in your speech about investing in small businesses, and creating Sallie Mae–type loans to help them out . . .".

"That's right," he said.

"But how do Sallie Mae loans help small businesses fight off the Cargills and the Wal-Marts of the world? Isn't the problem of small businesses rooted in their inability to compete economically with massive companies? Isn't this more of a fundamental problem in our economy that will take more than a few loan programs to fix?"

Dean paused, then nodded. "Well," he said, "there's not a whole lot the federal government can do about that."

What the hell kind of answer is that? I thought. "Well, what about reforming the corporation as a legal entity? How about requiring a unanimous vote of the board for mergers and acquisitions? The government has the power to change the structure of business, doesn't it?"

Dean frowned and considered the question for about three long seconds. And I swear he would have answered it, too, had not *Miami Herald* reporter Peter Wallsten suddenly pushed me aside and lunged at the candidate.

"Governor, getting back to substance," he said. "Is it true that you paint your own house?"

Getting back to substance? *Fuck you!* I thought.

Dean laughed. "Um, yes, it is," he said.

"Why do you paint your own house?" Wallsten asked.

Dean shrugged. "To save money, I suppose," he said. "I'm kind of a tightwad."

A dozen hands at once scrambled to write the word *tightwad*.

"Do you paint the inside, or the outside?" said Wilgoren, jumping in.

"Um, both," Dean said.

"Do you use a brush, or a . . ."

She made a gesture. "Or a roller?" Wallsten helped out.

"Uh, again, both," Dean said.

Suddenly I heard the voice of Colapinto yelling out behind me. "Governor!" he said. "Did you bring your harmonica on this trip?"

"No, I didn't," Dean said.

I sighed and slumped in my seat. In my notebook I wrote: "There is Waldo."

The next day, the morning after San Antonio, I finally got a chance to have a meaningful exchange with Dean. After Wilgoren woke me up, I quickly raced to my feet and shoved my way to the front of the pack. I felt embarrassed, because I was horribly hungover and reeked of vodka. Not only that, but I wasn't dressed as most of the other journalists were, and it suddenly struck me that I was about to address the possible future president of the United States unshaven and in a grimy Buffalo Destroyers T-shirt.

But what can you do? You don't get many chances to ask a direct question of a presidential candidate. I decided to lay off the serious policy questions, and just ask a simple question about something that had been bothering me.

"Governor," I said, "is there a reason you don't use the word 'peace' in your stump speech?"

Dean tilted his head and looked closely at me. Up close you can see in Dean's eyes, incidentally, that he is a person of not wholly insignificant intelligence. Short and stocky and with a doctor's scrupulously perfect hygiene, it sometimes seems as though you only have his full attention when the diagnosis is unclear, and this was one of those times.

"That's interesting," he said. "That's a very interesting observation. I don't use it, do I?"

"No," I said.

"I never noticed that before," he said. "That's something to think about."

I went back to my seat and fell asleep.

Four hours later, just after parting with Olivia Cobiskey, I was searching for an air-conditioned exit to the rally when I heard something new in Dean's speech. He was talking about Iraq and foreign policy, and he was saying that maybe as Americans we needed to reexamine what we mean by "toughness."

"Maybe we ought to think about being tough the way John F. Kennedy was tough, during the Cuban missile crisis," he said. "Kennedy stood down the joint chiefs and said, 'We're not going to war right now, we're going to try to find a better way. . . . Maybe it's tougher to stand up for peace than it is to stand up for war.'"

The crowd cheered.

Holy shit, I thought.

Jobs. Health insurance. Be a fan of breakfast again.

Here's a question that began bothering me about halfway through the Sleepless Summer tour. If you sell a candidate the same way you sell a cinnamon roll, *is* the candidate a cinnamon roll?

There's an awful lot of sales pitch in Howard Dean. It may not be the whole picture, but there's enough of it that it makes you scratch your head after a while, and wonder what the hell is going on.

Take Milwaukee, for instance. When the Grassroots Express landed and

we deplaned, the first thing I noticed was the setup on the stage in the airplane hangar where the speech was to be held: utterly gigantic American flag
in the background, a two-row, gender-balanced, multicultural grouping of
supporters standing in the foreground. While they waited for the candidate
to take the stage, the show people on stage all looked terrified, afraid to
move or make a face. Doing the math quickly, it looked like a suspiciously accurate statistical sampling of America: three blacks out of seventeen, two
Hispanics, etc. (There was even one angry-looking woman in glasses who I
could swear was supposed to represent lesbian America.) It was a horribly
painful scene: they looked like sausages nailed to a giant red, white, and blue
crucifix. It was the kind of thing that would make me puke blood from
shame if it were ever done on my behalf, but Dean bounded right up to them
with a big smile, like a kid jumping in the lap of a mall Santa.

The "I'd like to buy the world a Coke" group shot was only one of a number of grossly fake gags observed on the Sleepless Summer tour. There was
the Grassroots Express itself, of course. This was one of the things that I
found hard to reconcile with the widespread belief that Dean is "different"
and "not a typical politician." When the name to your campaign vehicle is the
Grassroots Express, while one of your opponents has a bus named the Real
Solutions Express and a candidate from a rival party (McCain) four years ago
had one called the Straight Talk Express . . . well, you haven't worked very
hard to be different. I interrogated O'Donnell and Enright about the author-
ship of the plane name, and both gestured silently in Trippi's direction. But
when I asked Trippi about it, the soft-spoken "man behind the candidate" (it
is very characteristic of the Democratic Party that its Svengalis all sound like
EST counselors) coyly denied responsibility for the name, saying only that its
origin was "just a bunch of people kicking an idea around."

There was the plastic grass on the plane, of course. Plastic grass! In about
the only astute observation I spotted in the daily newspaper coverage of the
tour, *USA Today* reporter Jill Lawrence noted that the ridiculous grass tufts
"looked like shallots."

There were other details. I noticed early on in the trip that whenever Dean went out in public, he rolled up his sleeves. But as soon as he was "relaxing" in private, he rolled them down again and buttoned the cuffs. I was fascinated by this detail (as was German reporter Waltraud Kaserer, who also noticed it) and for several days at each stop stealthily waited behind on the plane after the other journalists left, in order to try to catch Dean in the act of rolling up his sleeves. I was never once successful; he must have ducked into the bathroom to do it, or else somehow done it on the fly on the way out of the plane door each time. In any case, the whole thing was strange on a number of levels, not the least of which being the fact of a man who unwinds by buttoning his sleeves.

There were other details, including the odd fuzziness and vacuity of certain parts of Dean's stump speech. . . . It was not lost on some of us, for instance, that his wooden campaign slogan, "Take America Back," was also used by two other former Trippi candidates: Gephardt in 1988 and Jerry Brown in 1992. Much of Dean's public presentation, in fact, was a rehash of other Democratic campaigns. He makes a joke about Bush being "all hat and no cattle," which was a laugh line in Gephardt's campaign speech earlier this year. And his closer line, "You have the power! You have the power! You have the power!" (delivered in the style of Jesse Jackson's "Keep Hope Alive!" bit) was a Gore line in 2000.

The funny thing about this was that when I pointed out these behaviors to Dean supporters, they rarely failed to admit to being turned off by them. At best they were indifferent, distantly aware that these gags were being staged for some other mystical personage "out there" who would be convinced by them.

"Does that do anything for you, you know, seeing an ethnically mixed bunch of people standing in front of a big flag?" I asked eighteen-year-old Megan Colvin in Milwaukee.

She shrugged. "Well, no," she said. "But I think he's trying to say something about diversity."

"But," I said, "he's trying to say it to you, isn't he?"

"I guess," she said.

Michael Hurwitz was a Dean staffer at the rally in Falls Church. I found

him tending the back entrance to the stage, where, before the speech, the
multicultural poster group was milling about, waiting to go on.

"Let me ask you a question," I said, pointing. "How does this work? Does
someone on the staff say, 'I need two wheelchairs, three blacks, and a cheer-
leader'? Who does that job? And how do they pitch it to the actual people?"

He shrugged. "I think it's more like they come forward on their own."

Dean followers didn't need the trimmings; most were there because they
were anti-war and repulsed by the other Democrats who voted for the war. The
glitz was for someone else, and that someone else, I soon realized, was on the
plane with me.

As much as the reporters snickered about the campaign fakery, and occasionally cracked about it in print, there is no question that they were attracted
to the big-campaign symbolism like moths to a lamp. To be full of shit in
American politics is a signal to our political press that you are serious, and it
was quite obvious that the most transparently meaningless or calculating aspects of Dean's behavior were what most impressed the Sleepless Summer
press corps.

To wit: most of the reports filed during the trip focused on the size of the
crowds, the amount of money Dean has raised, the "feel of a general election
campaign" surrounding his appearances, and the sudden departure of his legendary "brusque, angry tone," which incidentally I never saw in the first
place. A great many of the conversations among reporters on the plane
centered around whether or not Dean had a chance to beat Bush, and these
speculations—called horse racing in the business—dominated the narratives
of most of the articles, many of which wondered aloud whether Dean was
"too far left" or would "moderate" his rhetoric in time for the real race.

When I asked the reporters on the plane what the value of this kind of reporting was, I got an interesting answer. No fewer than four journalists
replied to the effect that unless the electability issue was addressed, "someone like Kucinich" might get the nomination.

"Hell, if it came down to a battle of position papers, Dennis Kucinich
might win," laughed Jackson Baker of the *Memphis Flyer*.

"I think its value is that it helps to explain to the reader why I'm spending so much time with one candidate," said Mark Silva of the *Orlando Sentinel.* "He needs to know why I'm reporting so much on Howard Dean, as opposed to, say, Dennis Kucinich."

The next day, Silva ran a piece containing a quote from former Washington Governor Booth Gardner, comparing Howard Dean to Seabiscuit.

I was never much impressed by the "Howard Dean problem." To me personally, the whole issue seems ridiculous: I would vote for Count Dracula over George Bush. But it is a deflating thing to vote for a horse instead of a man. And "momentum" makes horses of them all.

*Once every
four years*   *Every damn day*

MANCHESTER, NH

4

CAMPAIGN DIARIES

In the fall of 2003, I spent several months living in a flophouse in Manchester, New Hampshire, trying on a severely limited budget to follow the progress of that first crucial primary race. During this time I wrote several pieces for The Nation, *culminating in a disastrous—and poorly written, I might add—profile of General Wesley Clark.*

These diaries cover the period prior to that fiasco that I spent in New Hampshire. Looking back, what is most interesting was how seriously I underestimated John Kerry. Watching him stumble around New Hampshire in these months, I would have bet my own life that he would never become the nominee. How he managed to win back the confidence of the campaign reporters, whom I had frequently seen doubled over with laughter every time he gave a speech, remains one of the mysteries of the campaign—and I'm sorry that I dropped off the trail during the period when this magical process took place.

September

In the distance we could see the destination: One Pace Plaza, the Pace University auditorium, the site of the third Democratic presidential debate. Actually getting it in our sights was important, because we were about five minutes away thanks to our inability to follow directions. Alex Zaitchik, the cheerful, boyish editor from the *New York Press,* was sweating heavily. He leaned over to me.

"I think," he said, "I have to go to the bathroom."

I thought about that. So did I, it seemed. Quite badly, in fact. We stood on a street corner searching for a place to go. Behind us, meanwhile, next to a park entrance, Howard Dean was giving a pre-debate speech to a giant crowd of supporters. On the campaign trail in the past few weeks I had taken to referring to Dean as The Fuehrer in my notes, because of the dictatorial confidence he had recently begun exuding, and the cult-of-personality vibe of his crowds. It was my little private joke, but now, as I heard his voice booming over the speakers, it struck me as not particularly funny. The Fuehrer was talking about *prison.*

I turned to Alex and tapped him on the shoulder. "Prison," I said gravely, "is the most expensive and least effective social service intervention we make."

"Prison is the most expensive and least effective social service intervention we make!" Dean's voice boomed out simultaneously.

Alex shuddered. "Holy shit," he said. "Don't do that!"

"Sorry," I said.

Alex pointed to a Starbucks across the street. We raced over there. Inside, there was a comically long line for the single public bathroom. We slid into it, trying to seem calm, and began waiting.

I tend to think of hallucinogenic drug experiences as being like criminal trials. The prosecution opens its case when you take the drug, which Alex and I had an hour before, in his office: a big pile of magic mushrooms for each of us. Then there is the intervening hour or so in which the jury hears the evidence. Finally, at the end of that hour, there is always that one moment when you know the verdict: innocent or guilty. Anyone who's taken these drugs knows what a guilty verdict means. Terror, panic, misery: a long sentence lasting many painful hours . . .

In the line at Starbucks I suddenly found myself shuddering, as though I'd been sliced with a razor, every time one of the clerks used the hissing steamed milk machine. The walls were oscillating unpleasantly. My skin was white hot and I was drenched with sweat. As I stared at the bathroom, still treacherously occupied after many long minutes, a surge of terror shook my body.

Will the defendant please rise!

"Guilty!" I said.

"What?" Alex said.

"Nothing," I said. "I didn't say anything."

Minutes later we left and made our way over to the debate. Protesters, demonstrators, and candidate supporters, all bearing signs, teemed in front of the entrance. People seemed to be rushing past us diagonally from all directions. It was neither a peaceful gathering nor a violent one, but more like the minutes after a shocking emergency, the scene after a large highway pileup. We put our heads down and went in.

"Hi," I said to the attractive young girl at the desk. "I'm Matt Taibbi, from the *New York Press*. We called ahead."

I smiled. What a relief; my voice sounded normal. She looked at her list. "Of course," she said, smiling back. "Here you are."

She handed me a big blue press pass, a reassuring stamp of social approval, that I quickly hung around my neck. To the left, through the metal detector, I could see wall-to-wall carpeting and a clean interior that almost certainly promised air conditioning. Maybe a change of luck was in the works.

No.

As soon as I got through the metal detector, Alex, already through, gave me the bad news. "They're not going to let us into the actual debate," Alex said. "We have to go to the press room."

The guard pointed. Four flights down a dark concrete stairwell.

I nearly fainted. I have terrible associations with trip drugs and steep descents. Nearly fifteen years before, I had been involved in a horrific experience, too sordid to describe fully here, in which I was arrested at the base of Mount Monadnock in New Hampshire after a tab of bad acid had prompted me to scream Mansonesque apocalyptic threats at total strangers near the mountain summit. (I had been convinced that I had been brought to the mountain to fight someone to the death.) I tried to escape the police and was chased down and pistol-whipped in the woods. They threw me in the cruiser, a golf-ball-sized gash in my head and my shoulders drenched with blood, and took me to the station. As luck would have it, as soon as we began driving down to town, the sun went down, and it was suddenly black outside. I remember quite clearly being convinced that this zooming car ride to jail down through the black mountain roads was actually my final journey down into the center of the earth, where hell was.

This wasn't that bad, but even to be reminded of that moment now was a very bad sign.

We stood at the entrance of the press room. "The military must have designed this place," I thought grimly. About 300 journalists were sitting glumly at SAT test tables in front of a colossal, Albert Speer–esque arrangement of gleaming televisions. Oppressive fluorescent lights everywhere, a vague sucking sound coming from the vents, burning shit-brown patches of gym floor poking out from under rented gray carpeting. And walking to and fro everywhere were nervous packs of the very ugliest people in the United States— the national press corps. Was it possible that all of these people had gone through the trouble of being accredited just to watch the debate on *television?* Where was the actual event being held? Mars?

One look was all it took. Alex and I decided to flee. We raced up the steps, the stairwell resounding with echoes. But at the exit we were stopped by the fat, splotchy-faced guard—your standard six-hit-dice dungeon monster.

"Where you going?" he barked.

"Um," I said. "Is there another room that we could go to? Maybe one more relaxing?"

He stared at me, confused. "The media room is downstairs," he said.

"But there's only *one room!*" I protested.

An official-looking woman with beady eyes, a nest of lanyards hanging from her neck, appeared from behind him. "It's big enough," she said, pointing back to the stairwell.

It did not occur to us then that we could have just ignored her and walked out the door. She pointed to the stairs, so that's where we went. "So that's how it is!" I thought to myself fatalistically, as we walked down. I was afraid to look at Alex; the last time I'd checked, he looked on the verge of tears. We settled into the worst two seats in the house, in the back and thirty feet from the nearest television, and returned to the business of "covering" the debate.

Thirteen more months of this, I thought.

Three weeks before, I'd arrived in New Hampshire on Sunday, September 14, beginning what I thought would be a long stint following the campaign. The big story that week on the horse-racing front was a dramatic shift in the balance of power in the campaign, as retired General Wesley Clark would announce he was entering the race later in the week. Simultaneous to the arrival of Clark was the rapid behind-the-scenes implosion of the candidacy of John Kerry. Only the week before, Kerry's hotshot communications director, Chris Lehane, left Kerry's camp amid the kind of bickering and open confusion that characterize a disintegrating campaign. Lehane, who had been Gore's spokesman in 2000 and whose hiring by Kerry had been considered a coup, was reportedly upset that the candidate had refused to take his advice and be more aggressive in attacking Howard Dean. When word of mounting tension behind the scenes leaked out to the press at the beginning of the month, the Kerry camp issued a statement, in Kerry's name, stating that "there will be no changes" in the staff.

But when Lehane's imminent departure leaked out a week later, Kerry characteristically issued a demented, nonsensical denial of responsibility for his "no changes" line, telling the *Boston Globe:* "Those weren't precisely my words. They were the words of a press release sent out."

Kerry is the only candidate on the campaign with a dependable talent for such McNamara-esque public statements, ironic (or perhaps not) considering his past: *Words were spoken. Press releases were sent out. Victory in Vietnam remains inevitable.*

The between-the-lines story in this story was that Lehane shares a political consultancy firm with noted political strategist Mark Fabiani, who would come out days later as one of the key advisors in the Clark campaign. Lehane didn't jump to Clark right away, but the implication was clear. Later in the week, Kerry's New Hampshire media coordinator, Kym Spell, would defect to the Clark camp as well.

That was the "backstory" to the campaign that week, I guess. Edwards was also due to formally announce that week, and perhaps the biggest underlying story was the impending September 30 deadline for the submission of fundraising data from the campaigns to the Federal Election Commission. The campaigns all openly treated this date as a kind of midterm exam in which a good showing was needed to convince backers to stay at the table. It would eventually turn out that a poor showing by Bob Graham in this first crucial test would be enough to knock him out of the race, making him the first victim of the *Friday the 13th*–style herd-trimming process that would eventually leave a succession of bodies all over New Hampshire, Iowa, and the Super Tuesday states.

I arrived in Manchester in the morning. It didn't take long to recognize the New England of my childhood (I grew up in various parts of Massachusetts).

Most people, when they imagine New England, think about old colonial homes, white houses with black shutters, whales, and sexually morbid WASPs with sensible vehicles and polite political opinions. This is incorrect. If you want to get New England right, just imagine a giant mullet in paint-stained pants and a Red Sox hat being pushed into the back of a cruiser after a bar fight. I found him minutes after my arrival.

I was looking for the Lieberman offices on Elm Street, the main drag in Manchester, when I ran into a pair of choice locals engaged in a Class A New England Domestic Dispute. Mullet was pointing a finger at Sparkly Barrettes, telling her to "get the fuck out of my face."

Barrettes grabbed her boyfriend's sweatshirt. "I just wanted to spend time with you alone tonight!" she wailed. "That's all I fuckin' wanted! Me an' you! Me an' you-u-u-u-u!"

She started crying. Mullet put his hand around her chin, then whispered something in her ear. They hugged, then jumped into an F-150 and drove off. A spiffily dressed black guy who was standing next to me, watching the scene, laughed.

"Love is a beautiful thing," he cracked. Immensely cheered by this scene—I was home again—I walked down the street, entered the Lieberman office, and registered to attend a Town Hall meeting later that night.

The location of Lieberman's office, and the rest of the campaign offices, is one of the first and greatest ironies of the New Hampshire campaign. Like pretty much every major New England town outside of the Route 128 ring around Boston, Manchester is a burned-out, postindustrial shithole of a city, a rotting hulk of an ex–mill town. If you've ever been to Lowell or Fall River or New Bedford, you know what the deal is here: big brick mills and factories that have been emptied out and converted to condos or malls or offices, usually at about 45 percent capacity. Huge chunks of the city are weatherbeaten, asymmetrical homes with cracking paint and rusted chain-link fences, and culture is a pretty steady mix of sub shops, karaoke and sports bars, bowling, and classic rock. In 95 percent of the city, the big shows in town at any given moment, year-round, will be booze first and then Red Sox, Pats, and Bruins games on TV. Only in one part of town does the pattern break, once every four years.

Like all burned-out American cities, Manchester has one showcase strip, complete with a few glitzy corporate-ish restaurants (like the Margaritas Mexican bar, a popular hangout for campaign staffers), a museum or two, an expensive and mostly useless concert arena (the Verizon Wireless civic arena, on Elm Street), the obligatory Internet cafe, and a selection of shops and boutiques for worthless knickknacks and other trash. In Manchester, this area is basically up and down Elm Street and then a few blocks over on a strip that runs along the Merrimack River, where the hollowed-out mill stores/condos are located. You'll find nice cars parked in these areas, SUVs with old Gore or McCain stickers on them (as well as the occasional vintage Volvo with a Dukakis sticker), and everything is in good repair, eminently reputable, and fit for the eyes of visitors.

This is where all the campaigns are. Gephardt, Lieberman, Edwards, and Kucinich are on Elm Street, while Kerry and Dean have bigger, swankier pads in the mills on the river. Braun and Sharpton aren't here yet, and Clark's offices would arrive in about a month.

It's like two different worlds. On Elm Street, the campaign is the big show, and at any minute you can run into a staffer who'll pass along that day's latest campaign gossip, like the Lehane business. If there's a campaign event in town, it's almost always in this area. But venture 200 yards from Elm Street where the actual people live, and you'll be hard-pressed to find a single person who's heard of any of the candidates. I did later find one, a twenty-nine-year-old named Chris Keith with long hair and a Slayer T-shirt. We were in Flo's Bar, a horrific dive a stone's throw from Elm that reportedly really fills up on the first of the month, when everyone gets their AFDC checks. Keith is a Dean supporter, and we talked politics animatedly for about a half-hour. I asked him if he could imagine someone like Dean or Dennis Kucinich coming in to Flo's.

"Shit, no," he said. "This is the worst fucking place in the state!"

We talked for a while longer, but then he got bored and split to go trawling for crack whores. By the time I left the place, he'd apparently found one. She was in her fifties and looked like a bog mummy. This is probably the way the election works for most of New Hampshire—a brief hassle in between Sox games and other business.

Some outsider candidate could probably score a lot of points just by setting up camp in a real neighborhood here. But none of them do. Headquarters has to be the fake place with no people. The backgrounds for their appearances are always Rockwell-esque portraits of rustic America, complete with statues, flags, people in work clothes, diner counters, etc. They never visit ghettos. When they want that effect, they simply imply it by fiat, a point made most starkly by the fake graffiti the Dean people concocted for the background of the candidate's Sleepless Summer speech in Bryant Park in New York.

This is a theme that I first began to consider on the Dean trip, the election as a kind of ritualistic piece of theater held exclusively for the consumption of upper-middle-class white people, for use in legitimizing a political process the rest of the country knows instinctively is a bunch of crap. It's an impression one can't avoid in New Hampshire, where I would later discover that you can go for weeks without seeing a single mullet at a campaign event. Instead, you exclusively see clean, well-groomed people in pristine locations, as I did at my first event, the Lieberman rally held at the New Hampshire Institute of Arts and Sciences, one hundred yards or so from Elm Street.

I was in an anxious mood at this event. Only an out-of-state senator, I thought, would schedule a Town Hall meeting in New England during a Patriots game. I'd ducked out of the game at halftime to catch Lieberman's act, which I'd never seen in person before. I expected it to be a revolting display of saber-rattling and self-important bullshit. It would exceed my expectations.

It started out quietly enough. The crowd was a mix of fleshy-looking college students in Joe T-shirts and what appeared to be respectable Jewish families imported from Weston or Newton or some other Boston suburb. In the center of the room, Lieberman's mother, Marcia Lieberman, sat quietly kvelling, a proud smile on her face. Rushing past her back and forth was Manchester Mayor Bob Baines, who was here to get a little face time for the national media. Baines was facing a primary vote in a few days, and I was worried for a while that he was going to break an ankle rushing to shake the hands of everyone in the room. The deranged smile plastered on his face brought to mind an Alaskan king crab.

The show really got started when Marcia Lieberman took the mic to introduce her son. Dame Lieberman, the height of a trash can, looks like Danny DeVito in a pearl necklace. I was too far away to see her makeup closely, but from a distance her face looked like a tight mess of grays and dark purples, as if it had been drawn with pencil and blood. After Baines introduced her to fanatical applause, she shook her head and then brought a hand to her breast, as though needing to catch her breath.

"I am so overwhelmed by this reception," she said, "almost to the point of tears. . . . Such incredible joy."

She brought a hand up to her eye and made a wiping gesture, as though holding back a tear. There was no tear, though. The crowd, about 200 people, redoubled its applause. The clapping lasted a good fifteen seconds. A number of supporters jumped to their feet.

Wow, I thought. That looks fake. I wondered if she cried on cue at other events, and made a note to check. Days later, a reporter would tell me that he'd seen the same act just before the election in 2000, on her birthday (Joe "surprised" her onstage with flowers), and again when Lieberman announced his candidacy this past year. Later on I went back and found this account of the 2000 birthday scene in the *Washington Post:*

> Joseph Lieberman then led the audience in a chorus of "Happy Birthday." As they finished, the candidate suddenly emerged from stage left carrying a bouquet of flowers. Someone pushed a three-tiered cake behind him on a cart.
> The audience saw the senator and began to cheer. When Marcia Lieberman looked around to see what the fuss was, she saw her son walking toward her. She put down the phone and hugged him. "Oy vey es mir," she said—Yiddish for "Oh, woe is me"—while wiping tears from her eyes.

Anyway, the crowd in Manchester was visibly moved. A few moments afterward, Mme. Lieberman introduced her son, who burst through a tight nest of Secret Service agents from the back entrance. Lieberman has a reputation on the campaign trail for being the most scrupulous of all the candidates when it comes to his security. Amy Hochadel, Dennis Kucinich's national field coordinator, would later recount to me a story about a meeting with union leaders in Iowa with Kucinich and Lieberman. In a closed room with no one but the candidates and the union people present, Lieberman kept his SS people right behind him at all times. "It was weird, like he thought one of the local chiefs was going to shoot him," she said. The Great Novelist in the Sky had done a good job when rendering the idiosyncrasies of this diminutive armchair imperialist.

Lieberman bounded to the stage, rubbed his hands, and took the mic. "Thank you, thank you," he said. "You know, having my mother introduced by the mayor of Manchester, with all of you people here. . . . It just hits me, you know, right here."

He jabbed his heart with his thumb. Then, smiling, he nervously dabbed his forehead with a handkerchief, cleared his throat, and straightened his tie.

The delivery was an amazing piece of schlock, pure Poconos comedian. I imagined the campaign slogan: "VOTE LIEBERMAN. TRY THE VEAL!"

It got worse. A few minutes later, Lieberman went into one of his stock themes, his biography. Of all the candidates, Lieberman and Edwards are the most enthusiastic when it comes to highlighting their humble beginnings. Both are proponents of the Mike Dukakis "I believe in the American dream; I'm a product of it" line. Lieberman's speech talks about a journey from poverty to the middle class. (Apparently the story stops before the part where he becomes a wealthy senator.) Smiling, he explained to the audience that he wasn't even aware that he'd been poor until later in his life.

"It reminds me of something I once read about that great ecumenical pope, John XXIII," he began.

Great ecumenical pope? What the hell was he talking about?

"He was poor, but he only realized that when he looked back later in life," Lieberman continued. "That's the kind of family I grew up in."

I was sitting next to Thomas Donovan, a local attorney who's running for the school board. "Did he just compare himself to the *pope?*" I asked.

He smiled. "Yeah, I think so," he said.

Minutes later, Lieberman built up his speech to a rhetorical summit, pumping a thumbs-up (Lieberman is the thumbs-uppiest of the candidates) at the crowd and shouting: "We have an *opportunity* to make the *future* better by *changing* the *leadership* of this country!"

The crowd erupted in applause. For a moment I was taken aback: I thought news that the Patriots had scored had somehow made its way into the building. The idea that one could inspire spontaneous applause with an all-star collection of dial-survey words seemed impossible, but it was happening. "Why are they clapping?" I asked Donovan.

He shrugged. "He's talking about leadership," he said.

I stood up and left in disgust. The next morning I scanned the news accounts in search of the headline: "LIEBERMAN COMPARES SELF TO POPE." No dice. Only one account out of a half-dozen around the country even hinted at it (Chris Keating of the *Hartford Courant* mentioned it in

passing); the rest opted for the hack-boilerplate approach that made Lieberman sound sane and sincere.

A quick note about campaign event coverage, by way of a comparison.
There is a passage in Nikolai Gogol's *Dead Souls* in which the author explains
the nuances of nineteenth-century women's education. Normally, he wrote,
it includes instruction in French, followed by training in manners and piano
lessons. But occasionally there will be an educational innovator who teaches
manners first, then moves on to French and piano. He concluded by describ-
ing groundbreaking new schools that will rebelliously begin with piano,
move on to manners, and teach French last.

Campaign trail reporting is the same three-headed beast. At least 70 percent of all campaign "event" coverage is a crude mishmash of three basic elements: candidate quotes, context, and man-on-the-street reaction. The basic
template looks something like this:

> Shithole, Faraway State (Wire Service)—In a mildewy auditorium run by the
> Elks or the Jaycees or some other local organization that is still considered
> prominent in this small, backward town delusionally convinced of its contin-
> ued relevance, Senator Egregious G. Liar outlined an ambitious plan for full
> health coverage of nearly all Americans today.
>
> "Under my plan, which will never be enacted if I can help it, citizens will re-
> ceive a tax credit that they can use to pay the high premiums imposed upon
> them by my chief financial supporters," he said, to uproarious applause.
>
> Liar arrived in Faraway State yesterday amid news of a new poll that shows
> him trailing surging Missouri Gov. Asyet Unindicted by a full 11 points. His
> campaign staff promised a new round of door-to-door visits that they say will
> help the candidate appear more accessible to the people he visited. Preposter-
> ous Moron, thirty-three, who teaches third grade in Shithole, was impressed
> by Liar's performance.
>
> "I thought he was a real straight talker," said Moron, who calls himself a
> member of A Party. "We need a fresh face in this race."

The rhyme scheme here is ABC, candidate/context/man-on-the-street.
Occasionally it is CBA and occasionally BAC. There are all sorts of variations.

But the one constant is that all three elements are always in there, and a near-constant is that they are in there to the exclusion of everything else. The more vital or revealing details are almost always overlooked.

The AP account of the Lieberman Town Hall was a perfect example:

CONNECTICUT SENATOR LAUNCHES "OPERATION: LIEBERMANIA" IN NH
By Holly Ramer, Associated Press Writer

When "Operation: Liebermania" landed on her doorstep, Kathleen Timbas was ready.

Notified in advance that Sen. Joe Lieberman would be campaigning door-to-door Sunday, she waited for the Democratic presidential hopeful with a list of questions scrawled on a legal pad. She squeezed in two—one about health care and another about the environment—before the senator moved on.

"I found it helpful," said Timbas, a financial analyst who favors one of Lieberman's rivals, former Vermont Gov. Howard Dean. "I'm not sure I got a solution on the environmental issues, but he helped lead me to some ideas I wasn't familiar with."

Though billed as part of "an all-out campaign blitz," Lieberman maintained his thoughtful, low-key style as he knocked on half a dozen doors in downtown Concord. Often, his young sign-waving supporters drowned him out with their cheer and chanting.

"Just another quiet day in the neighborhood," Lieberman joked.

But the senator later turned up the volume in Manchester for his first town hall–style meeting, where he clearly relished the standing ovations and frequent applause as he answered questions on everything from affordable housing to education to alternative medicine.

One audience member described a co-worker who questioned whether Lieberman, because he is Jewish, could be an effective mediator in bringing peace to the Middle East.

Asked how he would "answer such a racist charge," Lieberman spoke of his pride in his heritage and said the question should have been answered when John F. Kennedy, a Catholic, was elected president.

"I am convinced the question is not one's religion but one's policies—look at the difficulties George W. Bush has had," Lieberman said. "I'm convinced I can move the process further toward reconciliation than anyone else running for president."

Lieberman also repeated his criticism that Bush has underfunded homeland security, forcing communities around the country to lay off firefighters and police officers.

"That is about as foolish—I was going to use a stronger unpresidential word—as an army laying off soldiers in the middle of a war," he said. . . .

Lieberman also won praise from another Republican he met, Cliff Hurst of Manchester. Hurst said he supports President Bush, but admires Lieberman's strength of character.

"To me, that's the most important thing about a candidate," Hurst said. "He seems of all the Democratic candidates the most solid in his positions."

Incidentally, Lieberman's "low-key" style includes, in New Hampshire, a small fleet of new campaign vehicles, one of them a hideous PT Cruiser, emblazoned with gigantic pictures of the candidate's face. As for "thoughtful," there is a sign at the entrance to Lieberman's offices that reads, "BATMAN. SUPERMAN. LIEBERMAN."

The day after the Town Hall, Lieberman traveled to Claremont, a small town on the Vermont border about an hour and a half away. As a rare populous location in the western part of the state, candidates frequently visit there. And, like Manchester, it has its own safe locations for candidates' visits. There are two diners in the center of town, Dusty's and the Daddypops (also called the Tumble Inn Diner), and both are periodically besieged by invading candidates in search of photo ops. Daddypops, a vintage-looking boxcar-style diner, was an especially popular location. Its owner, Debbie Carter, told me that another candidate had hit her place a few weeks before Lieberman, but she couldn't remember whether it had been Dean or Gephardt. "It was one of them," she said. (It was actually Bob Graham.)

On the morning I arrived, I ate at Dusty's, which was packed, mainly because Lieberman was at the Tumble Inn. A guy in a flannel shirt next to me on the counter grumbled over his eggs. "They're there, so I'm here," he said. "Assholes." A week later, when Kerry visited Dusty's, I would find the same guy at Daddypops.

The previous evening I came up with what I thought was a sound way to avoid the classic three-headed-beast style of event reporting. The technique had the additional advantage of allowing me to not actually attend the event in question. I listened to Flannel Shirt whine about the Sox for a while, finished my omelet, and then, once I saw that Lieberman and his garish Joe-mobile (this one was a Subaru Intrepid) had left, walked over to Daddypops.

Inside, I found a young, bright-faced waitress named Amanda Harper at the counter. I explained that I wanted her and her co-workers to recreate the Lieberman visit as though it were a crime scene.

"You mean, like, where he left his fingerprints?" she asked.

"Exactly," I said.

She laughed, told me to wait a minute, then went over to explain the situation to Debbie Carter, her boss. The cook, an affable black yukster named James Fuskelly, overheard and offered his help as he worked on an order of home fries. Everybody seemed up for the project. Their resulting description seemed to me an improvement over the AP:

AMANDA: I guess the first thing he did was talk to these two guys in the first booth. They're the city directors or something.
DEBBIE: Yeah, the city directors.
TAIBBI: What, you mean like the selectmen?
amanda: Something like that.
DEBBIE: Just one of them. Guy Santagate, you know, he's the city manager. We call him Santa Gate. The other guy was Mark Aldrich. He's the local economic development director. They were waiting here for about forty-five minutes. They didn't look like they were enjoying themselves too much.
TAIBBI: Kind of drumming their fingers on the table, looking at their watches?
DEBBIE: Yes. You know, this was something they had to do, get it over with. Anyway, they talked to him for a while, then he moved on. . . . I guess he talked to me next.

JAMES: He gave her a thumbs-up first.
TAIBBI: A double thumbs-up?
JAMES: I'm not sure. I think it was a single.
TAIBBI: (to Carter) What did he say to you?
DEBBIE: Well, he said . . . he first said something like, "It's a nice place,"
and then he said this other thing that was kind of strange, something
like, "It's a nice relaxed atmosphere and you get the sense of it without
it being rehearsed." Actually no, I think he said "scripted."
TAIBBI: What does that mean?
DEBBIE: I don't know.
TAIBBI: How can a diner be scripted?
DEBBIE: I don't know. Actually you know I wasn't really paying attention
because I was worried about some customers that were trying to get in,
and they couldn't because there was this big crowd outside. Anyway, he
moved on. He was nice, though, I'll have to say.
TAIBBI: Who was next?
AMANDA: There were these two older ladies in the next booth, he talked
to them for a minute. Something about the minimum wage.
TAIBBI: Did he put his hands anywhere during this time?
AMANDA: I think he touched the top of the booth. You know, he put his
hand on the back of the seat and said something like, "Hello."
JAMES: I think he stuck his tongue out right around then.
AMANDA: Yeah, he sort of stuck his tongue out at some point.
TAIBBI: Like a joking stick-your-tongue-out?
AMANDA: Yes, joking. He stuck his tongue out and then it was like every-
body sort of laughed for a second.
TAIBBI: What was his tongue like?
AMANDA: (laughing) It was small and pink.

Everyone broke up and went back to work for a while. Later on, I asked
Amanda and James what Claremont was like. Both immediately had a lot to
say. "This town is dead," Amanda said, frowning. James added that he thought
the local Citizens Savings Bank ought to have been renamed the Senior Citizens Savings Bank. "This is a tough town. There's just nothing here at all for a
young person," James said. "If you want to go to a bar where there are actually
people your age, you've got to go all the way up to this place in Lebanon."

"It's horrible up there," concurred Amanda. "Although Perry's is worse."

James frowned and grew pensive. "I'll tell you, I went bowling twice. Just to do something. You know what that's like, to do something just to do something?"

I said I did. Later on I asked them what the local businesses were, what supported the town.

"There used to be some factories," Amanda said.

"Yeah. There was Tambrands," said James. "They made Tampax. But that's not here anymore. There were two paper mills, but one went out of business. And there was Goodyear across the river, but that's gone. I guess now," he concluded, thinking about it, "people mostly just sell stuff. Small things in stores."

James went on for a while. He was a really sharp kid, very bright and funny. In a just world someone would have swooped into town and signed a decree giving him a lifetime contract to be a chauffeur for the Swedish Bikini Team. But wherever it was that he deserved to be, he was here and you could tell he was troubled by the fact. He'd had a rough time in Claremont.

"When I was growing up here, I got arrested like six times, always for the stupidest stuff," he said. "I mean, loitering, minor in possession of alcohol, minor in possession of a nonnarcotic drug—that one I was just driving and there was a kid in my car who had a bowl in his backpack. Stupid stuff. Just try it. They can arrest you in this town for standing on the street. Six times I got arrested."

"And he's a good guy," chimed in Amanda.

"Yeah, exactly," he said. "Then I went to Manchester for five years and never got in trouble once. But then I moved back and in less than two years I've already been arrested twice, I'm on probation," he said. "I don't want to say anything, but I hang out mostly with black kids, and it's like the cops are following us around, looking for a reason. And meanwhile it's the white kids in town who are dealing all the crack. Seriously, come out with me sometime and stand on the street. You'll see."

I asked him if Lieberman had said anything to him.

"Yeah," he said, rolling his eyes.

"What did he say?"

"He said something like, if we don't have a strong military, then we don't have a strong defense. Something like that. And I was like, *what?*"

The next day, I decided to make the rounds at the campaign offices around town, leave a calling card as it were, and explain that I was going to be around a lot for the next few months.

It was an amusing exercise, because the offices were so different. The Kerry offices, a gigantic space with huge banks of telephones in a mill near the river, was easily the least pleasant of the lot. The staffers in there seemed overwrought and responded to the presence of a small-time journalist as though they had just been asked to co-sign a loan. A youngish blonde woman with tightly pulled-back hair and a bright preppie-yellow sweater—the kind of sweater that only women who have had early equestrian training would ever consider wearing—told me stiffly that she couldn't help me at all, and that I would have to wait until "Kym came back."

"Look, she's the only one who deals with the press," she said, clipping her vowels. "You're going to have to come back."

I would have been standing there a long time waiting for "Kym." Mme. Spell departed to the Clark campaign that very afternoon.

The Gephardt offices, on a nice fourth-floor office space on Elm, were incredibly clean, suggesting that the staff had had a lot of time to attend to housekeeping. It was empty except for New Hampshire State Director Erik Greathouse, who was exceedingly polite and a little bit sad. He offered any and all assistance, and suggested we go out for a beer sometime.

The Edwards office was hilarious. It looked like the Vanderbilt chapter of Theta Chi on the eve of a game against Florida State. The place was covered with debris—Nerf footballs, empty beverage containers, a medal commemorating participation in the "Virginia Beach Rock 'n' Roll Marathon." It was also completely empty when I got there: the whole staff was locked away in a room upstairs, watching Edwards announce his candidacy on CNN. Subsequent visits would reveal a mostly Southern staff that seemed to be perpetually bouncing off the walls, busy in every corner with magic markers and posters. Detecting a New Yorker, the Carolinians in charge of the office put me onto one of their few northern liberal types, a young Asian from Michigan named Tait Sye who had worked for Gore and in fact had worked under Lehane in the 2000 campaign. I would run into Tait numerous times over the course of the next few weeks, and he, too, offered to go out for a beer sometime.

An idea I had for infiltrating the Lieberman offices was already forming in my head, so I made it a point to avoid announcing myself as a journalist there. Ditto for the Dean offices; an unflattering article I wrote about the governor for *The Nation* had just come out, and I didn't feel too good about showing my face at Chez Dean just then. That left Kucinich, whose offices I visited last. It was the only visit I would make where I felt like I was on the same planet as the people working there.

There is something a little bit odd about the way most campaign staffers relate to the media. It's not something you can put your finger on right away. The best way to describe it is to say that any conversation you have with a staffer is likely to feel like a colloquialized version of campaign literature. In some cases you get a lot of shop talk, where the parties on both sides trade details about their professional hassles on the campaign trail; apparently journalists and staffers achieve a sort of intimacy through a kind of mutual exploration of their insider-ness. (HACK: "Last night was a nightmare. First they said they wanted 500 words, then it turned out they wanted 800. . . . Did you guys figure out that problem with the hotels?" STAFFER: "Yeah, we got a bunch of volunteers to handle the baggage. . . ."). This is kind of what it was like with Tait, for instance. He was telling me about Edwards's plan to hold one hundred Town Hall meetings in New Hampshire, more than any other candidate, and when I asked him how it was going, he smiled.

"It's been really cool," he said. "We did this one in some town up north, and we held it at this store that was like an old house with a big porch under an overhang that wrapped all the way around the building. You know the type? Anyway when we got there, there was this really big crowd, but then it started raining. At first we weren't sure of what to do, but finally we had the senator just take an umbrella, and he stood in front of the store and did his Town Hall while everyone else listened to him from under the overhang on the porch. It really came off well."

I could see in his eyes that he was recalling this scene with professional satisfaction. He seemed like a smart young man who was interested in his career and in doing well, and I was being invited to appreciate this. He was friendly and I sympathized. We didn't discuss what Edwards said during that Town Hall. When I asked about that later on, he handed me Edwards's policy paper, a sixty-one-page behemoth called "Real Solutions for America."

Later, I opened the booklet up. The first item I found in it was a section about reforming probation and parole. Apparently the senator believes that one of the most pressing problems of the criminal justice system is that not enough people are in jail. The booklet quotes him:

> In my view, the toughest, most important problem in our criminal justice system today is the early release system. We have 600,000 people leaving prisons each year. We have about 4.5 million people either on parole after jail or on probation instead of jail. . . .

I could probably still go have that beer with Tait, and maybe even stay friendly with him, so long as I didn't think too hard about things like this. But that is what it would take. I would subsequently observe, however, that almost all the reporters on the trial strove to maintain that surface friendliness with the campaign people—and pulled it off. Which says something in itself, I think.

It was different with Kucinich.

I'm not sure, at this stage, how the Kucinich people interact with other journalists. Among other things, they're probably not tested in this regard very often, as the congressman doesn't get a lot of intimate press attention. But it was pretty clear to me right at the outset that these were people who were highly interested not in the campaign process, but in their candidate's politics. I couldn't imagine, for instance, chatting with Amy Hochadel, the longtime Kucinich staffer who runs his New Hampshire office, about how the new posters were going over, or what kind of rig the candidate drove (Greathouse, for instance, rhapsodized at length about the fully loaded RV Gephardt had used in several appearances), or that sort of thing. She had other things in mind, and if we were going to get along, it was almost certainly going to be because we shared a point of view.

Hochadel, a pleasant, slightly crunchy-looking woman in her mid-thirties, worked in Kucinich's congressional office. In a phenomenon that I would observe all over the Kucinich campaign, she talked about her candidate with genuine reverence and with obvious personal loyalty. The Dean staffers I met, by contrast, were mostly all professional political operatives who were riding their fourth or fifth presidential horse. Hochadel's eyes lit up when she told me a story about how Kucinich had threatened to use eminent domain to seize a hospital in a poor neighborhood of Cleveland that a health conglomerate was planning to close. He used the same tactic with an electric plant, she said, ultimately saving both facilities. "It was a wonderful idea, and I loved it, but I remember laughing about it with Dennis," she said. "I told him that if we weren't careful, we were going to end up owning a hospital. But he said we had to do whatever it took."

I had never heard of an American politician threatening to seize corporate property before. Salvador Allende got himself shot for thinking like that. "Those are some pretty radical politics," I said.

"Yes, well," Hochadel said. "That's Dennis."

We talked briefly about the depressing state of affairs in the Democratic Party, then talked a little about Kucinich's chances. "The thing is," she said, "Dennis has been a huge underdog in every race he's ever been in. This is familiar territory for him. Every time he runs, no one gives him any chance at all and he never has any backers. But he goes door to door and as soon as people get a chance to hear him, they always go over to him. I mean, he's won five elections now. I know what the odds are, but I think he's got a chance."

There was no sense at all, talking to her, that her idea of *winning* was some kind of prize. She wanted Kucinich to win for a reason. It was the first spark of genuine idealism I'd seen anywhere in five weeks on the campaign trail. Later on, when I would spend a lot of alcohol-soaked time with other Kucinich staffers—a fun younger crowd, led by stately New Hampshire activist Richard Hendrick—I would find the same attitude up and down the staff. Almost all of them viewed the Kucinich campaign as something that would continue in some form or another, whether the candidate did well or not.

No sooner had I left Hochadel's office than I got a call from *The Nation,* assigning me a story about Kucinich. So I went back inside and made arrangements to travel with the candidate on a trip around the Bangor, Maine, area the following day.

Dennis Kucinich is not tall and he is not good-looking. In fact he is a somewhat ridiculous-looking man, tiny, so slight that he appears to be little more than a pile of rumpled clothes (he is given to boyish plaid short-sleeve shirts and a blue blazer, the costume of an eleven-year-old sent to church), little of him visible at all beyond a set of little hands, a pair of big ears, and a messy shock of black hair hanging over his forehead. But he does have one thing, and that is a kind of intense certainty in his voice. I would have said about his small stature that you could have knocked him over with a feather, except that you stop thinking this once he opens his mouth. Kucinich's air of conviction is so powerful and unmistakable that it actually gives him a physical presence.

There were about one hundred people gathered at the Pierce Memorial, a little square in downtown Bangor. Kucinich stood in the middle of them in a clearing, pacing back and forth with a microphone. He began by talking about his childhood, when he used to come to Bangor to visit his aunt and uncle, and recalled that he always used to buy a pair of Dexter shoes from the local factory. On the surface this sounded like a standard piece of campaign sweet-talk, but the nerd quotient in Kucinich is so strong that one can plausibly imagine him looking forward to buying Dexter shoes on a vacation. Then, commenting that Dexter was no longer in the area, he entered into a longish speech about visiting towns all across the country where there used to be factories and farms and businesses, but now were mostly ghost towns where it was unclear what people actually did for a living. I thought of Claremont.

"They used to make aircraft parts. They used to make car parts. They used to make cars. They used to make bicycles. They used to make washers. . . . And now," he said, pausing, "those communities aren't making those things anymore. All around America, you're seeing communities falling apart, because our economic base is falling apart. As the next president of the United States, I will address this question directly, and I will address it directly where a major part of the problem lies, and that is our trade policy. We have to understand that NAFTA and the WTO have led to a destructive undermining of the American economy!"

The crowd applauded politely.

"And as the next president of the United States," he continued, "my first act in office will be to withdraw from NAFTA and the WTO!"

He went on to talk about Iraq:

"When we were in Baltimore, in the last debate, you may have noticed," he began. "There was only one candidate who unambiguously and unequivocally said that it is time to get the UN in and the U.S. out. It is time *now, today,* to start! All the other candidates want to dodge this issue. Oh, there are candidates who voted for the war, and now say it's a bad idea. We have a lot of those. And there are candidates who said that they didn't approve of the war, but . . . we've got to stay the course. We've got to stay in there. I'm the only candidate who recognized, right from the beginning—led the effort in the House of Representatives, but saying today—that we have to have the UN come in and handle the oil revenues, the contracts, the building of a new government, and get the U.S. out of there!"

I raised an eyebrow at this portion of the speech. The conventional wisdom holds that Dennis Kucinich has no chance in this election, and though I generally loathe the horse-racing instinct in journalists, I had to admit that it was something I took into consideration.

I was expecting the Kucinich campaign to be the most depressing part of the election story—the honest man doomed to sparsely attended quixotic failure in a carnival of corrupt idiots. But in listening to him talk about Iraq, I had a vision suddenly of a scenario in which he might succeed. Say the war in Iraq continues to go badly, as it inevitably must, and maybe it takes a dramatic turn for the worse. And say all the other candidates, including Dean, maintain the same position they hold now, namely, that American troops have to remain there and remain in command there, even if international forces arrive. If Kucinich stays in as the only one favoring an immediate pullout, I thought, he just might get enough traction to make some noise in the election.

Why not? I thought. Stranger things have happened. Look at Eugene McCarthy. It only happens in extreme cases and only by accident, but occasionally a honest person can have some success in American politics.

The fantasy lasted about three minutes. But it was nice while it lasted.

Later in the day I got to talk to Kucinich for about an hour, in the back of a minivan, while he loudly ate from a bowl of udon noodles. We were on our way back to Bangor after a visit to the Common Ground Fair in nearby Unity, Maine, an organic farmer's fair. If there is such a thing as a home crowd for Kucinich, probably the only vegan ever to hold high office in America, it is an organic farmer's fair in New England. Being on assignment for *The Nation* in this atmosphere was like being a *Playboy* photographer in Cancun. It was actually a little unnerving. While interviewing a woman named Shlomit Auciello, who was running a tempura stand that both Kucinich and I patronized, a young man in a tie-dye shirt and a beard walked over.

"Hey," he said. "Did I hear you say you write for *The Nation?*"

"Well," I said, "occasionally. I'm a freelancer."

He shook his head in excitement. "Wow," he said. "Do you know Christopher Hitchens?"

I stared at him. "Dude, you need a girlfriend," I said.

He frowned, looking hurt, and walked away. In any case, the Kucinich interview was both awkward and extremely interesting. Among other things, we were about thirty minutes into it when it became clear that Kucinich thought that I was from the *New York Times*. Despite the confusion, which was embarrassing to both sides, I heard enough to convince me that Kucinich was not playing a part in public. Even in the safe confines of a leisurely lunch in a car full of his own people, he alternated between states of passionate defiance and seething frustration with the faux-opposition of the Democratic Party. He got especially hot when the conversation touched on the subject of trade agreements. At one point he got so upset that he reached into a bag at his feet and searched for the text of the NAFTA agreement. I told him I took his word for it, but he wouldn't rest until he found the actual document. I remember feeling extremely uncomfortable as this odd person bent over and rummaged around on the floor of the van:

KUCINICH: Okay, here it is . . . chapter 11, they have a whole series of side agreements!

TAIBBI: Okay.

KUCINICH: You have a whole series of side agreements, but they're full of loopholes. They're written that way! They're written so that you have the appearance of protections for labor, but not the fact. It's like it's a consistent thing, it's in everything . . . if you're talking about NAFTA or the Trade Promotion Authority, or whatever. For example, the Trade Promotion Authority, it has this section for environmental considerations. But they're not binding. You can put them in there, but they're not binding.

TAIBBI: It's just window dressing.

KUCINICH: It's just words. It's worse than window dressing, because you're putting something in front of people that looks fresh, and it's actually rotten. It's a consistent strategy by these people with these trade agreements that have considerations for the environment or whatever, then they create side agreements with so many loopholes that they're meaningless.

TAIBBI: But there are parts of the agreement that do mean something and do have teeth, but they all go the other way?

KUCINICH: Right. They go the other way. The agreements mean something in terms of protecting the property of corporations. Then they're real.

TAIBBI: And the other candidates are on the record explicitly pro-WTO, pro-NAFTA. . . .

KUCINICH: Absolutely! I mean, Dick Gephardt, his name was on the bill, it was the Gephardt bill that created the WTO.

TAIBBI: But he's the big union politician.

KUCINICH: I don't think even the unions know that Dick was the guy who created the WTO.

TAIBBI: Here's something I'm confused about. Why is it necessary for the Democrats to sell out the unions this way? Even from a practical standpoint, it seems like it would make more sense just to protect that demographic. I mean, this is theoretically their electoral base, right?

KUCINICH: Well, I can't tell you why they don't do it. I can tell you why I do do it. This is where I come from. This is my experience. The neighborhoods I come from are affected by this. I was at a meeting yesterday in Cleveland. We're trying to save this community hospital there. The second time in three years they've tried to close it. And it was very interesting. I could tell, generally speaking, which side of the issue. . . . I could tell who was advocating the closing just based on the way they were dressed.

TAIBBI: What, their shoes?

KUCINICH: I could just tell, just from growing up there. I *know* these people.

He had some great lines. When I asked him about the propensity of the other candidates to base their speeches around bunches of dial-survey words (*change, hope, opportunity, leadership,* etc.), Kucinich laughed. "It's the campaign version of spam. No wonder no one is interested in politics. Do you read spam?" Then, after a series of questions about the war on drugs, he segued into an exploration of corporate crime, coming up on the spot with a wild new proposal for corporate offenders.

TAIBBI: So a guy is driving around, he gets pulled over, he has a couple of joints in his bag or whatever . . . in the Kucinich presidency, what happens to this person?

KUCINICH: See, that's precisely the kind of thing where we need to be asking ourselves what we're doing, why we're prosecuting this person. It's ridiculous. You know who I'm interested in prosecuting?

TAIBBI: Okay.

KUCINICH: The guy who never gets pulled over, but has in the trunk of his car all the retirement assets of his corporation.

TAIBBI: Incidentally, he's usually a cocaine user. (Laughs.)

KUCINICH: (completely ignoring joke) See, there's going to be a shift in emphasis in law enforcement. I'm not interested in a country that pretends it's protecting the social order by incarcerating minor offenders. I believe that we need to strongly emphasize rehabilitation. (pausing) And I believe . . . we need to rehabilitate the guy who steals his company's pension as well.

TAIBBI: What, with a methadone program? Twenty-one days of greed therapy?

KUCINICH: Well, I think he or she would should be subject to rehabilitation.

TAIBBI: Just like drug court? You have to come in, have meetings with a counselor. . . .

KUCINICH: (staring off into the distance) After an appropriate time of service to society, he should be rehabilitated.

TAIBBI: So there would actually be counseling?

KUCINICH : It's an interesting thought. You know, I think behind greed is fear.

TAIBBI: Fear of not having anything?

KUCINICH: Right. It's like a lack of faith in oneself, in the ability to create the necessary wealth.

TAIBBI: So you think that it's a psychologically treatable condition?

KUCINICH: Well, I think that they should have access to rehabilitation if the circumstances dictate that they need it. . . . I mean, if you go to traffic court right now, you have to go to rehab. I don't see why you shouldn't in this case.

The next day, I followed Kucinich around New Hampshire. His first stop was a meeting with students at the University of New Hampshire (UNH). This was a much longer and more detailed speech than his Bangor appearance. Far from a standard stump appearance, Kucinich attempted to explain his candidacy as an extension of the humanist movements of Gandhi and Martin Luther King. He outlined his plan for the creation of a Department of Peace, explaining that his aim was a "fundamental change in the direction of society," in which "nonviolence would be an organizing principle." Quoting Jung, he said that his aim was to bring to the fore the "collective unarticulated conscious-ness" and the hidden, "shared aspirations of the community." He quoted from at least a half-dozen texts in the space of a half-hour talk: Barbara Marx Hubbard, Thomas Berry, Morris Berman, Emerson. . . . It was a remarkable departure from the dumbed-down, sanitized presentations of the other candidates—who would never give any audience, much less one full of teenagers, so much credit for their ability to think.

Later on, when I had to sit down and write my article about Kucinich, I found it difficult to balance my admiration for his idealism and lack of conde-scension with the unavoidable sense that he was doomed to play a tragic part in this idiotic process:

> The politics of Dennis Kucinich are easy to see but hard to describe, which is why conventional journalism, comfortable only with crass idiocies, has settled on calling him a leftist and burying him in the thirteenth paragraph. But to me the best way to describe Kucinich is to say that he seems to be the only candi-date who responds as an intellectually ambitious human being would to the problem of the presidency.
>
> When you think about it—and few people do—no great thinker or leader, no Thoreau or Bertrand Russell or Martin Luther King Jr. would look at the vastly complex problem of the human condition and see as the most urgent so-lutions incremental numerical adjustments of the type espoused by most can-didates. It is hard to imagine a Gandhi feeling passionate about a 30 percent tax credit for investment in renewable energy (Gephardt), or $66 billion for Iraq in-stead of $87 billion (Edwards), or a Community Oriented Policing Program ("COPS," a Kerry creature) that puts a few more cops on the streets. No, the great leader would see vast sicknesses to tend to, gross misapplications of hu-man effort, problems rooted not in numbers but in society's emotional priori-ties. And his solutions upon taking a great office would be of commensurate greatness: the elimination of war, the conquest of greed, the restoration of community.
>
> I'm not saying Kucinich is a great man. But he does think in these terms. He is clearly an intellectual who is measuring himself against history, not the other candidates. And it is this disdain for the other kind of ambition that has led observers to describe him as unserious.

The Kucinich platform is simple and unequivocal. Cancel NAFTA and the WTO. An immediate pullout from Iraq. Universal single-payer health care, a public program, everyone covered. His campaign literature is the size of a playing card. (The John Edwards "Real Solutions for America" pamphlet, in contrast, is sixty-four feverish pages of gibberish.) The message is a fairly recurrent theme of the campaign: the question isn't what fancy-sounding programs to devise; the question is whether you're going to take the first broad, obvious steps in the much larger fight. And the implication of the campaign, clearly understood by all Kucinich supporters, is that their man is the only one who is even engaged in the actual battle.

Therefore, you see a marked difference in the dynamic of the Kucinich campaign, as opposed to those of the other candidates. Many reporters in New Hampshire refer to the "summer camp" phenomenon on the campaign trail. "I first noticed it in 2000," said Laura Colbert of New Hampshire Public Radio. "In every campaign office, you have one older guy, and he's the counselor, followed by two dozen kids. Four years later, one of the kids is the counselor, telling stories by the campfire."

I spent some time in Manchester with some of those kids, many of whom have thought up cutesy tribal names for themselves ("Liebermaniacs" and "Deanie Babies," for example). Most were mealy college types in identically crisp white T-shirts who appeared ready to march with their candidate all the way to, perhaps, a wet T-shirt contest in Hilton Head. But it is not all that unusual to find someone who seems willing to go to his death, or the political equivalent of it, for Dennis Kucinich. These people are older and tend to have a permanent interest in politics; this is not summer camp for them.

"There's an old saying in martial arts, which is that if you fight to save your life, you die," said David Bright, the candidate's volunteer media coordinator in Maine. "You have to fight regardless of consequence. . . ."

The candidate talks gloomily about what will happen if—as appears likely, given the current polls—the vote should go the wrong way. "Unless we're motivated by principle in our voting, we walk into a mirrored echo chamber, where there's no coherence," Kucinich says. He sighs and repeats, "Where there's no coherence . . ."

Later in the piece I tried to contrast the theoretical Dennis Kucinich with the one operating in observable reality, the scene being the post-debate "spin room" at Pace University. To bring out the central problem I compared his helplessness in this demented atmosphere with the easy confidence of his Dostoyevskian opposite, John Edwards—the tall, bubbly bimbo without the faintest idea why he was running for president, but with all the physical equipment for the run:

> *No coherence* is exactly the term to describe the aftermath of the scene at Pace University, after the September Democratic debate there. Far underneath the auditorium, in the Pace gymnasium, 200 journalists are racing across the floor, circling candidates and their handlers like sharks after a shipwreck. There is pushing, shoving, shouting, people screaming at one another, and only very occasional fragmented questions about politics. At the edges of the fray you can find numerous foreign journalists shaking their heads in disbelief, stunned by the barbarity of it all. A Dutch journalist named Rik Klinkel is explaining to me how much better things are in the Netherlands.
>
> "Over there, you don't need to do this to get to a candidate," he says. As he speaks, he winds up and makes a violent elbowing gesture. Predictably, his demonstration results in his belting an Ohio newspaper reporter right in the eye. The man falls to the ground.
>
> "Ow, fuck!" he screams.
>
> "Please excuse me," the European says, extending a hand. The other reporter refuses it, collects himself, and runs away.
>
> In the center of the crowd, Dennis Kucinich is taking a beating. He has just had to endure two hours of a debate hosted by Brian Williams in which candidates who ran too long were interrupted by a game-show-style bell ("Somewhere at *Jeopardy!* they're wondering where it went," joked Williams unfunnily about the buzzer). It was intensely painful watching Kucinich try to read off, over the repeated protests of the *Jeopardy!* buzzer, the list of post-layoff executive payouts at Tyco, Delta, and Hewlett-Packard. "Delta laid off 17,400 workers. . . ." *Bzzz!* "The executive salary of the CEO went from $2.1 million to $4.6 million. . . ." *Bzzz!* "Tyco went from . . ." *Bzzz! Bzzz!* It reminded me of the death of Old Yeller. When I tried to ask Kucinich about the game-show format afterward, he waved me off, clearly pissed.
>
> "It was fine. It was fine. Whatever," he said.
>
> Minutes later, as he tried to escape the hall, he was assaulted by Comedy Central reporter Rob Corddry. Corddry was trying, satirically as it were, to

make a joke about the total incoherence of the spin room, and he was doing so by trying to ask Kucinich a question with a mouthful of peanut butter. Kucinich didn't get it. "What are you saying?" he said, annoyed.

But Kucinich deputy Paul Costanzo leaned over to whisper in his ear that this was Comedy Central, a good opportunity, and he should play along, etc. Kucinich clued in, then raced across the room to get Corddry a glass of water, to help him with the peanut butter. By the time he returned, the joke, not that funny to begin with, was many painful minutes old. The two glumly parted soon after, like motorists who had failed to revive a run-over cat.

Soon afterward I joined the scrum around Edwards. He was turning clockwise in a crowd of hacks and expertly batting away one question after another; he looked like Rafael Palmeiro at a home-run derby. When he caught *New York Times* reporter Rick Lyman standing openmouthed without a question ready, he cracked: "Hey, buddy? You just gonna stand there?"

Behind me, two female reporters cooed. "Wow," one said. "Just look at his tan!"

What I left out of *The Nation* article, of course, is that I myself had negotiated that scene with a head full of mushrooms. Not the kind of thing you want to admit to the editors of that magazine. Just after Edwards had brushed off Lyman, in fact, he'd turned to me. I tried to ask him about the *Jeopardy!* bell and made, I think, only partial sense.

"That bell," I said. "Wasn't it, you know, humiliating, don't you think it demeans the whole process. . . . I would have wanted to run offstage."

Edwards smiled. He was less than two feet from me and I made the mistake of taking a close look at him. His whole face seemed to be *breathing,* and under the beachy surface of his orange makeup I suddenly saw big blue lines appearing—radiating outward from his eyes and pulsating, as though they had a life of their own. I thought I might fall down.

"Well, I think they're doing the best they can," said Edwards. "You know, there are a lot of us, and they've got to find a way to get us all in there. . . . I think they're doing just great. . . ."

By the time he finished I'd turned my head to focus on a white spot on the wall across the room. It was a bad scene. My friend Alex was in a corner, his

head in his hands; he couldn't wait to escape. But I tried to stick it out in the
spin room scrum as long as possible. The tape record of that twenty minutes
or so after the debate is like a monument to human incoherence. There is a
long section of the tape in which I tried to engage the "pole girl" for Dick
Gephardt in a conversation (the candidates stood out in the crowd thanks
only to each being followed by a volunteer carrying a sign on a tall pole), but
the conversation doesn't make much sense; the only thing that stands out
is that she didn't want to talk to me. There are snippets of conversation with
Graham, who was standing almost alone in a corner, and a lot of heavy
breathing and shouting. Finally I decided to get out, but on the way I fell
straight into a Vegas nightclub act named John Hlinko and Josh Margulies.

The two affable brothers-in-law were the founders of the DraftClark
movement and had raised $1.9 million for the candidate, but no one wanted
to talk to them; surrounded by mobbed political heavies like Mark Fabiani
and Bruce Lindsay, they were standing by themselves making wisecracks to
each other. All they needed was a seltzer bottle:

HLINKO: Yeah, he married my sister. I couldn't get to my gun fast
enough.
TAIBBI: How's that working out, the whole family thing?
MARGULIES: We hate each other, but we like her.
HLINKO: It's hell. Hell. You know, we all make mistakes. But some of us
make huge, colossal, like just gargantuan mistakes.
MARGULIES: Well, she's pregnant. She's six months pregnant. So she's
got to be [inaudible]. I mean, I assume it's mine. I've been on the cam-
paign for seven months.
HLINKO: There was a pool boy coming around.
MARGULIES: Yeah, Paco, the pool boy.
HLINKO: I like Paco. He's always clean.
TAIBBI: You guys are like a vaudeville routine.
MARGULIES: Tip your waitresses.
HLINKO: We'll be here all week. We've got a two-drink minimum.
TAIBBI: Try the veal?
MARGULIES: Try the veal. That's good.

HLINKO: We'll have to use that.

MARGULIES: That's the second thing I've gotten out of the *New York Press*. The first, of course, is the remarkable selection of escorts in the back. It's like the whole back half. The front half is like news, a selection of clubs . . .

HLINKO: See, this is it, you alienate the *New York Press* . . .

MARGULIES: No, I'm serious, where else . . . I mean it's broken down, it's very specific.

TAIBBI: Now you guys are officially buttering up journalists.

HLINKO: Not at all. We're like the Straight Talk Express, version 2.0.

TAIBBI: Wow. That's like two campaign clichés at once. You guys are really learning fast.

HLINKO: Of course, we're big fans of the cliché. See, the thing is . . .

MARGULIES: I'll give you a third. Clichés were made.

HLINKO: Clichés were made. We take full responsibility.

From there the conversation devolved; reverting to their semiprofessional states, they tried to convince me what a great candidate Wesley Clark was. My anxiety quickly returned, and when I caught Alex sliding toward the door, I said my good-byes to the Clark twins and bolted.

Up on the street. The relief washing over us, Alex and I howled with laughter and quickly dived into a cab. The driver, an elegant Caribbean fellow named Oliver Maxime, asked us what was going on. We told him and he laughed. It all seemed good now. As we started to pull away I spotted Joe Trippi, Dean's campaign manager, rushing out of the building trailed by a young aide, looking desperately harried.

The tables were turned now. I rolled down the window and shouted.

"Hey, Joe!"

Trippi stared at me, not recognizing the face. Trying to ignore me, he crossed the street in front of our cab.

"Who is that man?" Olivier asked.

"That," I said, "is Howard Dean's campaign manager."

Olivier rolled down his window and shouted.

"Sir!" he said. "How is Howard Dean doing?"

Trippi whipped around in horror. "What?"

"How is Howard Dean doing?" Olivier repeated.

He shook his head. "I don't know!" he said.

Trippi's assistant quickly leaned over and whispered in his ear. The look on the Dean campaign manager's face expressed unmistakable discomfort. Was it possible that *black cab drivers* in New York recognized him now? Had this process officially gotten out of his control? Recovering himself, he gave a thumbs-up.

"He's doing great!" he said. "Just great!"

Monday, October 20

I am the only candidate running with the breadth
and the depth and the length.

—John Kerry, addressing Every Child Matters seminar, University of
New Hampshire, October 20

The double-entendre factor on the campaign trail is proving to be larger—and broader and longer—than expected. Kerry's size-is-important pronouncement today was about the third or fourth truly good one I've caught so far. Kucinich had a fine one a few weeks back. While talking about John Ashcroft, he tried to make a statement about the invasiveness of the Patriot Act, but got caught in the middle and had to repeat himself. "Patriotism is not about peering into every ass . . . about peering into every aspect of our lives," he said.

A few days later I caught a speech by Michael Moore at the Rolling Thunder Fair in Manchester. Moore was talking about the Republicans doing "a lot of crack . . . a *lot* of crack." It was probably only a double entendre for me, because I was sitting behind him. Moore is a man who should probably avoid certain words in his speeches—or wear suspenders.

I caught Rip Van Kerry—half his audiences are always asleep—at Durham today, where he had a pair of events at the university. A gag I had planned for him failed. I first got the idea when I talked to a Dusty's diner customer in Claremont. He was an old guy in orange camouflage and he was shaking his head.

"Guy comes in and takes one look at me and says, 'Were you in the service?' And I'm like, these are orange. I'm a *hunter.*" He laughed. "Next thing you know, he's talking about Vietnam."

So I bought an Army baseball cap, a POW-MIA T-shirt, and a stopwatch. My idea was to cross paths with Kerry in the guise of an ordinary voter and time how long after the handshake it would take for him to mention Vietnam. When I reached UNH today I found that the POW T-shirt was missing, so I only had the hat on for the Every Child Matters conference.

When I got to the back, I ran into an acquaintance, Aaron Houston of the Marijuana Policy Project. Houston's MPP chapter is about the only genuine grassroots activist group (unless one counts the Kucinich campaign) that is taking a permanent interest in the campaign in New Hampshire. The other main activist groups are the Every Child Matters folks, devoted to children's issues, and the Service Employees International Union (SEIU), mainly focusing on health care, both of which heavily poster and flyer almost all the main campaign events. The MPP, however, is the only group interested in things like sabotage and high-wire political actions. They meet regularly and organize heckling campaigns against the pro–drug war candidates, in particular John Edwards. I see them everywhere and they're a breath of fresh air. At the Kerry event, I found Houston slumped in the back of the conference, a questionnaire hanging limply in his hand.

"They're screening the questions," he said. "I can't get in. No marijuana questions today."

He noticed my hat, and asked me what was up. I explained.

"You're shitting me," he said.

I assured him I wasn't. He bent over laughing.

"So get this," he said. "I used to be in ROTC, right? Anyway it was earlier this summer and it was hot, so I got an old-school army haircut, really high and tight, you know? And we went to an event at Derry where we were going to be picketing Kerry. I had on some aviator glasses, too. Before the event starts, Kerry spots me from a long way off and comes over to me. And he's like, 'Gee, were you in the service?' And I say, 'No, Senator, actually, I'm here picketing you.' And he slaps his head and says, 'Of course. I remember you now.' "

He wished me luck. I needed it. It was all I could do to stay awake during Kerry's talk. Of all the candidates, Kerry is the worst when it comes to the Nixonesque rattling off of statistics. Every time I hear Kerry speak, I think of Nixon's famously incoherent line about "crime today is growing nine times as fast as the population." What did that mean, anyway? Thirty-five years later, no one has any idea. Kerry is the same way: right from the start you get buried under a blizzard of numbers he has memorized like favorite nursery rhymes, and only afterward—if you're still awake—do you think to wonder what they meant. My notes on his UNH speech read, in part, as follows:

> The 4 major pollutants. . . . The three great teachers in life (one of which is "teachers") and the 2 most critical ingredients in drug prevention . . . introduced to 15 kids in a brownstone in New York. . . . Over 20,000 graduates, and we're in 43 states and 142 towns . . . bottom 40 percent earn as much as the top 1 percent . . . 0–8 instead of 0–5, it's not just the after-school programs, it's ALL of them (looping thumb, tracing full circle at ALL) . . . 47 percent of 19,000 and that's daily, that's a daily figure . . . 100,000 sex abuse cases last year. . . . Right here in New Hampshire. . . . Right here in New Hampshire. . . . I remember having colic as a child. . . . How is this possible in the richest country in the world?

At times Kerry would drone on in such a steady monotone that the audience wouldn't catch it when he slipped up. At one point he castigated Tyco for moving its address to Mexico, then two minutes later explained that we can't allow Tyco to move its address to Bermuda. Then he went back to Mexico again. No one blinked. No one was listening.

There are a lot of buffoons on this campaign, but no one, at this juncture, is a bigger joke than John Kerry. I have yet to run into a person outside his campaign who does not bring up Kerry's legendary waffling ability the very first minute his name is mentioned. Later that afternoon, when I stopped into the Kucinich offices to say hello, I ran into Adam Sachs, the campaign's

Massachusetts coordinator. I told him I'd caught a bunch of Kerry events that day.

"Oh, him," he said. Then he licked his finger and stuck it up in the air.

And before that, I was speaking to Richard Hendrick, the Kucinich press guy, on the telephone, and was arranging a time to meet him for a beer. "How about this afternoon?" he asked.

"Can't," I said. "I've got Kerry."

"I'm sorry," he said.

"It's okay," I said.

Hendrick explained that he'd just had to moderate a showing of *Hearts and Minds,* the Vietnam anti-war documentary. He recalled the scene where the vets threw their medals on the steps of the capitol, then mentioned Kerry's not-infamous-enough story about throwing not his own medals, but the medals of a World War II vet who asked him to throw his for him. "That's like one hundred times worse than 'I didn't inhale,'" he cracked. "The guy is unbelievable."

Even Houston, at the UNH event, seemed subdued. "Actually Kerry is on our side now," he said. "He's against raiding the medical marijuana clinics this week. But, you know, with him, he could change at any time. So we're just here to make sure he doesn't flip again."

At the close of the UNH deal I waited, stalker-like, at the exit for Kerry. But at the last minute he ducked through a side door, flanked by his glum-looking staff. I will not miss him tomorrow.

Big news this morning: Lieberman and Clark have pulled their campaign operations in Iowa. Lieberman looks fucked to me. He has to finish at least third in New Hampshire in order to stay in.

Tuesday, October 21

Kerry, the bitch, escaped my clutches again.

I had him this time. I really had him. It was very nearly the perfect scenario. He was scheduled to do a "downtown walk" with ever-mugging Manchester Mayor Bob Baines at 12:15. It was a close call for me because I had an assignment to catch Wes Clark on an absolutely identical "downtown walk" in Nashua at 11:30. I made it a point to get what I needed out of Clark quickly, then, at about noon, got in my car and raced twenty minutes north back to Manchester, screeching around Granite Street onto Elm just in time to see an army of Kerry posters, followed by an army of Gap-model-looking journalists, bearing down the home stretch of Elm Street. Kerry himself had just disappeared into the Harley-Davidson store. I imagined that that would have been a particularly nauseating scene, given that Kerry is a self-described Harley fanatic. That very morning, in fact, the *Globe* ran a cock-sucking brief highlighting that fact, pointing out that onetime *Easy Rider* star Dennis Hopper was among a number of supporters who had raised over $100,000 for Kerry.

Doing the math in my head quickly, I realized that Kerry likely had only one restaurant left on his route—a little place called the Merrimack Diner. I dashed in and sat at the counter at the front of the place. They *always* stop at the counter first and they *always* talk to the first guy at the counter. I had on a green Army sweater and my Army hat. Quickly summoning the necessary props (coffee, newspaper; the two-day stubble was already in place), I settled myself in and waited for the avalanche.

A fellow journalist proved to be my undoing. A TV cameraman showed up early to shoot some B-roll of the diner. He got behind the counter, right near where I was sitting, and began shooting the soda fountain and the coffee machine. As he was engaged in this dreary activity, Kerry entered. He was tall and beaming and, in a crisp blue shirt, radiated helpless stupidity. I "looked up" from my newspaper and caught his eye. He started to walk toward me . . . and then the cameraman knocked something over farther down the counter (I think it was a spoon).

In the instant it took for Kerry to turn his head toward the disturbance, the wave of people carried him beyond me. He did a loop around the spacious restaurant, and I was sure I was about to catch him on the rebound, when at the last minute he and his staff ducked out the emergency exit!

But there is still plenty of time. I will get him this week, guaranteed. There is an AFL-CIO gig up in Whitefield this weekend; he will not escape me in that town.

The Clark event was bizarre, to say the least. In a driving rain a smallish group of reporters gathered in front of the Nashua City Hall and waited for the candidate to arrive. Clark staffers monopolized the one sheltered area under the City Hall entranceway, grumbling about the weather's effect on the candidate's health. Clark had been scheduled to give a major address on the economy today, but it was scratched because the candidate is sick and has no voice. He has literally been quiet as a mouse for over a week now. To compensate, the staff has apparently been scheduling seen-but-not-heard-type events like this one.

While we waited, I made a new friend. Hiroaki Wada of the Japanese newspaper *Mainichi,* an affable-looking fellow with a stringy beard and an impossible accent, sat glumly under an umbrella, his hood drawn tight. I introduced myself and we immediately laughed our way through the Japanese business-card-exchange thing. Wada even taught me the bow. He had only recently come to the United States and was shocked at the insanely protracted nature of our electoral process.

"In Japan, prime minister elections—two weeks," he said, shaking his head.

I had spotted him yesterday at the Kerry event and asked him what he thought.

"Ah, very dull," he said. "I try to follow him."

We chatted for a while. He seemed a little overwhelmed by the process and I could sense as we spoke that he was probably trying to fish some quotes out of me for his piece. As a former foreign correspondent, I knew this drill: *any* native was good copy, even a fellow reporter. At one juncture he began to ask about something he'd heard in Washington.

"What about the Clinton people, perhaps, yes, Hillary enters the race?"

I laughed. "That won't happen," I said.

"No?"

"No," I said. "That is something that the right-wing radio stations invented in order to scare their people into donating money to the Republican Party."

He frowned. "I see. Why?"

"Why not?" I said.

Clark himself, when he arrived, looked confused and hyper. I must have been standing too close to the curb because he bolted straight out of his minivan with a hand extended and gave me a shake. He had a bony hand. He then plunged into the crowd and went straight ahead and then, apparently deviating from the script, rushed into City Hall. Staffers Bill Buck and Jamal Simmons raced after him.

"Wait," Buck shouted. "What's the deal here? Where are we going?"

The crowd of reporters raced in after him. By the time I got inside, Clark, gerbil-like, had reversed course and plunged back outside into the rain. He then took a sharp left and bolted down Main Street, the reporters racing after him.

I stopped and talked to Buck for a moment—made a formal interview request—then left.

Much later in the afternoon I went back to Nashua and did the crime-scene technique with one of the businesses he visited, a little bakery called the Patisserie Bleu. It was perhaps not as interesting as some of the other places I'd hit on the campaign, but it did produce one delicious detail. Owner Jacqui Pressinger described her confrontation with the general:

PRESSINGER: And then he said something about how much he liked Nashua. . . .

TAIBBI: Had he ever been here before?

PRESSINGER: I didn't get that out of him. But he said it reminded him of some small town in Texas.

TAIBBI: Texas?

PRESSINGER: And then, um . . . and then he got an "everything" bar, and then he came over here and was whispering to me and the other girls. . . .

TAIBBI: Because his voice is gone.

PRESSINGER: I don't know.

TAIBBI: Yeah, he's got laryngitis or something.

PRESSINGER: Anyway, he was whispering that he had a sweet tooth, and his favorite dessert was a Napoleon.

TAIBBI: (laughing) His favorite dessert is a *Napoleon?* That's so appropriate!

PRESSINGER: (laughing) I didn't even catch that, until you mentioned it.

TAIBBI: That's really funny.

PRESSINGER: And then he started talking about West Point.

TAIBBI: Because he was first in his class there.

PRESSINGER: Yeah.

TAIBBI: Did he tell you that?

PRESSINGER: No. He was just talking about them eating Napoleons at West Point or something.

TAIBBI: (flabbergasted) Wow.

PRESSINGER: A cute story. I like pastry stories!

Are Napoleons part of the curriculum at West Point?

Saturday, October 25

Grade A political doublespeak on display today, at the New Hampshire AFL-CIO conference way up above Franconia Notch, in a town called Whitefield.

The setting was a beautiful, *Shining*-esque luxury manor called the Mountain View Grand Resort. The place was remote, lavish, all old wood and luxury, surrounded by snowy mountains—a perfect setting for a mass homicide. There were about 150 representatives of New Hampshire locals that came out to hear four of the candidates live (Kerry, Dean, Kucinich, and Clark) and one via phone (Gephardt). Each candidate had a half-hour to speak and answer labor-related questions. But there were some nonlabor subplots to the campaign that surfaced in the early stages of the conference.

Earlier in the week, Howard Dean had done a media buy in New Hampshire, running what the media characterized as an "attack" ad pointing out that on the Iraq issue, "The best my opponents can do today is ask questions today that they should've before they supported the war."

That doesn't seem to me to be an attack ("If you elect Jones, niggers will run wild in the streets!"), just a statement of position relative to the other candidates. . . . Only problem was, it wasn't correct. Kucinich, of course, led the anti-war movement in the House, and opposed the vote. And Jesus, Al

Sharpton . . . I was standing under him listening to him call out Bush in front of 400,000 people at the March on Washington in February.

Anyway, immediately after the ad hit the airwaves, Kucinich called foul, threatened legal action, and demanded that Dean pull the ads from the airwaves. This kind of proactive move by Kucinich greatly cheered his supporters: I happened to be at the opening of his new offices in Portsmouth on Friday when he announced to his people that he was challenging Dean on the matter. There was nervous laughter in the room when I suggested to Kucinich that he should also have protested the hideous tan sweater Dean wore in the ad.

"I mean, Larry Bird wouldn't have worn a sweater that ugly," I said. Kucinich smiled and turned away. My sense of humor only bats about .240 with the candidate.

Anyway, Dean surprised everyone at the conference when he stood up and began his remarks to union leaders by pointing out that "Dennis did, of course, oppose the war," and in fact spent a few minutes giving Kucinich his props. (He ignored Sharpton.) It seemed an odd time to address the issue and reporters spoke to him about it afterward, in the parking lot outside the hotel. A reporter from, I think, WMUR in Manchester asked Dean if he planned on pulling his ads.

"Well, we're not going to alter the ad schedule," Dean hissed.

Translation: *maybe* we'll pull the ads, but *no*, not because of Dennis Kucinich. Dean had smoked his apology inside, but once outside, he blew it out without inhaling.

It got better. After a little more badgering he mumbled something about not, of course, having wanted to suggest that Dennis Kucinich had supported the war. But as he hopped into his car, he added, "Well, I'm not really sure that's what I said, anyway."

Another fine demonstration of disingenuousness came from Clark. One of the questioners at the conference was a videographer from WMUR named Ryan Murphy. Murphy's union was currently having trouble getting a contract from management: it was a mini-version of the infamous Wage

Rage NABET dispute between NBC employees and GE. Murphy asked each of the candidates the same question: would they participate in a boycott of a WMUR debate if the station did not give its workers a contract?

Two candidates, Gephardt and Kucinich, scored beautifully on this question, which incidentally is the perfect kind of question to ask a candidate: make them take a stand, yes or no. Gephardt, by phone, said:

"I come from a labor family and I was taught to honor a picket line. I won't cross a picket line, for a debate or anything else." The word *debate* dripped with contempt as he spoke. I'm not a Gephardt fan, but it was a good moment for him. The crowd cheered.

Kucinich, who along with Gephardt was the star of the conference, also did well with that one, answering, "Well, yes, of course," right away to Murphy's question. He added: "I mean, this isn't a situation where I have to wring my hands and worry what my corporate sponsors think. Of course I'll boycott it."

But Clark fucked up badly. At the conclusion of Murphy's question, he pointed and said, "Well, let me ask you something. Has management sat down with ya?"

Murphy sighed. He'd just answered that question ten seconds ago. "Again, General, we've been in negotiations for nine months."

Clark nodded. "Well, I think that management ought to sit down with you and work this out. And I'm going to follow up on this. But I'm 100 percent behind you."

Outside, the WMUR guy repeated the question, but put it a little differently. He asked if Clark would boycott *if the other candidates* also boycotted.

"You betcha. I'm with you one hundred percent on that one," he said.

I made a comment to the reporter that this was tantamount to asking if Clark would not debate himself if all the other candidates boycotted, but he ignored me.

"General," I said. "What if the other candidates *don't* boycott? Then what will you do?"

"Well, we'll see what happens," he said.

"Gephardt and Kucinich have already agreed to the boycott," I said. "Why can't you just say yes right now?" I asked.

He smiled. "We'll take a look at this," he said.

There was some other weirdness in Clark's presentation. He seemed confused about whom he was speaking to. To a labor conference he brought a couple of VFW boosters in bright red jackets, who flanked him as he entered. Then in his speech he kept dropping military metaphors all over the place and talking about the sense of unity in the service. "When you're in uniform, you're part of a team," he said. "And we always had this sense that the generals weren't any better than the soldiers. . . ."

Was Clark implying that the *workers* were like *soldiers?* It sure seemed that way, and it definitely went over badly. It got worse. Early on, he talked about how being in the service had allowed him to "be all he could be." Then he repeated himself later on: "Every part of this society has to get the support that they need to *be all they can be.*"

After the conference I asked him about this. "General," I said. "Are you really going to make 'BE ALL YOU CAN BE' your campaign slogan?"

He smiled and gave me a nudge, clearly thinking I was with him on this one. "It *is* my campaign slogan."

My flophouse home in Manchester is beginning to take up a lot of my time and astonished attention. Both because I have no money and because I wanted to live hard while on the campaign trail, I took a room in the down-and-outiest flophouse in Manchester, a little rooming house (the "Walnut St. Rooms") about five blocks from downtown. Once upon a time, this place was owned by a former prison worker, and it was a sort of unofficial halfway house for the recently released. One of the tenants, a onetime race car mechanic named Curt, told me that he used to do a sweep every day in search of the shanks and knives that the other tenants hid in the common areas of the building. Because of frequent parole inspections, the ex-cons couldn't keep weapons in their own rooms.

"I'd find shanks in the freezer, taped to the fire alarm, every fucking place you can imagine," he said. "The guys would get into it and I'd just slide under the table and out the door. I tried not to get to know them too much, but they just kept after me. Then one night there's a knock on my door. I open it up, and this nasty-ass hooker kisses me right on the mouth. And one of the parolees is standing behind her and he says, 'Look what I got for you!' "

There's new ownership, and it's a little better now, but even now we have several parolees in here, an ex-con released after five years for assault with a deadly weapon, a few junkies. Two weeks before I arrived, there was a heroin OD upstairs. The sight of the junkie's body being removed still haunts the fifty-two-year-old schizophrenic who lives above me: Patrick carries a flashlight around the house to shine on the "spirits."

Anyway, I bring this up now because we all had a surprise in the house last night. Earlier in the week, one of the tenants upstairs had been taken away by police, and the rumor in the house was that he had been busted for selling drugs to kids at a nearby school. No one worried much about that. "Shit, I wish he'd sold *me* drugs," said Jay, the above-mentioned ex-con. But last night it turned out we were wrong. The tenant had actually been arrested not by the police, but by the FBI, and not for selling drugs, but for robbing five New Hampshire banks. The news was greeted with much hilarity in the plywood-paneled communal kitchen, where everyone goes every day to eat microwaveable dinners and drink enormous amounts of Budweiser.

"Hah! What an idiot!" said a young skinny guy named Jason, recently released from heroin rehab. "What kind of a moron robs five banks in New Hampshire—and *stays* in New Hampshire?"

"Worse than that, he stayed here," said Curt. "If I did that, I'd be sitting in the highest point of the state, looking down the whole time. Just looking straight down."

The bank robber is apparently now sitting in a federal facility in Dover, and he's looking at 125 years. He left some stuff behind in his room.

"Tons of these weird computer CDs," said Curt. "Buy without a down payment. 'All about mutual funds.' Stock market safe havens. He was looking to *invest*." He laughed. "I guess he wanted to be a real financier."

Saturday, November 1

Hilarious headline on the front page of the *Boston Herald* this morning: "Kerry Blasts Dean over NRA Backing." Why hilarious? Because the accompanying picture was of Kerry standing in an Iowan field with an orange vest on, a big rifle on his shoulder, looking contentedly upon a pheasant he'd just shot.

I would like to say that John Kerry is the only candidate spineless and stupid enough to blast an opponent for a gun-friendly position on the same day he invites journalists to follow him as he shoots defenseless animals out of the air, but this just isn't true. I have actually already observed this behavior several times on the campaign. Clark does this midspeech whenever he brings up guns. He often talks about his experiences as a kid searching his house early for Christmas presents, coming upon the family gun, and not touching it. The story ends up being, at once, about the traditional love of guns within the Clark family and the need to keep guns away from children. Something in there for everybody, as it were. That said, Kerry is the only person to do this kind of thing in giant font on the front page of his hometown paper.

Kerry must be calling in some favors with the home field media. There has been a blitz of mostly friendly stories about him in the two Boston dailies lately. A front-page story in today's *Globe,* written by a person named Patrick Healy, breathlessly portrays Kerry as a kind of reluctant, soft-spoken JFK with a mild ideological consistency problem. There were some priceless passages in the piece. Healy begins a section about Kerry's Iraq policies by saying, "The war has been a particular frustration for the senator." Funny, I would have thought that the war was particularly frustrating for the people on the business end of it. Then Healy moves on to quote the senator:

"My position in a nutshell [is], I believe Saddam Hussein should have been held accountable, and I think it should have been done right, and if I'd been president it would have been done right," Kerry said. "One simple sentence. There you are."

This convoluted passage screams for somebody to point out that this is exactly what Nixon was saying about Vietnam in 1968. Nixon had a commercial about Vietnam during that election that was eerily similar in tone to Kerry's "simple" sentence. The voice-over read:

"Never before has so much military, economic, and diplomatic power been used as ineffectively as in Vietnam."

As Joe McGinniss wrote in *The Selling of the President 1968:* "The war was not bad because of insane suffering and death. The war was bad because it was *ineffective.*"

Healy's piece finished up the three-headed format with a man-on-the-street quote, in which a seventy-four-year-old Korean War veteran named Doug Kelley compared Kerry to JFK. Kerry's own staff couldn't have done better.

The accompanying photo, by Laurie Swope, depicts a heroic-looking Kerry sitting, face bathed in angelic white, talking to ("connecting with," in the language of the article) a bar patron in Portsmouth. The senator looks like a cross between God and Santa Claus in the picture.

I remember Swope. I was there in Portsmouth that day, following the candidate around in a gorilla suit. The thing had been sitting in my trunk for months and I had gotten frustrated enough to start wearing it to events, as a sort of protest. In Portsmouth, I also kept trying to get into the background of Swope's pictures. Among other things, I was faintly hoping for a caption that read something like:

AROUND THE BUSH: *John Kerry and a gorilla address voters in Portsmouth, NH. Kerry, left.*

But it was not to be, because Kerry staffers kept intercepting me everywhere I went, covering my gorilla face with a Kerry poster. One, a prim, WASP-looking post-college type, swooped down on me less than ten seconds after my arrival.

"You must be a journalist," he said. It was a joke—he was trying to say something cheeky about journalists, to a crazy person. . . . He straightened up with gross surprise when I told him he was right.

"Uh-huh. *New York Press*," I said, handing him my card. With the rubber gorilla hands, digging the card out of my bag was a cumbersome process; it took about ten uncomfortable seconds.

He examined the card. "Uh, okay. Why are you here in a gorilla suit?"

I shrugged. "When your candidate stops being full of shit," I said, "I'll stop wearing a gorilla suit."

He nodded and walked away. For the next ten minutes, as Kerry made his way down Market Street, I had a lot of company. A few security types came over, just to let me know they were there—"How's it going?," that sort of thing. Nonetheless, they let me drift behind within six feet of the senator. I made a point of not reaching into my bag.

I was getting bored, just letting the tape run, when suddenly Kerry himself whipped around and walked up to me. It took me by surprise, an admirable show of backbone: confront the situation head-on, don't just let this hairy creature trail behind you and mess with your concentration. "So, what do we have here?" he asked, shaking my hand.

"I'm press," I said.

"Who are you taping that for?" he said.

"*New York Press*," I said.

"All dressed up?" he said. "Halloween?"

I reared my head back. "What do you mean?" I asked.

"Your costume," he said, pointing.

"What costume?" I said.

Watching a big-league politician do the math in these situations is an interesting thing. Kerry took about a second after my answer to determine that absolutely nothing positive lay in the future of this conversation. He whipped around, found a veteran in the crowd with an Army pin on, and stepped right toward him.

"Now there's someone in my club," he said, grasping the man's shoulder.

Later on, as I sat with the gorilla suit half-off (pant legs on, unzipped chest hanging down), smoking a cigarette after the "downtown walk," I caught that first Kerry aide talking on his cell phone and arranging a dinner with his friends. The conversation was centered around trying to find a place that would accommodate his picky girlfriend. "Well, she wants some place that has barbecue," he said. "But you know, her idea of barbecue is probably like *calamari*."

Monday, November 3

Sometimes you have to wonder—what exactly is it that separates a "real" candidate from, say, a lunatic who dreams of the presidency from the confines of a rubber room? It ought to be that the real candidates are the sane ones, respecting the awesome power of the presidency, with a sober understanding of the task before them. Because if that is not true, if the converse is the case, then that would mean that the asylum is the outside world, while the sane are locked up like madmen, left with nothing but hopeless fantasies.

Today was "registration day" in New Hampshire, a quadrennial milestone in the presidential election process. This is the day when the secretary of state's office in Concord opens its doors for anyone with a desire to run for president and a willingness to pay $1,000 for the privilege. Traditionally this is an opportunity for the press to fill 600 words and a photo slot with a bland account of this or that major candidate showing up to put his John Hancock on his application form (the press loves these Capra-esque scenes of Mighty Power Brokers submitting to the reassuring terrestrial civic rituals), the account ending with a bemused summary of the various no-name weirdos who also show up to throw their hats in the ring.

I showed up early to meet the Other Candidates. I briefly considered putting my own name on the ballot, but $1,000 was out of my range. I would have to be content with mere Journalism. I expected a parade of demented egotists, clinical cases, and perhaps a man or two in a chicken suit—in other words, a caricature of the actual slate of major candidates. I was almost right, but within that "almost" there was room for a little revelation.

The secretary of state's office was a bustle. There was a small crowd of middle-aged female clerks rushing to and fro, rolling their eyes and sighing like exhausted nursery school teachers. Paula Penney laughed when I asked her how her morning had gone so far—it was ten o'clock.

"Oh, yeah," she said. "We've had five already. Look, they're onto you."

She pointed. In the hallway, several funny-looking men were peering in, obviously aroused by the presence of a journalist. A vessel into which insane theories could be poured. I sucked it up and took out my tape recorder.

Harry Braun . . . with him I'm going to skip ahead to a description of his platform, because his physical appearance is impossible to capture otherwise. Braun, a scientist and energy consultant (he ran a massive wind power project in Arizona) who once ran against John McCain for Congress as the Democratic nominee, is running for president on a platform of saving the world through the construction of a massive matrix of sea-based wind power plants. He calls them "windships" and in your first minute with him, he'll hand you an ornate color illustration of one of those ships. They look like massive free-floating square riggers, something out of Jules Verne. Now here's the key thing. Braun's windships produce hydrogen. His whole vision of humanity's bright future is centered around hydrogen energy; he has plans for cross-country underground pipelines, hydrogen tankers, hydrogen-run homes, cars. . . . You can ask Braun about something as far away from energy as the prison system, and he'll be talking about hydrogen within two minutes. But the weird thing is that even within these monomaniacal parameters, he . . . makes sense!

"Hydrogen is completely inexhaustible," he said. "You'll never run out. So we're going to make the United States energy independent, so that we don't have to import oil from Iraq, or anywhere else. It suddenly changes our entire foreign policy, which has been driven by oil for the last sixty years. That's why we support dictatorships, even though our foreign policy people say we support democracy. It's like the Indians all over again. We say we want to help you, but in fact we just want to rob you. . . ."

Physically Braun is a character from the 1940s brought magically to life. He wears a crisp three-piece pinstripe suit and elegant gold-wire glasses, and carries a long black umbrella with a mahogany handle, which he frequently pointed for emphasis in conversation. His hair is the whitest of white, and it would seem impossible to imagine a germ existing anywhere on his person.

"We've mass-murdered a lot of innocent people for oil," he said. "We need to have a new administration. We need to bring our troops home from these countries, because we don't need their oil. We need to build windships. We will employ millions of Americans to do it. . . ."

He ruffled in his burgundy briefcase and took out pictures of hydrogen-prototype cars, homes, "cold" pipelines. As I watched his pink hands and his white hair, it struck me. He *looks* like hydrogen! He is the pure, light element, brought to life in human form!

Braun was nuts, but only slightly nuts. There was no doubt in my mind that he believed in the science of his proposals, and I suspected, given some of my readings on the subject, that much of what he was talking about might even have been feasible. When I brought up the Davis-Besse nuclear power plant in Toledo—a little-known burgeoning environmental disaster story—Braun seized on the subject and recited to me the entire sorry history of that plant, down to the number of inches worn away from the containment dome. He knew what he was talking about.

And as I listened to him, I wondered: why is this person automatically dismissed as a lunatic? What could be more natural than a scientist running for president, taking a case directly to the people for the funding of a massive, revolutionary investment in world-changing science? The campaign is a time for national discussion—why can't it be about science? Why does that kind of vision have to take a back seat to this dreary, confined dialogue about tax policy and abortion rights?

The other thing that struck me about Braun was his idealism. His political dreams imagined the awesome power of the presidency as a means of ridding the world of all its problems. None of the "real" candidates ever gives off even a whiff of this quality. Even the sincere idealism of Dennis Kucinich is a relatively fractured and limited thing in comparison, occasionally rising to something sweeping like a Department of Peace, but more often than not bogged down in resignation to the limitations of the system. In the voice of Kucinich one hears the frustration of years of committee battles, and the hope of depressingly elusive, long-sought minor victories. It dims his bulb a little.

Not so with Braun. His bulb was very bright, and it burned with pure hydrogen power. It was really too bad that he was crazy—just crazy enough to keep him safely hopeful in his bubble, and also just crazy enough to insulate him from ever being taken seriously.

"It's much safer, hydrogen. . . . People say, well, what about the *Hindenburg?* What most people don't realize is that two-thirds of the passengers and crew survived. And the thirty-five people who died in that accident?"

He raised an eyebrow.

"Yes?" I said.

"Thirty-three of them jumped," he said triumphantly. "And they died from the fall."

I frowned. "They would have died, though, wouldn't they?"

"No!" he said. "They jumped out, died from the fall."

"Yeah, but," I said. "Wasn't there this spectacular, ghastly fire?"

He shook his head. "It was all . . . look," he said. "Hydrogen is the lightest element in the universe. The ghastly fire you're talking about was above the gondola. There wasn't anybody above the gasbags. They were all below the gondola."

"Okay," I said. "But if the gondola had been above the gasbags, they would have died, wouldn't they?"

He thought about that. "Yes, they would have."

We parted amicably. In the ways that mattered, he was certainly less crazy than John Kerry or Wes Clark.

On my way out, I ran into another candidate—and this was a very different kind of encounter. Ten minutes after talking to Bob Haines, in fact, I sat there with my tape recorder, wondering whether I was now obligated to turn over my interview to the Secret Service as evidence. It was a real moral dilemma.

Haines is a visible figure; I see him everywhere in Manchester. He is a frumpy Texan in a cowboy hat whose clothes are always wrinkled and imply even at a distance a barely concealed catastrophe of stinky underwear. This was the chicken-suit contingent in the candidate mix, and I wasn't particularly interested in talking to him. But he cornered me in the hallway and gave me a convoluted and mostly incoherent biography. Through heavily pepper-minted breath he explained that he had already run twice, but so had Ronald Reagan before he won. He wasn't interested in telling me his platform. I was about to walk away when he grabbed my elbow. He literally grabbed my elbow. And then he said:

"Texas . . . is not big enough for the both of us."

"You and Bush?" I said.

He nodded. "The White House . . . is not big enough for the both of us."

I smiled. "You could share it," I said. "You on one side, he on the other. So long as you had separate beds, it'd be okay."

He frowned. "No," he said. "It's High Noon in New Hampshire."

"Okay," I said.

"It's High Noon in New Hampshire," he repeated. "You get my drift?"

"High Noon. Right," I said, wresting free.

I started to walk away. He called after me. "You ever see *High Noon?*"

"Yeah," I said. "Gary Cooper. He shoots the bad guys in the end."

"It's High Noon in New Hampshire," he said for the third time.

Penney, the clerk, had walked out into the hall in the middle of this and followed me down the stairs. "Yeah, he's a strange one," she said. "He's been arrested a bunch of times."

"For what?" I said.

"I think he was waving a gun around in Manchester. Something like that."

TOGETHER
THEY ARE LEAD-
ING US ALONG A
ROUGH ROAD WITH
SHARP EDGES, AND
WHILE WE MAY ARGUE
ABOUT WHERE WE ARE
HEADING, WE HAVE NO
CHOICE BUT TO FOLLOW,
BECAUSE
A nation fights as ONE.

5

FALL/WINTER 2003–2004

The Influence of Reality Television
Reality Television Before World War III

Excerpt from William Shirer IV, *The Rise and Fall of the United States* (Putnam, 2037). From the chapter entitled "The Anschluss Begins."

In the years before the campaign of outright territorial expansion began, entertainment had begun to play an increasingly important role in American society. The evolution of American television entertainment advanced most particularly on two fronts. The first was an increasing emphasis on a celebration of law enforcement and the military in the prime-time drama genre.

As discussed in a previous chapter, this trend reached its peak in 2008, when eighty-nine of the ninety-three original drama and situation comedy shows on the four networks had law enforcement themes, with ABC's *CSI: Binghamton* and CBS's *Coast Guard Dogcatcher* leading the ratings. It is perhaps fortunate that the nuclear holocaust wiped out all video records of the leading children's show from that year, a puppet vehicle called *FEMA Presents Armed and Prepared*—although some survivors still recall it vividly.

The second trend in American television during this time was the continual blurring of fantasy and reality, and a muddying of the lines between news and dramatic programming. The trend began innocently enough when the networks, in a cost-cutting move, produced dramas that featured ordinary people engaged in idiotic and demeaning contests of strength on faraway islands, with the participants voting one another out of the game. It progressed with shows like *Extreme Makeover* (2003), in which self-hating neurotics volunteered to be mutilated by plastic surgeons for the entertainment of the public.

In a parallel development, politics during this time began increasingly to resemble reality programming, in particular the elimination-survival shows. The 2003 election of the action star Arnold Schwarzenegger to the governorship of California was of particular importance as a pioneering precursor to full-blown reality political programming.

No single television show, however, was to have more influence on the terrible events to come than *Extreme Fascist Makeover*, launched in 2007. The appearance of this inspired piece of programming is one of the more unlikely subplots of the American tragedy. It was conceived by a onetime political dissident named Matt Taibbi, whose late conversion to the imperial cause has caused him to be judged very harshly by history; indeed, his very name would become a synonym for *traitor* in languages all across the planet. In his memoir, *Why Not? Diary of a Collaborator*, published shortly before his execution, he describes the origins of the idea:

> I tuned into the news on CNN just after watching an old rerun of *Queer Eye for the Straight Guy*, and found myself troubled by the drab appearance of President Bush and his lieutenants as they walked through the ruins of Damascus. . . . It occurred to me at that moment that America was a strapping fascist hunk, straining to get out but trapped in the frumpy wardrobe of a Jeffersonian democracy. And I thought to myself: "There's a TV show in this."

Through family connections, Taibbi managed to get a proposal into the hands of David Collins, an executive producer for Scout Productions, which had produced the gay-makeover show *Queer Eye*. Negotiations ensued, and finally Taibbi and Scout convinced the John Birch cable channel to produce a pilot with former congressman and Fox anchorman Joe Scarborough engaged as on-air talent. The first program, a "fascist makeover" of President Bush and the Oval Office, was to have far-reaching policy implications for years to come.

In the program, five fascists of various types—one Le Penite, one German Nazi, one Italian blackshirt, one Spanish Falangist, and an offensive coordinator for the Nebraska Cornhuskers—"made over" the Oval Office and Bush in the areas of "fashion, grooming, food and wine, interior design, and culture." In his memoir, Taibbi describes the transformation:

> We took Bush away to be fitted for epaulettes. . . . When he came back, he found that we'd painted the White House jet black and covered it with scary vines. . . . The fence posts around the presidential residence were adorned with human heads, which he quickly recognized, to his delight, as belonging to Democratic congressmen. The walls on the inside were covered with his presidential portraits, while on the front lawn there was a raging bonfire fueled by portraits of his predecessors. On his desk, we'd left an executive order for the cancellation of elections. . . . We asked him what he thought. He laughed. "This is amazing," he said. "Laura is going to love this." Then this little abashed smile came on his face, and he wiped one of his eyes. That was the money shot. The show was pretty much off and running from there.

The show was an immediate hit, and subsequent episodes featured makeovers of the U.S. Constitution, Reed College, Cuba, and the Sundance Film Festival, among others. In one of the highest-rated and most rebroadcast programs in the history of American television, *Extreme Fascist Makeover* spent a half-hour tackling the *New York Times*—and ultimately, in what must be seen as a humorous gesture, left it exactly as it had been.

Historians who blame the subsequent "makeover" invasions of Europe and Southeast Asia on the show are at least partly correct, though the true blame for these later wars should probably rest elsewhere. Certainly the merging of programming and policy was a drawn-out, gradual process that began long before the show's appearance, and was considerably advanced even by then, though most Americans were probably not aware of it.

It is an undeniable fact that for more than a decade before the big wars, the chief trend in all television programming was a kind of growing uniformity of the broadcast aesthetic—in which all events, no matter how disparate in character, were produced in an identically salable style loosely identified as *good television*. Wars were thus covered in the same splashy style as football games (complete with colorful commentary), while elections were indistinguishable from ad campaigns, and televised trials were given the same glitzy graphics and segues as police shows. As the post-war historian Fritz Werner wrote:

> Throughout the later prewar period, what was successful politics was seldom not also successful television. . . . And with the lines continually blurring between fantasy and reality on the air, and with the medium's rapacious quest for marketable new taboos to shatter, it was probably inevitable that successful television would eventually itself become successful politics. *Extreme Fascist Makeover* was nothing if not good television.

The fate of Taibbi is one of the more curious footnotes of the nuclear wars. Captured and castrated by Dutch guerrillas in the Californian campaign, he was for many years displayed in a cage in an Amsterdam zoo, which mistakenly identified him as late-era Bush administration Propaganda Chief Jonathan Franzen. When the body of the real Franzen was discovered in the arms of another male corpse in a bomb shelter on the island of Réunion, Taibbi was forced, under torture, to reveal his true identity. Victorious humanity was astounded at its good fortune in unearthing this notorious war criminal, and a sensational international show trial ensued, culminating in his public electrocution.

As he awaited sentencing, Taibbi managed to pen his memoir. Today it stands as an ultimate testament to blind careerism. Even as he faced death, he managed to write more than 200 pages detailing his failed efforts to sign actress Eliza Dushku to the show, and in the end he confessed only to having "furthered stereotypes." But history knows differently.

One Penis, Under God

The Candidates Believe the Children Are the Penis

David Hasselhoff has nothing on me. My reindeer-nose-red 1994 Grand Am is now the ultimate campaign trail vehicle, a souped-up T-72 of political journalism. Just take a look at the equipment inside.

A short list of items in the trunk: one full army uniform, complete with West Point hat; a gorilla suit; two cervical collars, one in 3.5-inch size, one the full 4-incher; a stretch black pinstripe suit, three sizes too small for me; a plastic briefcase containing two dozen minicassettes and a booklet of Beyoncé stickers; a CD of pet clip art with 6,000 pictures of dogs; the complete works of Devo; and some other unspeakable items related to personal hygiene for use in emergency situations.

Additionally I have, behind the passenger-side visor inside the car, an auxiliary set of gorilla hands. At some later stage of the campaign I'll be able to explain what all of this is for; I really can't get into it too much right now. But there is one new piece of equipment that I'd like to discuss. I broke it out two weeks ago. It's a white sailor hat covered with marks from a black magic marker. Residents in New Hampshire can guess what this is all about because it is a tribute to a New England sports legend, the great Bruins goalie Gerry Cheevers. Cheevers used to carve a notch in his mask and color it black every time the thing saved his life. He played a long time and by the end of his career, you almost couldn't see any white in it. He was scarier than Jason.

I wear the hat every time I watch a candidate speak. And every time he

---

October 28, 2003, *New York Press.*

mouths the phrase along the lines of "It's about creating jobs," I make a black mark. In two weeks, I have almost three dozen marks. The last one came at Wes Clark's "major economic address" at the UNH-Manchester campus the other day ("That is why we need to do whatever is necessary to create jobs . . ."). John Kerry, I've observed, is good for two marks per appearance.

With a few notable exceptions, the speeches of the candidates are a revoltingly dependable mishmash of about nine or ten clichés. This is political oration written with a fork; you take a dozen or so key words (*challenge, hope, opportunity, leadership, security,* etc.), arrange them on a bed of lettuce, and serve them up one after the other in between statistics-laden bitching about the Bush administration. The rest of the presentation is pretty much all window dressing: flags, slogans, pins, tallness, a tan, a backdrop of mute ethnic minorities. And unless you've lost your voice (as Clark did last week), you punctuate the whole thing with a lot of shouting, hysterics, and goofy gesticulations—pound your fist and do a looping double thumbs-up at the phrase ". . . for our *children!*" The next day, the *New York Times* calls it an "impassioned address."

Hopefully someday a dedicated taxonomist will make a full map of campaign cliché phyla. I've tried to get a start, but it's a monumental task. The complete catalogue would make a great drinking game for campaign trail journalists; one beer per cliché would leave us all wasted by 11 in the morning. Here's a short list of some of the candidates' more laughable habits:

Right here in ———! The absolute king of campaign speech clichés, it's as though the campaign were an elaborate homework assignment in which the teacher told all nine students, "Write a stump speech containing the phrase 'Right here in New Hampshire!'" Every last one of the candidates does it, even Dennis Kucinich, who normally uses an exponentially smaller number of clichés than the other candidates. Again, Kerry is the master here. In the last speech of his I caught, at UNH-Durham last Monday, he did it twice (e.g., "Right here in New Hampshire, President Bush made a promise to deal with the four major pollutants. . . ."). During the debate in New York a month ago, Al Sharpton delivered a beauty: "Right here in Queens," he said, "we read Bush's lips. He lied." The debate was held in Manhattan.

Americans for America! A few weeks ago, I went into the chamber of commerce in Claremont, New Hampshire, and asked where I could find the Gephardt campaign offices. A woman named Alicia Beck, the executive director of a community-development association called Main Street Claremont, laughed. "It's on the fourth floor, I think," she said. "Just go up there and you'll find it. It probably has a sign that says 'Americans for Gephardt' or something."

Actually the sign said, "Guaranteed Health Care for Every American."

All the candidates have the "America" slogan front and center, and the way each of the candidates approaches this hideous prerequisite says a lot about their campaigns. Probably the driest is "Dean for America," although that one is a little weird, too. (Is that what America needs? More "Dean"?) Edwards's "Real Solutions for America" is, like the candidate himself, roundly mocked by journalists for its hand-up-your-skirt cheesiness. The Clark slogan is appropriate for a babbling, senile old codger in the last death throes of a terminal ambition-sickness: "New American Patriotism." (A Clark staffer snapped at me last week when I asked if it was in opposition to the Old Foreign Patriotism.) And the Kucinich effort, "A Prayer for America," might as well be a sign that says, "Dump My Books."

The penis test. Campaign oratory has worsened considerably since the advent of the dial survey—that hideous research technique in which test subjects are asked to turn a dial to one side (favorable) or another (unfavorable) in response to words spoken by candidates. The results of these surveys guarantee that certain words will be repeated ad nauseam, often forced into places in the text where they don't belong, to fit some kind of mandatory quota.

Curiously, traditional Democratic dial-survey words like *compassion* and *healing* have given way this election to "tough" Republican words emphasizing strength and fatherly qualities. Last week I did a test to see if any candidate could give a speech without using some combination of the following words less than a total of one hundred times: *challenge, responsibility, leadership, hope, values, opportunity, principles, future, patriotism, protect, tough choices, change, action.* Turns out I overestimated things—slightly. I don't have the final results yet, but it looks like the average for a stump speech is actually about fifty. (The Clark address last Wednesday came in at sixty-one.)

If you ever want to pass an amusing half-hour, download a candidate's speech and use the find/change function to replace all of those words with the word *penis*. The results will tell you pretty much everything you need to know about modern political speech. Here are some samples:

Clark, October 22: "The New American Penis is not just about matters of war and peace; it's about jobs and penis and penis right here at home. It's about taking penis for our shared penis. It's about reclaiming what's been lost, but also about building a better penis for all our children."

Dean candidacy announcement, June 23: "The Americans I have met love their country. They believe deeply in its promise, our penis, and our penises. But they know something is wrong and they want to take penis. They want to do something to right our path. But they feel Washington isn't listening. And as individuals, they lack the power to penis the course those in Washington have put us on."

But the best penis I've yet encountered was a Lieberman speech on September 15 in Manchester: "We have a penis to make the penis of our country better by penis the penis of this nation!"

Stuffed on Thanksgiving
In Baghdad, the Fourth Estate Buys the Fake

It was a media event without precedent—an elaborately staged production in which a small group of journalists was literally kidnapped, flown into a war zone, stuffed headfirst into the ass of a Thanksgiving turkey, and then made to flap its arms for the amusement of all humanity when the commander-in-chief blew into a kazoo. A more dramatic example of Stockholm syndrome has probably never been shown on television.

There are going to be a lot of Bush-haters out there who will be tempted

---

December 2, 2003, *New York Press.*

to evince disgust at the "shock and awe" Thanksgiving trip for the obvious reasons: the stage-managed sentimentality, the humiliating spectacle of our commander-in-chief whizzing in and out of Baghdad under cover of darkness like a campus flasher, the billionaire president's simultaneously hilarious and sickening appropriation of poor-person language in asking for a "warm meal somewhere."

This is wrong. If we are to be honest with ourselves, we must admit that this stunt was certainly the closest thing to physical courage that George Bush has ever publicly demonstrated. Not that it isn't tempting to make light of some of the "hazards" he faced ("The president encountered and witnessed traffic for the first time in three years," White House Communications Director Dan Bartlett told reporters), but there's no denying that the trip was a serious logistical achievement and not without real risks. Even if he were only following the orders of his pollster, Bush should at least be given credit for not shitting his pants in the line of duty.

It's Bush's job, after all, to lead us into disastrous foreign-policy adventures and then try to sugarcoat them with mawkish, grandstanding publicity stunts. No one should be upset with the president for doing his job. What we should be upset about is the national press corps behaving like PR agents, which is what happened last week.

Rather than tune out and tell the president to pay for his campaign ads like all the other candidates, the entire American media rolled over and covered the stunt at face value, even after the administration made it clear that the only journalists they would invite along would be the ones who could be counted on to portray Bush as a cross between Christ and Douglas MacArthur.

Take Terrence Hunt of the Associated Press, one of the thirteen journalists selected for this courageous exercise in editorial independence. When finally called upon to file his surprise-guest story, Hunt, perhaps moved by his Mesopotamian surroundings, described Bush in mythical tones:

> At that moment, President Bush strode forth from the wings in an Army track suit emblazoned with a First Armored Division patch. The bored crowd shot

from their seats and whooped. As he surveyed the crowd, a tear dripped down the president's cheek. . . .

It may very well be that in the age of Plutarch, kings not only wept over conquered horizons, but also were said to "stride forth from the wings." From reading Hunt, you'd never know that the vocabulary of executive entrance has advanced in a less hysterical direction since then. But such literary trumpet calls were about par for the course for the major dailies, which followed a peculiar pattern in their coverage: first gushingly swallow Bush's PR stunt whole on the front page, then later freak out about what they'd done in pusillanimous, self-hating analysis pieces somewhere deep in the bowels of their news sections.

The *New York Times* was a great example. America's paper of record was one of dozens of publications around the country to run Hunt's piece on its front page, and for the *Times* this in itself was already a kind of gross public surrender to the White House. After all, the reason they'd had to resort to leading with a shoddy wire-service report was that its own correspondents, like CNN's, had been conspicuously disinvited to the Air Force One adventure.

That this was in retaliation for unfriendly Iraq coverage was obvious. The White House has been quite open about its use of tactics like these for some time now. Citing concerns about the "filter" through which the ostensibly cheerful news from Iraq was reaching ordinary Americans, Bush last month bypassed the major networks to give a series of eight-minute interviews to local television stations. CBS called it the "public relations equivalent of a declaration of war."

Similarly, Bush last spring passed over *Washington Post* reporters Mike Allen and Dana Milbank at the notorious prewar press conference, apparently in retaliation for a *Post* Iraq story entitled "Taking Liberties with the Truth." And *Houston Chronicle* White House reporter Bennett Roth was frozen out for months after asking an untoward question about Bush's daughter.

So how did the mighty *Times* react to being forced to take its turn at being publicly slapped in the face with the proverbial presidential rubber chicken? Well, first it dutifully followed the New York tabloids in splashing Bush's Julia-Child-holding-the-turkey pool photo on the front page. Then it ran Hunt's piece underneath, below the loving headline, "Surprise Guest Makes It Worth the Wait."

Then, inside, at the very end of a spineless analysis piece, it had its own Washington bureau chief, Phillip Taubman, whisper the faintest of third-person protests to reporters Jacques Steinberg and Jim Rutenberg:

> Mr. Taubman said he respected pool protocol but questioned why the press corps traveling on Air Force One could not have been enlarged somewhat, given the gravity of a visit by the president to Iraq on Thanksgiving.

This, folks, is how the press fights back in America. If the *Times* had any balls at all, it would have answered Bush in kind—either by ignoring his nauseating trip entirely, or, even better, by burying his turkey picture under a page-19 feature about Belgian anti-fur activists. Instead, it invited its readers to sit in on the pathetic spectacle of its editors and reporters timidly complaining to *one another* about having been left out of the fun.

The *Washington Post* also complained, even though it had been included on the trip. Mike Abramowitz, the paper's national editor, ventured to the *Times* that the abduction of its reporter Mike Allen to a foreign country, and the confiscation of his cell phone, had perhaps in some mysterious way disrupted the editor-journalist relationship. "I don't feel entirely comfortable with that," Abramowitz said. "I prefer to know what our White House reporter is doing." Meanwhile, the *Post* dutifully ran the Julia Child photo and all the rest of it on the front page.

Outside of America, the response to Bush's stunt was universally savage and unrelenting, with the London-based *Independent* leading the way (front-page headline: "The Turkey Has Landed"). Many papers chose a Caesar theme to lampoon Bush: the headline in the Lebanese *An-Nahar* paper hissed,

"I Came, I Saw Nothing, but I Will Conquer." Other papers were less flippant in their condemnation: the Barcelona daily *La Vanguardia* prosaically commented that "George W. Bush does not attend the funerals of soldiers killed in Iraq, but has dinner in Baghdad with those who dream of coming home alive."

Only in the States did reporters swallow the whole thing without irony. Even when Bush pissed in their professional faces, America's intrepid journalists did not blink, instead seeming glad for the attention. Here is how *Newsday* described one particularly delicious scene:

> Soon they touched down at Andrews Air Force Base, Md., taxied into a hangar where another Air Force One jet was waiting, and climbed out into the white and noisy, brightly lit space. [White House reporter Mike] Allen looked up and saw Bush at the top of the plane's stairs. . . . He paused, and holding his thumb and pinkie apart at his ear in the symbol for the cell phone, he mouthed, "No calls, got it?"
>
> In case they did not, the president, with good humor, made the "cut" sign across his throat.

I'm not sure a real journalist would have found too much "good humor" in that scene. Then again, how could a real journalist have gotten on that plane?

Fascism Is the Answer

On January 4, the *New York Times* ran a lengthy article about the image problem of the Democratic Party. Written by James Traub, who, I suppose, is an authority on such things, the article sought to answer the question of whether or not the Democrats could convince voters that they were the party of strength, or whether they were, as Traub put it, still "lost in a funk of pacifism." Here is how the article leads off:

January 13, 2004, *New York Press.*

A few weeks ago, I asked Howard Dean how, given his vehement opposition to the war in Iraq, he felt he could overcome the Democrats' reputation as the anti-war party. "I think you're still in the old paradigm, which says that they're the party of strength and we're the party of weakness," Dean admonished me as I sat across from him on his campaign plane. The chaos in Iraq, he said, had upended the old stereotypes. In John F. Kennedy's day, Dean pointed out, the Democrats enjoyed the reputation as the party of resolution. "I think this may be the year to regain it, oddly enough," Dean said.

I laughed out loud after reading this paragraph. The humor here was in imagining the reaction of Noam Chomsky to the article's very premise. Here was the *New York Times,* vilified by the right as the great Trojan horse of leftist propaganda, writing an iconic piece whose premise held that the Democratic Party—the Democratic Party!—needed to *overcome* its anti-war reputation. And there was Howard Dean, almost universally described in the media as the next incarnation of Leon Trotsky, *agreeing* with this premise.

Dean did not say, "There's no shame in being thought of as the anti-war party. The only problem is that we're not really anti-war." Instead, what he said, essentially, was, "We're not really anti-war, never were, in fact, and I intend to show the American people how tough we really are!"

His plan? To sneak around Bush's right: "Our model is to get around the president's right, as John Kennedy did to Nixon," said Dean. The article goes on to celebrate the party's decision, made after the successive defeats of Adlai Stevenson, to campaign on the threat of a "missile gap" with the Soviet Union. Traub is careful to note that such a missile gap never existed, and that this campaign tactic was little more than a cynical play on the paranoid fears of Cold War America, but he nonetheless celebrates this strategy for helping John Kennedy ride into power. Similarly, he blasts George McGovern for stupidly following his conscience in the matter of the Vietnam War, an unforgivable blunder that led to a historic ass-whipping at the hands of Richard Nixon. Traub concludes his article:

Strong and wrong beats weak and right—that's the bugbear the Democrats have to contend with. George McGovern may have had it right in 1972, but he won Massachusetts, and Richard Nixon won the other 49 states. McGovern recently said that he is a big fan of Howard Dean, whose campaign reminds him very much of his own. Dean may want to ask him to hold off on the endorsement.

Anyone who wants to understand why the Democratic Party (barring a catastrophic implosion by the Republicans) will never win another major election in this country need only read this article. It correctly identifies the core problem of the party, which is this: voters are repulsed by weakness. What it fails to get right is the fact that the party, as currently constructed, will never be able to get around this problem. Why? Because weakness is inherent in the party's ideology.

There are only two ways to appear strong. One is to stand for something. The other is to kick ass. Today's Democrats most emphatically are not equipped to do either.

On the standing-for-something front, that question was settled long ago. Nothing can be more obvious than that the current Democratic leadership considers actual principle a laughable electoral weakness. This was demonstrated most forcefully a few weeks ago when Hillary Clinton joked about Mahatma Gandhi having worked in a St. Louis gas station (on January 3, Hillary prefaced a Gandhi quote by saying, "He ran a gas station down in St. Louis"). If Gandhi were running in this race, the Democratic Leadership Council—bet on it—would be warning of a McGovern-like landslide defeat. Democrats consider strength to be the skillful capture of swing votes via the tactically precise execution of a fuzzy policy of standing for nothing at all, as in the case of Bill Clinton.

As for kicking ass, forget about it. Any party that has to roll up its shirtsleeves and pleadingly show off its biceps to James Traub is doomed from the start. The way to show voters that you are strong is to walk into the room with James Traub and punch him in the face. Then, as he crawls around on the floor picking his teeth out of the carpet, you ask him: "What was your question again?"

Such a display would doubtless trigger all kinds of press reaction. But there certainly wouldn't be any more 7,500-word treatises on your "toughness" problem.

The Democrats' problem is that they are trying to counter the actual, admirable viciousness of the Republicans with a cheap imitation of viciousness. Both parties are equally unscrupulous, but the viciousness gap will remain real and unbridgeable—until some changes are made.

I think it is high time that we all admitted that outright fascism has a lot to offer American society, and the Democratic Party in particular. Not only would it be an enormously successful electoral strategy, but it would also be vastly superior as a governing principle to the halting, pusillanimous, fake fascism of the Republican Party. Just think of the benefits of claiming the presidency on the following platform:

World Domination

This would be the centerpiece of the new domestic policy of the Democratic Party—and I stress the word *domestic*. Because it is here that the fatal weakness of the Republican Party would be laid bare.

As it stands, the Republicans are tougher than the Democrats because they will not hesitate to bomb the hell out of anyone, provided that the target cannot meaningfully fight back. But here's the thing: the Republicans are not interested in ruling other countries, any more than they are interested in ruling the United States. All they really want to do is make money. They only use military force insofar as it is necessary to (a) extract another country's resources, and (b) ensure that these countries become and remain markets for American products. Beyond these parameters, they're amazingly squeamish about using the military.

A Democratic candidate can expose this weakness easily by announcing a blunt post-election plan. On his first day in office, he signs an executive order declaring every person on earth to be a citizen of the United States. Around the world, the offer is made: any person who wishes to have American citizenship can go to the nearest embassy, have his photo taken, and be given a passport.

In three weeks, the population of the United States would triple. Perhaps even quadruple. Within a year, we would be larger than India and China combined. Europe, the last holdout and the last serious threat to our preeminence, would quickly be reduced in comparison to a tiny, castrated banking haven on the order of Liechtenstein or Switzerland. All that would remain is the tedious process of liberating our people from tyrannical rule around the world.

While it is true that resettling the impoverished American diaspora in the homeland would have some initial desultory effects on the North American job market, these would be offset by new opportunities abroad as "native" Americans travel in search of investment opportunities, adventure, and self-actualization in the new states, which would simply retain their old names: "Oklahoma," "New Jersey," "Bangladesh." A period of spectacular and global economic expansion, rivaling that of the late 1800s, would surely follow.

Cultural Cachet

Never again would anyone say that Americans do not appreciate soccer. Our reputation as a vast monolingual wasteland would be quashed forever. Overnight, we would become the largest and most diverse, tolerant, intellectually advanced country in the world.

Full Employment

All hands in the New Democratic America will be needed for a massive investment in public works. This was, of course, a successful platform for the Democratic Party once before, in the age of FDR. But America has since turned sharply against Tennessee Valley Authority–type socialism, and rightly so. It very much approves, however, of socialism centered on weapons production. How can we justify spending money on such luxuries as bridges and schools and alternative energy plants here at home, while our people are suffering under imperial rule abroad? What we need is a massive investment in advanced weaponry, ships, aircraft, and medical supplies for the armed services. A quadrupling of the defense budget would be more than sufficient to guarantee a high-paying job in the defense sector for every man, woman, and child on the American continent. Furthermore, our enlarged military would provide education and training opportunities for everyone who wants it, eliminating the need for our vast, wasteful, and anachronistic public university system.

Trade

In one fell swoop the Democrats could end the problem of jobs moving overseas—because there will be no more overseas. All trade will hereafter be domestic trade.

Again, this would lay bare the ragged poverty of the old Republican isolationist ideology. They would rather see American children working for 10 cents an hour in places like Indonesia than commit the resources needed to liberate them. Also, there would be no more of this backdoor robbery of American sovereignty through such treasonous bureaucracies as the WTO (the authors of which, incidentally, would immediately be captured, sent to military prisons, and, after a cathartic series of public confessions, executed). All other persons belonging to organizations or states claiming jurisdiction over American trade policy would also be subject to capture and imprisonment.

Social Unrest

Any fascist domestic platform for the Democrats would have to include a plan to permanently imprison 1–2 percent of the population as undesirables—that is to say, maintain the current prison population. But the Democrats would simplify the process by allowing police to imprison citizens at will, without charging them with anything. This would put an end to the idiotic, indirect process we currently call the War on Drugs, which is not only time-consuming, but also has the additional negative consequence of inspiring an actual criminal subculture. Instead, we could simply promulgate an official policy of jailing the poor. Soccer moms and NASCAR dads—both crucial electoral blocs—would heartily approve, and the country would be safer. Morally, it would be a wash.

But the centerpiece for creating a New Democratic Majority is how to use the military. If we accept the premise that campaigning against war is impossible—and even Howard Dean admits that it is—then it's silly to lack a specific plan for *how* and *where* to attack. The Republican idea, echoed by most Democrats, is to sit around, wait for some dubious justification for the use of force to present itself, and then trot out some incoherent cover story on the eve of attack. What's so tough about that? Why take the long way around? It's time to make the world safe for America by making the world America.

Prickless for President
The Smooth, Flat Space Prevails in New Hampshire

And so the reader may judge for himself what the major's position was when he saw, instead of a nice-looking, well-proportioned nose, an extremely absurd flat space.

—Nikolai Gogol, *The Nose*

Gogol's great nightmare stories would never sell in today's America. To appreciate a story like *The Nose*—about a petty philistine bureaucrat who wakes up one morning to find his nose missing, forcing him to go chasing it around St. Petersburg—the audience probably has to have at least a theoretical fear of castration.

January 27, 2004, *New York Press.*

We don't have that here in America. Having no penis is part of what being an American is all about. The population readily accepts this as a fact of its own experience, and in fact even expects it of its leaders. Just look at New Hampshire.

There is probably no more reliable predictor of electoral success in this country than the absence in the press of "prodding-edge" imagery surrounding the candidate. Show me any candidate who is routinely described in the *New York Times* as being "pointed," "bristly," "thistly," "blunt," "blistering," or "sharp," and I'll show you a loser. *Testy* (derived from an old French word meaning *head*) and *upstart* are also evolutionary relatives of these terms.

Then there's *prickly*. "Prickly" is the kiss of death for any major politician in this country. Jerry Brown, in his presidential run, was prickly. Viagra spokesman Bob Dole, ironically enough, was prickly. Then, of course, there's the great Kaiser Prickhelm, Howard Dean, who in recent weeks was blasted into space dust because of his unapologetic prickliness.

"Prickly" is fatal. I have yet to find a politician who survived it. John McCain, probably the highest-ranking prickly person in the American political establishment, is still a senator, but his prospects for the White House grow smaller all the time.

Dean's battle with "prickly" was so drawn-out and painful that it ultimately took on the character of a Stalinist show trial, in which he was dragged out before the national jury and forced to publicly confess his prickliness. This sordid drama reached its climax in a January 3 *New York Times* piece by Rick Lyman entitled, "As the Race Turns Hot, What About Dean's Collar?"

Lyman's piece was bursting with dangerous-penis imagery. Such words as "bulging" and "jabbing" appeared alongside thinly veiled double entendres such as "The salient aspects of the Dean temper mentioned by those who have witnessed it are that it flashes quickly and then disappears" and "It always blew over pretty fast."

The piece built to a dramatic flourish:

"At one point, Dr. Dean used 'prickly' to describe his temperament for a reporter, then seemed to regret the choice when the word was repeated to him."

" 'I can be prickly with the press corps,' he said. 'I'm not usually prickly with other people at all.' "

What is amazing about this passage is that Lyman here is implying that *prickly* is a word Dean chose all by himself. What Lyman failed to mention is that Lyman himself had described Dean as "prickly" in no less a place than a *front-page headline of the Sunday New York Times* less than two weeks before, in the December 28 article, "From Patrician Roots, Dean Set Path of Prickly Independence."

In any case, Lyman got his confession, which allowed him to slip in yet another hilarious double entendre, one incidentally used quite frequently on these campaigns. He quoted a Gephardt press release as saying that Dean's gaffes had "underscored the fact that he is not equipped to challenge George Bush."

Newspaper readers should be aware that mainstream political journalists tend to write using matched pairs of adjectives. For every "fiery" politician, one will be "calm"; for every "shrill," there is a "self-assured"; for every "glib," a "folksy"; and so on. "Prickly" and "pointed" are wedded to two very specific antonyms, and it is these two that are surging to success in the Democratic race: *smooth* and *nuanced*. In any important race, the candidate with the pointy edges will be juxtaposed against the more desirable offering, whose personality is described as having pleasing flatness; instead of thorns, he has mere depressions in an otherwise glassy exterior. Nuances.

John Kerry and John Edwards have been battling for the "nuance" tag throughout this campaign, and it appears Kerry has the high ground now. (Kerry had a hell of a time getting there, though; for months last fall, he suffered through articles that asked questions like "Nuanced—or Squishy?"). Take this passage from the AP's Calvin Woodward, about the Iowa results:

"But in the first votes that matter in the 2004 presidential election, Iowans opted for the experience, steady demeanor and nuanced positions of Kerry, 60, and staggered Dean's upstart campaign."

Two days before the New Hampshire primary, the *Times* also chimed in: "Mr. Kerry has often struck more nuanced, politically cautious positions."

Dean's failure to understand the strength of "nuance" has cost him this campaign. Early on in the race, in fact, while sitting atop a nearly twenty-point lead in New Hampshire, he had the nerve to dismiss Kerry as being "too nuanced." That was back when he probably still thought that the candidates and their supporters actually decided their own fate in America. He failed to understand the aerodynamics of politics in our current media climate. The candidate must have nothing on his person that creates drag, or he will not fly.

The candidate, in short, has to be prickless. This has nothing to do with whether or not he has an actual, functioning biological penis. Nothing about Howard Dean suggests that he's packing a whale under there. It's more about a compact the candidate must enter into with the political and media establishments. He must show that he can keep it in his pants. He must show that he understands that in the public sphere, there is only one big, swinging dick out there—the media itself. If he refuses to accept this, he inevitably suffers the same fate Howard Dean did: they will cut his balls off, stuff them in his mouth, and send him staggering down Main Street for the amusement of the public.

Roundedness is an important concept to understand when one tries to address the nature of censorship in this country. Only in very rare cases is something actually prevented from appearing on TV or in the newspapers. The more important censorship is indirect and centered almost entirely around subtle differences in tone. You can get all kinds of things on television, but on balance, pretty much all content has to be rounded enough at the edges, unthreatening enough to the corporations ruling the airwaves, to serve competently in its only important role: a medium to sell advertising. Since the only real action that takes place on television is the sales pitch, it stands to reason that no other action of competing realness will ever be allowed on air.

That's what this election is all about. The political establishment does not want any sexual competitors out there. The major party candidates exist as vehicles for furthering the status quo—just as programming exists to sell ads. I'm not sure what Dean's crime was, since politically he was not all that different from the other candidates. It might have been that he opposed the war.

It might have been that he subverted the party structure through his treason-ous attempts to raise a war chest by appealing directly to the electorate. Whatever the specific offense was, the general offense was clear: he unzipped his little Vermont fly and wouldn't zip it back up again.

Now he's toast and we will have Senator Flat Space as a candidate. Stands for nothing, says nothing, does what he's told. In other words, he's "equipped" to challenge George Bush.

Odd Man In
Dennis Kucinich Is Nobody's Fool

Last Friday, after seeing a gloating *New York Times* editorial published the day before about the Democratic primaries entitled, "And Now There Are Two," I called the campaign offices of Dennis Kucinich. I wanted to express my con-dolences on the death of their candidate. I assumed something terrible had happened both to him and to Al Sharpton; probably the two had been hit by a bus, or mauled to death by circus lions at a Jefferson-Jackson Democratic Party dinner in Sheboygan, Wisconsin. . . . We Americans are a stoic people, we like to grieve in private, but on this occasion I thought I would at least make the gesture of calling and offering my support.

I never reached Sharpton, but at the Kucinich offices, I was greeted with a surprise. The candidate was not dead at all. He was living and breathing and, apparently, still eating organically grown produce.

"He's absolutely fine," said Jon Schwartz, Kucinich's media radio consul-tant in Washington. "He's fit as a horse. We're expecting him to throw 250 in-nings this year. He's wearing out our catchers in Winter Haven right now, as we speak."

Actually Kucinich was campaigning somewhere in Minnesota, which, like New York, has a primary coming up on Super Tuesday, March 2. To prove that reports of his candidate's death were greatly exaggerated, Schwartz

February 24, 2004, *New York Press.*

ended up putting Kucinich on the phone. On Saturday, I spoke to Dennis for about a half-hour as he drove through greater Minneapolis.

Before I get to that conversation, there are a few things about the campaign of Dennis Kucinich that I think are worth mentioning.

There are a lot of people out there who are inclined to laugh at this candidate. A few do so because they genuinely find him laughable, but most do it because they see him being laughed at in the news media. In this country we generally take our cues about whom we can safely laugh at from the mainstream press, and for the most part we laugh at the weak, the earnest, the sincere, the emotionally vulnerable. We laugh at people who are fat and ugly or who work as temps or at McDonald's because none of us wants to admit that we're not the ripped six-pack guy on the cover of *Men's Health* or a member of the Sharper Image target market. We're cowards, afraid of admitting to being who we are, and we laugh at people on the margins to avoid being identified as outsiders by the remorseless center.

It's the same with politics. Over and over again we have been told, in a million different ways, that a certain kind of idealism is actually childish weakness, and that the only pragmatic way of approaching life upholds force and commerce as the chief engines of social organization. That is why we laugh at people who use words like *peace* and *community* but praise as tough, responsible leaders anyone who's willing to drop the most mother-of-all-bombs on defenseless foreign populations. We laugh at a person who uses the word *peace* for the same reason that we laugh at the person who works as a temp or at McDonald's: because we're afraid of being lumped together with him. We're afraid of being the proverbial punchline to the proverbial Dennis Miller joke about John Lennon and Joanie Baez and that goddamn Cat Stevens song "Peace Train."

I will never forgive America for what Dennis Kucinich went through this year. Because he has had the audacity to call for an end to all wars, to announce plans for the creation of a Department of Peace, to question the very culture of viciousness and intolerance and crass commercialism that rules our public discourse, he has been labeled a lunatic by nearly every "responsible" press organ in this country and cruelly mocked to a degree that no civil society should allow an honorable man to endure. The *New Yorker,* that revolting beacon of glib, self-satisfied affluence, runs a cartoon showing Kucinich sweeping to victory in a primary held on Mars. The *New York Times* first angrily demands that he not waste any more of our time, then actually physically disposes of him after the passing of some self-imposed fictional electoral deadline. Even the more genuinely funny and more intelligent people in American public life—I'm thinking particularly of Tony Kornheiser and Michael Wilbon—can't resist savaging Kucinich whenever they get a chance. All because he's funny-looking, and because he uses the word *peace* without kidding.

I am a Dennis Kucinich supporter because I believe America's greatest problem is its incivility, its intolerance to new ideas, its remorseless hatred of weakness and failure, and the willingness of its individual citizens to submerge their individual cowardice within the vicious commerce-driven standards of our national self-image. George Bush is a terrible president, but he is merely a byproduct of these wider national tendencies, which exist outside of him and independently of him. And these tendencies are symbolized exactly in the laughter directed at Dennis Kucinich. To vote for Dennis Kucinich, I believe, is to vote for man's right to publicly be who he is and not be ridiculed for it. If we are peaceful people, it is a vote for our right to merely be who we 'are.

This is not a small thing, because we are in danger of losing that right in this country. If you are the wrong kind of person, even the *New York Times* would have you disappear from the stage entirely. That is why it is important to understand this vote not as a pragmatic choice for a winner, but as a passionate act of self-preservation. We must stand with the man who is taking all the abuse that most of us are too afraid to take in our own lives.

Well, enough of that. Getting back to the conversation with Kucinich on Saturday: I found the congressman in what appeared to be a good mood, as he negotiated the *New York Times* afterworld. Because I'm interested in this question personally, I first tried to ask him what he thought the reasons were for the media's persistent calls for him to leave the race. After all, he's not spending *their* money. But he seemed less interested in talking about the reasons why the press insists on thinning the herd than in pointing out why it's important to ignore them. One interesting point he made was that being ignored by the press was not automatically a bad thing.

"It's like being covered by corporate cops," he said. "I mean, they certainly didn't do Howard Dean any favors. . . . So this idea of having a press corps cover you relentlessly may be overrated."

He went on to suggest that even regularly consuming media can be as bad for you as being covered was for Howard Dean. "The thing is," he said, "if you depend on the media for your life, for approval, then you end up being bound by its logic. I don't, so I'm not."

Kucinich wrapped up his remarks about the media with a classic Kucinichism, taking a moment to expound upon the reasons why people in the media who behave this way should be treated with compassion. One would call this a common rhetorical technique of his, except that most of the time when he talks this way, he appears actually to mean it. This time was no exception.

"[People in the media] have a terrible cross to bear," he said. "Let's look at it from their point of view, okay? What a great responsibility they take on. They have to decide the fate of the world every day. They have to be able to tell people who their leaders should be, what the right decisions are to make . . . and it's very hard to do that, it's hard to be able to make those decisions."

He went on: "You have to remember that this is kind of a throwback to another era, when there were vast amounts of people who could barely read, who couldn't really make decisions on their own. So they had to be guided. So what a difficult position to be in, to know that you always have to guide people as to exactly what to think. . . . So you have to have compassion for people in that situation."

Regarding the upcoming primary, Kucinich was fairly unequivocal when asked to name the main issue that distinguishes him from the remaining candidates in the field.

TAIBBI: Leaving Al Sharpton aside for a moment, in what way can you say that you present a real alternative to George Bush in a way that John Kerry or John Edwards does not?

KUCINICH: On the war. You know, both of them have the unfortunate occasion of having parroted the president's position on weapons of mass destruction. And not only parroted it, but in the case of Senator Kerry, greatly embroidered and embellished it. Just look at his speech, I think it was October 9, 2002—he goes into tremendous detail about the weapons of mass destruction, he is tremendously detailed about the threat. And then for it to have turned out. . . . What a great concession, to admit to having been fooled by George Bush, and then calling this a qualification for the presidency. . . . (Voice trails off, goes silent.)

TAIBBI: Um . . .

KUCINICH: (returning, thoughtfully) I mean, perhaps it is a qualification for the presidency, and what does that say? I was never subject to the rarefied atmosphere of the Senate, but as the ranking Democrat on a congressional subcommittee devoted to national security, I never saw any proof that there were weapons of mass destruction.

TAIBBI: But a lot of us who were on the outside, who didn't even have the privilege of being in Congress, we supposed automatically that this whole weapons-of-mass-destruction business was a pretext for an invasion that was planned all along for other reasons. Is that correct? Is the idea that they were fooled a little strange to begin with?

KUCINICH: Of course it is. And of course that's what was going on. But there were a number of things that went into this, that played a part. One of those things was the whole dramaturgy of the constant threat, the lions and tigers and bears, oh my, and that was played up. And then there was the realpolitik search for hegemony in the region. And on top of that there was the posturing of various political leaders who were engaged in this ridiculous struggle to look tough. So this raises the question of what category of person you want your president to be in. That's not to say that the others aren't fine people in their own right. But it does say that when we entered a war that was totally unnecessary, that . . . I challenged the White House, I challenged the members of my own party, I challenged the media. And they did not [act] and so having given in to the administration on the war, it made it impossible for the party to challenge the White House on economic issues.

TAIBBI: Wasn't the vote that Kerry and Edwards made also just generally an endorsement of the whole idea of preemptive war?

KUCINICH: Absolutely. It licensed preemptive attack.

TAIBBI: Because when the newspapers today talk about the vote that the two senators made, they generally discuss it only in the context of their having believed there were weapons of mass destruction. But wasn't there a larger issue, which involved lessening the standards for going to war?

KUCINICH: Yes—but again, what are the implications of their having *believed* there were weapons of mass destruction? It's not just about a vote, the vote was what it was, but what information did they have? It just raises the question—what were they thinking? I mean, if they were fooled by George Bush—who else would they be fooled by?

Good point.

In case you haven't seen Kucinich in a debate or haven't read this in the newspapers: he is the only candidate in favor of ending the for-profit system of health care and replacing it with free, universal, single-payer health care. When I asked him how this compares with Kerry's plan of making the Senate health plan available to everyone, he explained: "The Senate health plan is a government-subsidized for-profit health plan. I'm talking about eliminating those for-profit costs entirely. Plus my plan covers everything—dental, mental health, ambulatory care . . .".

"Wait a minute," I interrupted, "the Senate health plan doesn't have dental? Or mental health?"

"Oh, no," he said.

"So what does John Kerry do when he falls down and breaks a tooth?"

Kucinich didn't laugh. "I can't speak for John Kerry, but I'm sure he can make other arrangements. He probably has another plan."

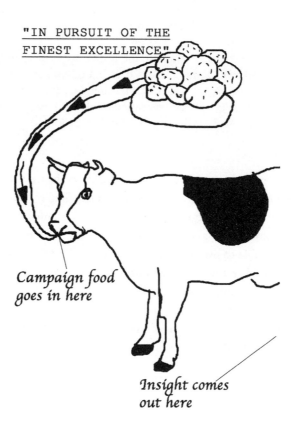

"IN PURSUIT OF THE
FINEST EXCELLENCE"

Campaign food
goes in here

Insight comes
out here

6

FEED THE BEAST

On the Campaign Trail, No One Can Hear You Scream

This article appeared in much shorter form in Rolling Stone, *and covers a difficult period in February and March 2004 that I spent on the Kerry campaign plane.*

It wasn't until the day after the Wisconsin primary, after five days on the campaign trail with John Kerry, that I found it—the perfect metaphor for campaign journalism.

Just outside of Wausau, Wisconsin, in a little town called Merrill, there is a state-of-the-art dairy farm called Van Der Geest Dairy. It is one of the most advanced milk-producing facilities in the world. In a gigantic, gleaming, airplane hangar–sized building, far cleaner than a barn full of cows could ever reasonably be expected to be, some 3,000 head of cattle move continuously through a mechanized cycle of milk production.

The journey starts in the rear of the building, in the "holding area," where the cows rest, eat, and drink. They lie in comfort on individual-sized sand beds that spill out into a small river of feed that is continuously refilled by machine. In this area the cows are free to get up, walk around, get a drink, and socialize. It is clean and kept at a uniform temperature.

The cows gravitate on their own to a sort of concrete purgatory in between the holding area and the milking parlor. When enough of them are collected in this area, a giant iron bar called a "crowd gate" lifts up on a track from the front of the area, moves backwards, and traps the cows from behind. It then begins advancing forward.

Eventually the cows are trapped from the front and the back like sardines, and will stand there for many long minutes at a time, lowing and jumping on top of each other, even shitting all over each other. They are now desperate to race into the milking parlor the instant the door opens.

When the cows are finally wedged into individual-sized milking stations, sensors in their collars tell the central computer that they are in place. A long bar appears from the side, pushing and locking them into diagonal wedges astride one another, like cars in a parking lot. Finally, a group of mostly Mexican dairy hands runs up and down an alley below the cows and affixes electric milking machines to their udders. The machines detach automatically when the cows are milked.

It only takes five sets of hands to milk 500 cows per hour.

In the milking parlor the waste flows in a dense brown stream and disappears through a grate in the floor. It is chemically treated and filtered and then sent out, millions of gallons a month, to lagoons.

I nearly lost my mind on the campaign trail. It was close.

I hovered in and around the Kerry campaign for nearly a month—from before the Wisconsin primary to sometime after Super Tuesday—but I'm going to begin this account in the last week. That was when I was pushed over the edge. That was when a reshuffling of the seating on the campaign plane landed me next to a remarkable figure named David Hume Kennerly.

Kennerly, *Newsweek*'s ace photographer, is one of the exalted personages on the campaign trail. He and *Time* photographer David Burnett are a matched set; they have known each other for over thirty years, going back to the days when they worked in Vietnam at the same time, and both are veterans of presidential campaigns dating back to the days of Nixon. They are the Obi Wan Kenobi and Darth Vader of American political photojournalism, with the likable, unassuming, quietly creative Burnett as Kenobi and the bombastic Kennerly the obvious Vader.

Both are legends, but Kennerly has the additional advantage of being a legend in his own mind. On his website (www.kennerly.com), which he seemingly directs everyone he meets to visit, the "About David" section starts off with a bang: "Internationally recognized as one of the greatest photographers of his time, David Hume Kennerly. . . ."

When I was first seated next to Kennerly at the beginning of March 2003, on a leg from Columbus, Ohio, to Atlanta, I had no idea who he was, and wasn't particularly interested. I had my own problems. A normal human being concerned with maintaining his sanity is going to have a difficult time on the campaign trail. In many ways it is like being trapped in a monstrous, three-dimensional voice mail world, like a voice mail amusement park ride, designed by Satan, that never ends. At each stop, the candidate makes an appearance and it is the same thing over and over again:

"To hear my timid, preposterously compromised position on trade, press 1."

"To observe me in a vigorous public display of my manly athletic inclinations, press 2."

"To hear me unconvincingly assert my place in a tradition dating back to Truman, Kennedy, and Johnson, press 3."

And at each new stop you're frantically pressing zero, trying to get a human being on the phone, and all you get is the same recording: "I'm sorry, I didn't understand you. To hear these menu options again, press 1. . . ."

Beyond that, the behind-the-scenes "Boys on the Bus" story—the traditional color angle to the campaign trail gig—is similarly a dead end. Every journalist who tries this story (including, most recently, Joe Hagan of the *New York Observer*, who viciously wrote up this same crew of Kerry journalists I was traveling with) inevitably tries to describe the culture of the plane as a poisonous nest of cliquey, elitist snobs who ruthlessly enforce a primitive, high-school hierarchy—*Heathers* meets *All the President's Men.*

I looked for this story—it would have made my life easier if it was true—but it simply wasn't there. The reporters on the plane are, with a few exceptions, quite friendly. Mainly they are exhausted and grimly focused on the grueling logistical problem of continually Feeding the Beast, a task that in the modern media age of round-the-clock content has become so demanding that it doesn't leave much energy for individual arrogance or pretentiousness, even if the inclination were there.

About the only obvious cartoon personality I ever encountered on the campaign trail was Jodi Wilgoren of the *New York Times*—and she was less of a personality than simply a very loud person with an enormous ass. On the Kerry plane, the most-maligned figure was probably Wilgoren's colleague at the *Times,* David Halbfinger. I wanted to hate this harried, Dustin Hoffmanesque figure, but even he seemed more tragic than villainous. He appeared to be in a constant state of unrest and the look on his face suggested a man who just *knew* that thirty years down the road, he would still be two hours from deadline.

Once, at the airport in Buffalo, he stopped on the way into the plane, kneeled right in front of me on the tarmac, pulled out his computer, and started typing something. He couldn't even wait the thirty seconds to get into the plane. . . . About the worst thing you could say about him is that he was the kind of person who one hundred years ago would have yelled at his servants; if the roving Soapbox Internet server was down for even thirty seconds at any time during the trip, you could expect him to appear instantly to freak out about it.

But as far as insight goes, this was not much to work with. Early on in the trip, I began to suspect that the real story on the plane was not so much the individual characters, but the collective personality of the group. There was something fishy about it, something unnatural even beyond the obvious in the way it and the campaign staff coexisted. But I couldn't put my finger on it.

Nor was I the only one to notice. Alexandra Pelosi, the quirky HBO documentarian who inspires highly ambiguous emotions among the press crew because of her habit of shooting video of them on the job, mentioned it one night on a plane out of Milwaukee.

"Yeah, there's something weird about all of this," she said, waving her hand across the plane. "If you could get at it, you'd have something, but what is it?"

Alex had been on the campaign trail for an entire year in 2000 and this time around has been on since last summer; the campaign process was her subject, and she hadn't figured it out yet. I had maybe three weeks at the most. Finding oneself thusly engaged in a seemingly hopeless quest to nail down 5,000 words' worth of *there's something fishy about this* can be a deeply stressful predicament, particularly when you never stop being aware that this investigation is costing someone about $10 a minute.

That was what was going through my head when they seated me next to the legendary Kennerly. I was frustrated and depressed, alternatively fantasizing about committing acts of terrorism and teaching English to underprivileged inner-city kids—anything that wasn't this assignment. About the last thing I wanted to hear was an impassioned soliloquy on the theme of journalistic accomplishment.

The bald, white-bearded figure leaned over to introduce himself. . . .

It went on for two hours. There were the heroic 'Nam stories, the stint as Gerald Ford's personal photographer, the 1968 and 1976 campaigns, the Pulitzer Prize. . . . Kennerly left the business briefly in the 1980s to make movies; he produced a 1989 made-for-TV film called *Shooter,* surprisingly the story of a photojournalist in Vietnam that starred, among others, a young Helen Hunt.

"Helen's great, really great," he said. "She was a really sweet kid. Now, the guy they got to play the character based on me. . . ."

I signaled to the stewardess for a drink. She ignored me. Kennerly went on and within a short time had turned his laptop in my direction. He had an entire archive of his photos from a recent trip to Central Asia with Donald Rumsfeld, his old buddy from the Ford days. He described each photo individually, clicking and opening each one with a tap of his finger.

"This one's really great," he said. "I like this, the way he's looking out the window of the helicopter. There's like this weird *concern* on his face. You can see, he gave me really great access the whole trip."

Jesus, I thought. Who would want "really great access" to Donald Rumsfeld?

He went on. "Oh, yeah, this one is great," he said. "You see how he's standing in the middle of all these soldiers? It's kind of like, you can't tell which one is Rumsfeld at first."

There must have been 500 pictures. The minute hand raced around. The stewardesses served dinner and took it away. I only managed a few bites. Each time I would lift my fork to my mouth, Kennerly would open up a new picture. It actually became quite funny after a while.

For the next two days Kennerly would occasionally reappear at just the right time with some pointed, unsolicited piece of advice.

On the tarmac in Atlanta the next morning, the campaign staff pressed 2 on the keypad and produced a football for the manly candidate to throw around.

Kerry does the sports-on-the-tarmac thing a lot. It looks great on television, but in person the effect is surreal.

It happens suddenly, without warning. The whole of the press crew will be standing in line at the ass end of the plane, getting swept by the Secret Service, when suddenly the polished figure of Kerry—this gleaming, toothy, larger-than-life creature with a Christoff haircut—will appear out of nowhere and commence his photogenic ballet, technically playing with other staffers but in reality performing quite in solo. It is like watching an unusually gifted moose perform a figure-skating routine. And the instant that happens, all of the photographers and cameramen will drop everything and run full speed to completely encircle him, so that he has to both catch and throw the ball from inside a closed loop of humanity furiously taking his picture.

If he has to run to one side to catch the ball, the entire crowd of journalists travels with him. From a distance this looks like a bit of biological phenomena, like viral cells attacking a drifting mitochondrion.

I had nothing else to do—what is there to do in that situation?—so I decided to get in on it. I signaled to Kerry and ran a pattern across the concrete. The receiver is supposed to look at the quarterback's eyes, but all I could see was that TV smile. The Candidate turned and gracefully hit me right on the hands. The cameras followed, then moved on as I threw the ball to a staffer.

Back on the plane, I wrote in my notebook: "Throws tight spiral." What that knowledge was good for, I had no idea. But there it was.

Suddenly Kennerly came back to the seat, fresh from snapping the football show. He put his hand on my shoulder.

"Hey, you caught a pass from him," he said.

I shrugged. "Yeah," I said. "He throws a nice ball."

"Well, congratulations," he said. "I hope somebody got a picture for you. You'll probably be on the news tonight." He snorted. "Hey, good for you. That's nice."

He patted my shoulder again. The look on his face was priceless. It said: *Someday, kid, if you're lucky enough to keep this job, you too can spend your golden years running like a rodeo clown after a millionaire aristocrat with a football.* The balls on this guy, I thought.

The next day was the best. In Orlando, after a Town Hall event (one of the two main species of candidate appearances, the other being the rally; in the Town Hall, the public gets to play the voice mail game), I was sitting in the press filing room, picking at my lunch. The post-event files were always a tricky time for me because while the daily press was working, I usually had little to do. Early on in the trip I found a solution to this problem—more on that later—and managed to not be there at all most of the time. But when I was in the filing center, I always looked like an ass, flipping through *Sports Illustrated* while all around the press feverishly sent its Urgent Message out to the anxious world population.

I was just about to take a bite of grilled marinated flank steak when Kennerly dropped his equipment on the table next to me.

"Well, at least you're getting fed," he said.

"What?" I asked, halting my fork.

"I don't know how you're story's going to turn out," he said. "But at least you're getting some good food."

I had two thoughts right away. The first was, *fuck you*.

The second was, hey, that's funny. They just fed us an hour ago. Why am I eating again?

Soon afterward, I stopped eating. And suddenly everything started to make sense.

The traveling press pool is a high-class cage.

It takes a while to see it, but once you do, it's hard to miss how completely U the Important National Pundit are sealed off from the outside world. On a typical day you awake in your hotel and very early in the morning—six or six-thirty is a typical hour—have to bring your bags down to one of the campaign "sherpas" or "shepherds," who arranges for its delivery to the plane. After that there is usually a half-hour or so in the hotel lobby. Then it is a bus to the airport, a security sweep on the tarmac, a flight to somewhere or other, then another single-file trip to the bus, which takes you straight to the event.

I didn't notice this at first, but very often, when the press bus arrives, there is another handler waiting right at the bus door. When you step off the bus he is literally pointing in the direction of the press filing center, normally a concrete room somewhere deep in the ass of whatever building the event is being held in. In case you miss that, there are always big paper arrows on the ground pointing you in the right direction, with signs that say things like "PRESS FILE." At one stop in New Orleans, these arrows were plastered for a stretch leading a full 200 yards between the outdoor area where Kerry's speech was being held and the Cajun restaurant the campaign had converted into a filing center.

"Yeah, it's funny," said Evan Richman, the affable photographer for the *Boston Globe*. "When you first get on the trail, you think: why are they treating me like an idiot? But then, after about a month, you're like—okay, this way, huh?" He mimicked lowering his head and following the signs.

At the event you do have free roam of the place. You can stay in the special walled-off press area, or you can mingle with the "public," that is, the people who came to the event. The idea that this somehow represents contact with the outside world, however, is a little problematic. After all, these are all people who came to see the candidate. They have that in common. And the setting is, of course, completely artificial. Everything is scrupulously clean and shiny and ready for television. Behind the candidate there is usually a platform where a statistically representative sample of the human racial gene pool is standing in a cheerfully supportive pose. The people.

After the event you go back to the file room, and file. From there it is the same routine as before: bus, plane, bus, event, bus, plane, bus. At the end of the day, often very late in the evening, you arrive at a ridiculously expensive hotel where a big fluffy bed with no fewer than five down pillows is begging you to plop down and collapse. There is never quite enough time to get a full night's rest. Ordering your wake-up call, you begin the next day on exactly the same schedule.

The isolation is so total that during some stretches the journalists, like prisoners, actually have to search out little cracks in the system just to smuggle in cigarettes. Among the staffers on the Kerry campaign, the preferred method is to send the baggage sherpa, a cheerful, sleep-deprived soul named Pat Shearns, to make runs during the events. Poor Pat often sleeps less than two hours a night. He hopes to have a few days off before November.

From the point of view of the journalists, the whole process could easily be done virtually. The flavor of the individual locations ends up becoming a source of black humor, a trade joke, usually delivered from behind the windows of a moving bus.

Riding through an ugly section of Milwaukee, after we flew in from Las Vegas:

"Wow, Milwaukee sure isn't Las Vegas!"

"This isn't Milwaukee. It's *Milwaukee Hotel*—in Las Vegas!"

Once, I was trying to sleep in the bus, when Martin Kasindorf, the *USA Today* reporter, perked up in the seat in front of me.

"Hey, look," he said. "An alligator."

That was how I knew we were in Florida.

From inside this hermetically sealed universe, the cream of the national political press corps somehow has to come up with oceans of insightful material. Photographers take 500 pictures a day. Most reporters have to file at least once a day, sometimes twice; the wire service people often have to do more than that. At each stop, the Beast is waiting in that filing room to be fed. But with the gathering of material needing to take place literally at the speed of existence, how is this possible? Where can the information come from?

Answer: they have to feed it to you.

The spread at the filing center in New Orleans was about par for the course: massive in scale, with a local flavor, so you know where you are. There was boiled crawfish, crawfish étouffée, red beans and rice with sausage, ratatouille, braised catfish, bread pudding, and rolls with parsley butter. Praline cookies. Fresh-brewed iced tea. The speech that day was to contain an escalation of anti-Bush rhetoric, something about the president's foreign policy being really reckless and irresponsible.

The food looked great, but I wasn't having any. I had stopped eating from the campaign trough two days before. In fact, I had stopped going to events altogether. Previously it had been an occasional thing, but now it was an official policy. Rather than stay in the high-class neighborhood where the events were always held, I made it a point to seek out the bad neighborhood full of nonvoters that was always precisely a half-mile away and personally deliver the message that I didn't give a shit about their lives.

In New Orleans Kerry's speech—the coin flip produced a "rally," not a Town Hall—was held outside, at the Seaport, in the heart of the Latin Quarter. Walking out of the area straight down Conti Street, you have to pass through about five blocks of tourist shops full of plastic voodoo skeleton souvenirs, rubber masks, and aprons bearing messages like "New Orleans: Don't

Fuck with the Chef!" Then the shops melt away into bars and daiquiri stands, and from there the bars turn into warehouses—and finally you pass by a French cemetery, and just behind the Winn-Dixie is a stark dirt lot full of low-rise brick buildings.

This used to be Storyville, the birthplace of jazz—onetime home to Jelly Roll Morton and Louis Armstrong—but now it's the Iberville housing projects. This place is so rough that I wasn't there two minutes before a kindly black policewoman named Sharon Cager zoomed up in her cruiser.

"Are you lost?" she said.

"No," I said, flashing my tags. "I'm press."

She looked at me as though she smelled rotting cheese. "What the hell are you doing here?"

"I'm covering the presidential election," I said.

She took about twenty seconds to think about that. "Yeah, right," she said. "And you know where you are?"

"The projects, right?"

She shook her head. "You're going to get jacked up in here," she said.

She drove off. I started going door-to-door. As was usually the case, it took a while before I found anyone who planned on voting in the next election. The approval rating of politicians in places like this hovers somewhere between Stalin and athlete's foot.

"I don't like to use the word *hate*, *hate* is a bad word, but sometimes that's how I feel about them. I don't believe a word they say," said Lethia Guishard, a sixty-year-old woman and longtime resident of Iberville. "A stray dog deserves better than what we've got. Look at what we have to live with. There used to be a bleach factory right behind here. A lot of folks in this neighborhood got real sick. There'd be sludge from the factory running into the street and the kids would have to walk through it to get to school. Then there was a fire there, and we were just lucky the wind was blowing the other way that day. We tried to get them to do something about safety, but every time I went to City Hall, they'd just send out a different person to tell me they were busy.

"Now they're going to close this place up and we're all going to be moved somewhere else," she said. "As it is, we get subsidized utilities, but the next place that's not going to be happen, they tell us. I can't even find out what's going on. Our councilwoman, Jackie Clarkson—she's a Democrat. She's the mother of Patricia Clarkson—you know, the actress? I keep going to her office, but, like I said, every time I do, they send out someone else to tell me to go away. I mean, she represents the Quarter, too, so who are we? Like I said, a stray dog deserves—"

"Excuse me," I said, looking at my watch. "I hate to interrupt, but I've got to go."

"What?" she said.

"Look, this is all very interesting," I said, "but I'm *working,* you understand? And I've got to get back right away. I might miss John Kerry playing Frisbee."

She stared in shock. "Playing what?"

"Actually, he prefers football," I said. "And he's pretty good at it. You should see it, he throws a really nice ball."

She nodded. "Oh," she said. "Okay. Well, nice talking to you."

"Take care."

Back at the Seaport, the event had broken up and a large contingent of the campaign staff had gone exploring, ending up on Bourbon Street, where they bought large quantities of Mardi Gras beads and king-sized Hurricane cocktails. There was a lot of laughing and stumbling around, and there was one reporter—I wish I had gotten a picture—who was wearing what appeared to be his weight in beads and standing in perfect contentment, with his lips stained bright red from drink. The party continued on the plane, where Kerry himself even got into the action, tiptoeing into the press area to catch some beads.

"Do I have to flash for these?" he said, smiling.

"Show us your health plan!" someone shouted.

Everyone laughed. "Well, it starts with twelve steps," Kerry quipped.

Drunken conversation overheard on the bus that night in Houston:

"It's too bad we didn't stay behind in New Orleans."

"Yeah, we know New Orleans."

"We know it *too well!*"

A wrong turn in Houston the next morning forced me to accelerate this increasingly ridiculous routine. At the Houston Community College in the well-heeled Bellaire suburb, I took off due north the instant the bus arrived, but quickly found the way blocked by that great nemesis of campaign journalism: train tracks. I doubled back and ran full-speed back to the event, where I found a Dennis Kucinich supporter named Gary Hardy standing and vainly trying to hold up a giant "Peace" banner in the wind. (It kept blowing down, despite three people trying to hold it up.) I explained my situation to him and he immediately packed me into his car and drove me a half-mile in the opposite direction, to a Central American barrio called the Southwest district. This time, there was practically another country sitting right in the shadow of Kerry's Town Hall event.

At an open-air flea market we jumped out of the car, and with Hardy's help—I don't speak Spanish—I quickly practiced what journalism I could. A nineteen-year-old named Eleu Aguirre was wandering out of the car parts stand where he worked.

"Do you know who's running for president?" I asked.

He nodded. "Boosh," he said. "And—Kennedy."

Hardy prompted him. "You sure about the Kennedy thing?"

He snapped his fingers. "Oh, Kerry!"

"What are your concerns this election season?" I asked.

Hardy translated. The answer came back: "The security is good."

"The security is good in this country?" I said.

"No," Hardy said. "The security is good at this flea market."

"Fine," I said. "Noted. What does he think of gay marriage?"

Hardy translated. Aguirre stared up at us helplessly.

"Come on, out with it!" I said. "Gay marriage! What do you think?"

This time Aguirre looked up at both of us in plain fear, then slowly backed away.

We stopped four or five more people, and it was the same story each time. No one was going to vote, or had ever voted, because they had no resident papers, and no one had anything at all to say about the election. It simply didn't matter here. The president was like the weather: sunny today, rainy tomorrow. One store owner declined to talk about the election, but pointed to a shelf full of religious articles.

"Okay," I said to Hardy. "Tell him I'll get the plastic Jesus. How much?"

"He says it's not Jesus, but St. Christopher, and it's five dollars."

"Whatever. I'll take it."

St. Christopher in hand, I sped with Hardy back to the event, which was breaking up. The menu included pasta salad, tossed salad, lox, strawberries and melon, bagels, muffins, danishes, croissants, pumpkin bread, fried chicken cutlets, roasted potatoes, scrambled eggs and tortillas, barbecued salmon fillets, sautéed asparagus and carrots, pear tarts, mixed fruit tarts, chocolate-covered strawberries, raspberry tarts, and an assortment of breakfast tacos. Additionally, each of the journalists had waiting for him, at his writing station in the filing center, a batch of fresh-baked chocolate chip cookies, wrapped in bandanas patterned after the American flag.

"Once, in Iowa, we didn't feed them often enough," Kerry staffer Lars Erikson explained. "And they got grumpy. We can't have them grumpy."

One of the things that people should be aware of, when they read campaign coverage, is that the "man-on-the-street" interviews in the articles almost never take place on the actual street. Reporters come into contact with the population mainly in two ways. The first is through the rectal-thermometer avenue of polling data, which incidentally almost always reflect the responses "of those who intend to vote."

The second is mainly the man-on-the-street interviews of people at or around the events, which are almost always in certain kinds of neighborhoods. Whether the rest of the people are edited out or simply not seen, something jumps out at you when you actually look at all of these interviews. The responses are always of a certain type: yea ("I just like his straightforwardness"), nay ("You didn't feel like he was knowledgeable"), or undecided ("I've been waffling between him and Edwards").

You never see answers like "I think they all suck" or "I'm not voting, and I hope they all die in a fire." If you only go by the news coverage, all of America votes.

This is borne out numerically. You can search a long time before you find a nonvoter-on-the-street in major news coverage. Halbfinger hasn't interviewed one this year. I went back to mid-December and found twenty-eight straight men-on-the-street in his pieces who fell squarely within the three usual categories.

How about Jill Lawrence of *USA Today*, that muckraker who lately announced to us that the people have now firmly decided that the chief issue in this campaign is "electability" as opposed to "likeability"? Sixteen straight since the new year.

It's not so much that the reporters are ignoring an important issue in the voter participation story. The issue is *how* they cover it: from which point of view, and with what emphasis. This massive, unceasing amount of coverage is aimed exclusively in one direction—at this exquisitely stage-managed soap opera of the American democratic process, where all of America looks clean and hopeful, and everybody in the picture believes. It becomes a never-ending advertisement for the health and functionality of the system, and within the parameters of that advertisement, the candidates are quite incidental.

All that really matters is that the reporters are kept on a steady diet of the he-said, she-said routine that passes for politics inside the bubble: you, sir, are soft on defense and won't spend enough on intelligence! No, sir, it is you, sir, who is soft on defense, and won't pay enough for body armor! (This was actually the current theme between Kerry and Bush that night in Houston.) And once the exchange of shots that day is safely recorded, everyone goes home to a five-star hotel and tries to sleep off the poached salmon and sea scallop fajitas and blackberry crème brûlée they just ate at the "office" cafeteria. Democracy works! America is doing just fine!

If large numbers of people are turned off politics and election coverage in this country, it's almost certainly because they are reluctant to consume the waste products of that singular process the campaign represents: a bunch of rich people talking to each other. It's the worst show on television. And it's on all the time.

From the very first moment I stepped on the plane, I knew I was in the presence of profound ugliness. It was a tangible, visceral thing that I was conscious of every minute, like cold air or a bad smell. It was not an amusing kind of ugliness, not kitschy like a Brooklyn social club full of mobsters. This was something modern and clean and scaly and something that on some level was a serious ideological threat to people like me, that is, small-time losers. But what exactly the source of it was, it was impossible to say. And I needed to find that source, because that was where the story was.

You could see a few things around the edges. There was the paranoia, for instance. It is almost impossible to cram sixty or seventy people in an incarceration-type setting, add about 500 gigawatts of constant deadline stress and high-stakes political expectation, and have not a single person utter so much as one incautious word, say one interesting thing. Everybody on the campaign plane is terrified of everybody else, as frightened of speaking their minds as the citizens of an Orwellian dystopia.

The candidates, naturally, are terrified of the reporters. The reporters are terrified of each other (people like me being the chief reason) and also of losing favor with the candidate. The staffers are simultaneously afraid of coming across as too stiff and of being too loose with their tongues, so they split the difference—palling around with you now, buying you that second beer if you ask, but watching both you and themselves like a hawk the entire time. There is no In Vino Veritas on the campaign. Even the most junior staffer learns to be able to keep his head straight after the fifteenth shot. And every conversation you have with anyone is a Defcon 5 affair, because everyone knows that anything they say could end up on HBO or under a Philip Gourevitch byline within ten minutes—or, more to the point, in Alex Pelosi's documentary six months later.

Not even the stewardesses and the pilots are unaware of this dynamic. They keep their mouths shut and hand you that extra bag of peanuts. One plane we were on had recently been chartered by the Celtics. A stewardess who confided in me that then–Celtics rookie Marcus Banks spent most of the time in the back of the plane watching DVDs asked me not to ask any more questions about her clients. It is like being trapped in a zoo exhibit with no shelter from the crowd, where the penalty for touching your own genitals is death. Everyone therefore walks with their arms at their sides, and pees with no hands.

There is the insular nature of the assignment, already alluded to. There is the shallowness and idiocy of the stump-speech/wire-feed reporting format, which reduces the entire exercise to a sort of rolling sports story—again, already alluded to by hundreds of others who've been there. There is the financial excess, the waste, the fact that the reporters on board are participating in the projection of a fake version of reality. And last but not least, there was the issue that I believed for a while was most important—the idea that the campaign was little more than a permanent commercial advertisement for an elite political consensus, a commercial that served its purpose even if you were denouncing it. Say what you want, just so long as the attention is focused in the right direction.

But all of these concerns were ethereal, theoretical. There was nothing you could see and feel on the campaign plane that would capture the inherent cruelty and absurdity of the whole process. Every conceivable original angle on the process that one could take from within the confines of the plane had not only been done, but done, as things are done in our media, to death—turned into a cliché that had been swallowed up and assimilated as a legitimate if quirky ingredient in the whole excellent affair. Any kind of dissenting commentary on the electoral process was actually celebrated by the mainstream media, as a prime example of the First Amendment working in all its glory. There was simply no way to talk about the media effect in terms of its quantitative character, other than to physically juxtapose the 1,000 credulous campaign pieces against the one or two articles in minor publications that wondered pissily if the whole thing was not just a giant load of elite hogwash. This is done in places like the FAIR website, and no one much cares.

For over thirty years now, since the publication of such books as *The Selling of the President, The Boys on the Bus,* and *Fear and Loathing,* it had been accepted as a given that the press itself plays an enormously important role in the process. Even if you wanted to argue, as I did, that the behavior of the press during the campaign was the dominant factor in guaranteeing that only certain kinds of ideologically acceptable candidates could appear in the general election, such a story would shock no one, because it's already "out there," as a "thing." More than a dozen times on the Kerry plane, I had reporters ask me: "So, you're doing a *Boys on the Bus* thing, right?" The original *Boys on the Bus* raised a few eyebrows, sure, but no one anywhere is threatened by a *"Boys on the Bus* thing" now.

I was having a tough time in particular because I now found myself working for a magazine that was spending thousands of dollars a day for me to watch this whole business unfold, and the only original conclusion that I could reach was that participating in the campaign at all was counterproductive, and that the only way to really express the horror of it in a proper way was to reject it openly and entirely, that is, to not be there. The story, it seemed fairly clear to me, was everywhere but the plane—in the neighborhoods that the campaigns never visited, in the issues that were never discussed on the air, in the minds of the millions of people who were too sickened by it all to vote and who never visited the rallies. But the campaign scrupulously avoided any physical proximity to those people, those places, those issues. And even if I wanted to confront one of the candidates about it, I had to do so shouting over a dozen other reporters who had other things on their minds.

Another factor, one that should not be overlooked by those who wonder how it is that so many campaign reporters could remain so narrowly focused on such a small range of issues for so long throughout the race, was money. To have regular access to the candidate requires a sponsor with a very deep pocket. The best way to have that regular access is to be one of the regulars on the plane, and to be in the "pool." In any group of reporters on the plane, there is a sort of rotation of a select few who follow the candidate to places when it is not feasible to bring everybody on the plane along. There are always a few pool reporters (one photog, one print guy) who follow the candidate in his bus while the rest of the reporters stay on the press bus; at smaller events, say when the candidate visits a small factory or school that is not equipped to handle the whole national press corps, he just brings the pool with him. Later, the "pool guy" will go back to the bus and tell the other reporters what great insights the candidate delivered in these private times. The pool guy therefore gets the casual access to the candidate, gets to talk to him in easy conversation, and gets to have a shot at philosophical speculation with him. But not everybody gets to be in the pool. You have to be a lifer to get in there.

I once asked Lars Erikson, the Kerry staffer, how it was decided who was in the rotation for the press pool.

"Well," he said, "the pool is really reserved for outlets that make a lengthy commitment, who've been with us for a long time."

"Okay," I said. "What if *Muhammad Speaks* wants to be in the pool? Would that be okay?"

"Well," Lars said, laughing. "We could make a special arrangement for, uh, him [he said the word *him* like he was spitting out a snail] maybe once or twice, but in general, to be in the rotation, he'd have to make a commitment, like a six-month commitment."

By my calculations that would make it about a $350,000 ticket. He didn't look worried.

The strain of being unable to capture that one scene that described all of this was quite literally driving me crazy. My editor at *Rolling Stone,* Will Dana, kept calling me while I was on the road to ask how things were going. I kept lying to him, until finally, in a moment of particular desperation while laid out in a Boston hotel, I sent a letter proposing a series of different takes on the story. I'm not going to get into the specifics of the letter, but essentially I proposed four or five conventional methods of handling the story, one of which included the outright surrender of simply doing a standard "candidate profile" of John Kerry. The response to all five proposals was basically "Let 'er rip."

It wasn't the editors' fault; they had no idea how desperate I was for something more specific, nor could they have. I sat looking at the words *Let 'er rip* for about an hour, wondering histrionically if my life was over.

At that point I gave up trying to come up with a sound way of approaching the campaign trail from the inside. I was relegated instead to taking steps to preserve my actual sanity. I needed, purely for the sake of keeping my own head straight, to simply *behave* in a way that made me feel like I was not participating in the process. My writing career, I assumed, was over. What was important now, apart from upholding the grim professional responsibility to file something to this magazine, was to preserve my dignity as a citizen, to not be a paid accomplice in this campaign fiasco.

Meanwhile, my personal life was unraveling. My relationship was falling apart, as every phone call I made home was a caricature of a mawkish, tiresome, self-indulgent failure pleading for approval in the wake of incipient defeat. Even worse, I was unable to communicate on the phone the maddening nature of life on the plane.

"Every time he finishes one of his speeches, everybody runs to the filing room and starts *writing something!*" I'd shout. "Like they take it seriously! Do you know what I mean?"

"I know, Matt, I know. . . ." Masha would say. But I could hear, over the phone, that she was playing Asteroids on her laptop as we talked.

Like all depressed people, I was becoming a burden even to my loved ones. No one wanted to hear what I was going through, and rightly so. I got stony "Yeah, right. Uh-huh" silence every time I made suggestions to parents and friends, from the comfort of my five-star Boston hotel, that it was perhaps time to quit journalism and join the Peace Corps, feed the hungry, teach underprivileged children. . . .

I was all alone. I was fucked. I was locked in a death battle with life and I was firing back with two fists of nothing. From time to time on the trip, I went through the melodramatic process of planning my suicide, fantasizing about leaving my hanging, naked body in a Westin suite for pasty-faced Kerry aide David Wade to find . . . a few times, I got fairly far along in my plans, although I remember that in at least one case I cut them short to watch a Celtics game.

Then, one morning, just as we were leaving Boston, I hit upon the idea of going on a hunger strike. I was going to be on the plane, but I was not going to accept food or anything else from the campaign. If I was going to die, I was going to starve to death right in front of everybody. That would be even funnier than leaving my body for Wade to find. Just the simple act of exercising some willpower in some direction gave me something to focus on. And so, for the rest of my time on the campaign—nearly seven days—I didn't eat one bite.

I still had no story, but I started to feel better.

By my second-to-last day on the campaign trail, I was nearly deranged with hunger. I looked like a madman and the stewardesses on the plane, who were initially amused by my refusals of food, were beginning to look at me queerly each time they passed by with a full cart of snacks. Equally disturbing to them was the fact that I would then get up and follow behind, dutifully writing down every single food item they were passing out. I had reached a point where the only aspect of the campaign that I felt needed seriously to be documented was the specific menu on each of the six or seven meals we were fed per day.

I was due to leave the campaign on a Monday. On the Saturday before, I was outside an event in Houston when I got to chatting with one of Kerry's press handlers, David Morehouse. I was surprised to learn that Morehouse had been the director of strategy for the Office of National Drug Control Policy in the White House in the mid-1990s. He had been the chief deputy to General Barry McCaffrey, which made him one of the highest-ranking narcs in the country at that time.

In the state I was in, this collision with an ONDCP operative struck me as extremely meaningful, especially since it was the second such meeting I'd had in less than a week. Just days before, as I stood fighting depression during Kerry's Super Tuesday victory speech, I'd encountered another such person.

As Kerry began his speech, I stared at the podium with blank eyes. And just then, someone behind me to my left tapped me on the shoulder.

I turned around. A short, bald man with maniacal eyes extended his hand, breathing loudly through his mouth.

"Isn't this great?" he said.

"I guess," I said.

"Bob Weiner," he said.

I shook his hand. "Matt Taibbi," I replied.

He smiled proudly. "I'm with the Office of National Drug Control Policy," he said. "Well, I used to be, anyway. Used to be the communications director. I worked with *Barry McCaffrey!*"

"Oh," I said, recoiling a little. "No shit."

"Yeah, no shit!" he said. "What do you do, Matt?"

"I'm working for *Rolling Stone*."

"Oh," he said. "Good magazine. We did some things with you folks a couple of years ago."

I was in such bad shape that it suddenly seemed entirely possible that the ostensibly countercultural *Rolling Stone* was in some kind of cooperative, collusive arrangement with the White House drug czar. It later turned out that Weiner was referring to some *RS* pro-legalization article that he had provided dissenting quotes for. But at the time I didn't know this, and the Orwellian realization that I myself might be indirectly working with the drug-enforcement apparatus just bounced harmlessly off my flatlined psyche.

"Gosh," I said, "that's nice. The thing is, Bob, I'm not feeling too well right now. . . ."

"Yeah, it's a good magazine, despite it all," he said, ignoring me. Then he waved his hand in the direction of the podium. "But you know what's great about this?"

"No," I said honestly. "What?"

"We're going to have a president with sense again," he said. "This current guy is a disaster. Right now, all domestic law enforcement goes through

Ashcroft and Ridge. It's all about terrorism now. I mean, the War on Drugs isn't even a priority!"

"Wow," I said. "That's just self-defeating."

"Thank God for Kerry," he said. "It's going to be like the old days again."

I stewed over this meeting for days. So, when I found out about More-house, I made a decision. I decided that as a gesture to every person who'd ever been busted for possession in this country, I would eat a ton of acid, then dress up in a Viking costume, interview Morehouse in a state of plain derangement, write about it in a gigantic national magazine, and, well, fuck him. It wouldn't be much of a gesture, but it was something.

I bring a Viking costume with me everywhere I go. You just never know when you might have a need in this area. I used to use a gorilla suit, but over time I found it was generally too hot to wear on the job, particularly indoors.

I made the decision as we flew from Houston to Jackson, Mississippi, where Kerry was scheduled to speak at a black school called Tougaloo College. The night before the event, the whole press corps went out to a blues bar in Jackson and whooped it up. Not having eaten in five days, I was blitzed after half a beer and only vaguely remember David Halbfinger coming up to me and talking cheerily about how great the "blues music" was in the bar. Then I remember inviting Evan Richman, the *Globe* photographer, back to the hotel bar where we were staying and trying to involve him in some kind of deep personal conversation about the business. Richman, a nice guy, was polite, but bugged out to his room at the first appropriate opportunity, leaving me to face the angry stare of the bartender who wanted to close.

The next morning, I got up, had a cup of coffee, and promptly ate two hits of acid I had been keeping in my wallet. I had bought them from a girl on Roosevelt Island, New York, before the trip in case things went well and I had the luxury of taking a hit or two toward the end just to see what eating acid and talking to John Kerry was like. The acid, she explained, had been sitting in her apartment for about a year, so she had no idea if it was still any good. "If I were you," she said, "I'd eat more than one. They're not fresh."

So I did. Then, as I waited for them to take hold, I calmly put on my Viking costume. It was an absurd getup, with a giant horned helmet, a big furry shawl, a breastplate, and furry liners for my "boots," which were actually a pair of Kmart sneakers. Then I sat in my room watching *Sportscenter*, waiting for it all to take hold.

It took about forty minutes. By the end of that time I was having trouble reading my watch. Deciding that it was better to be early than to miss the whole thing, I simply grabbed my notebook and headed downstairs to the lobby to wait for the bus.

On the way down, I shared an elevator with a Secret Service agent. He took one look at me, then observed the diamond-shaped Secret Service press badge hanging in front of my furry shawl.

"Hi," I said.

"Hey," he said, nodding. No reaction. He had clearly been trained for this kind of thing.

In the lobby, the first person to spot me was Jim Loftus, the only human being with a sense of humor on the Kerry staff.

"Who-oa!" he said. "Nice costume!"

"Yeah," I said.

"So, what's this all about?"

I shrugged. "Why not?" I said.

He nodded. "Right, right," he said. "Why not? I could give you an answer, why not."

"Yeah, but don't," I said. "That might spoil . . . your relationship with the press."

"Fair enough," he said. "Wanna smoke?"

We went outside and had a smoke. The cigarette, I remember, tasted like peanuts. From there we filed onto the bus. Some of the other reporters asked me what was going on, and I just shrugged. Meanwhile I was beginning to have serious motor skill problems. The sheer logistical difficulty of keeping track of my few items of equipment—tape recorder, notebook, pens—was occupying all of my mental energy. When we got to the actual event, I sought out what

I thought was a quiet place on a riser to the side of the event; most of the reporters were using the riser that faced the candidate, so I was all alone and safe, or so I thought. But as we got closer to the time for the speech, I found myself suddenly surrounded by Tougaloo's gospel choir, a large squad of black musicians who placed a keyboard and a set of microphones right in front of me. Everyone in the crowd was black as well. I could hear people whispering across the hall. Then, suddenly, as happens with these drugs, an evil voice spoke to me from somewhere inside my head.

"Don't shout *nigger*," the voice said.

The thought would not go away. For some twenty consecutive minutes I sat, helmet on, sunglasses shielding my eyes, furiously writing in my notebook: "I will not say 'nigger' out loud. I will not say 'nigger' out loud. I will not say 'nigger' out loud. . . ."

Finally I became afraid of what might happen if I stayed in the hall and went outside, where I sat under a "tree," which was actually a bush about four-and-a-half-feet tall. Two small black children playing catch with a tennis ball stopped to stare at the Viking under the bush, then moved on. Meanwhile I tried to distract myself by reading a book I'd bought the night before, Jon Gruden's *Do You Love Football?* The Bad Thoughts disappeared as I found myself engrossed by the book, which at the time seemed to me the greatest novel ever written, something like a cross between *Ivanhoe* and *Remembrance of Things Past.* In one section, Gruden described how as a young man he had been taught by his father, also a coach, that it was important to be good "on the board," that is, to draw perfect X's and O's on the blackboard. As a result, he had spent much of his junior high years not paying attention in school and instead just drawing pages and pages full of perfect O's in his notebooks.

I started filling my notebook with O's. By the time I heard a cheer from inside the event that signaled that Kerry had come onstage, I had about three pages of perfectly round O's.

I didn't even hear the speech. I had to reconstruct it later from the tape recording. Kerry was talking, I knew, but I wasn't listening. The tape record indicates that at one point, in an attempt to connect with this down-home, southern crowd, Kerry whipped out his folksy side. Talking about his plan for getting out of Bush's economic mess, he said: "I remember something my mama told me. The first rule is, when you dig yourself into a ditch—stop digging!"

The only break in the O's in my notes comes from that moment. "Why dig yourself into a ditch?" I wrote. Then I went back to the O's. There were several pages more before I spotted Morehouse drifting around in the press filing area. I went over to him.

"Hey, David," I said. "Hello."

He looked at me. "Nice getup," he said.

"Uh-huh," I said. I was going to play this straight, though, just make it a normal interview. No jokes about the costume; just get right into it.

"So," I said. "You were with the ONDCP in Clin—in second . . ."

"In what?" he said.

"In the second—in the Clinond—"

I was unable to pronounce the phrase *In the second Clinton presidency.*

"In the what?" he said.

I wiped my brow. "You were in the ONDCP in the sec—in the Clinton—"

"Okay," he said. "In the second . . ." He was trying to help me out.

"In the term—in the second Clinton . . ."

"In the second Clinton presidency?" he said.

"Yeah, exactly!" I said. "Thanks."

"No problem," he said. "What's with the costume?"

"Did you have anything to do with any of the ONDCP public service announcements back then?" I said, ignoring him.

"Yeah," he said. "What's with the costume?"

"Oh, this . . ." I said. "What about that stuff where there were messages in shows like *Friends* and stuff about kids not, uh, taking drugs?"

"No, that wasn't me," he said. "That happened after I left. Although I was there when it was just being considered."

"This costume is just . . ." I began. "I was like, why not, you know? You ever feel like that?"

"No," he said.

"So you did other messages?" I asked.

"Yeah, lots of public service announcements," he said.

"What about the fried egg thing?" I asked.

"Yeah, there was the fried egg thing, some others," he said.

"The fried egg thing," I repeated, nodding.

"Yeah," he said.

"The fried egg thing," I repeated.

"Yeah," he said. "Most of it was all about prevention, you know, rather than the punitive aspect."

"It's tough to get kids to stop doing drugs," I said. "They think a little weed is like nothing, and then next thing you know, they're out of their goddamned minds."

"Yeah," he said.

It went on:

TAIBBI: Now, were you the strategic planner at the ONDCP the whole time?

MOREHOUSE: No, I was an aide . . . what was my title the first time? I was the Defense Department representative.

TAIBBI: Nice. So what was that, like interdiction, planes. . . ?

MOREHOUSE: No, that wasn't what I did. I was an aide—an aide to the drug czar.

TAIBBI: Barry McCaffrey!

MOREHOUSE: No, the first one. Lee Brown. When I went back the second time, though, I was the director of strategy for McCaffrey.

TAIBBI: (horns nodding) Gotcha!

Once that interview was over, I raced out of the room and sat down again under my bush. An awesome feeling of relief washed over me, though I was not sure what the source of it was, since actually I had accomplished nothing. When it came time for everyone to file back onto the bus, I hopped on, the drug having evened out, and just basked in the nice afterglow that comes with positive hallucinogenic experiences—the pleasurable feeling of spring air on the skin, an enjoyment of the slow passage of time, the feel of thick book pages flipping in my fingers. As I pored through the rest of Gruden's masterpiece in the air en route to Miami—that night's destination—a *Newsweek* reporter came over and plopped down in the seat next to me.

"So, what's all this about?" she said. "The rest of us want to know."

I shrugged. "I think I'm . . . not cut out for this kind of work," I said.

"Fair enough," she said. "Well, good luck."

She got up, leaving me alone again. I was still a loser in this crowd, but at least, I felt, I was a loser on my own terms. Previously I was one of them, a beginner, but a twit; now I was a twit, but at least not one of them. When we reached Miami and I felt the warm night air, I actually felt like going for a swim.

Campaign reporters have a tough life. It's tiring as hell, and there's never enough sleep. Some reporters go through long stretches, weeks if not months at a time, where they never have a day off, never sleep in their own beds. You feel lousy most of the time: they feed you eight times a day, and you spend most of your time sitting on your ass, which incidentally is usually housed in clothes that haven't been laundered for quite a while.

And the rest of it—the plush hotels, the four-star food, the hobnobbing with senators and governors, the best music acts in the city coming out to play for you everywhere you go—for most of the reporters it's a mirage. All that bling bling is on a company card. The instant you rotate off, the instant you take that cape off, you go back to being just another guy, wherever it is that you actually live.

On my final night on the campaign, the Sunday after Super Tuesday, a number of the reporters gathered on the pier outside the plush Westin Diplomat Hotel in Hollywood, Florida, just outside Miami. Several of the reporters were going to be leaving the trail, so some of the rest had arranged a send-off. Jim Loftus stood up to give a speech in honor of one of the departing crew.

Loftus, incidentally, is Kerry's best advertisement for the presidency. He is that rarest of creatures in politics: a political operative with a personality. He reminded me a little of some nightclub owners I've known in the Third World—always had a story, never surprised by anything, gets a kick out of it all. You could have an unguarded conversation with him at any time of the day, which for a reporter on the campaign trail is like having an adult who's always around to buy for you at the liquor store.

"Okay, everyone," he said, clearing his throat. "Okay. Now, all of us here work for big, evil corporations. We all know that. But not all of us here can really aspire to being big and evil. Some of us really have to content ourselves with being little and evil."

He gestured to the departing journalist. "And I think that [he named him] here really exemplifies that quality: small, and evil."

He raised his glass.

"Let's drink to the small, evil people," he said.

I raised my beer. Hear, hear.

7

SPRING/SUMMER 2004

You Say You Want a Tivo-lution?
When the Whole World Is a Giant Commercial, There's Nowhere to Hide

I was in San Antonio over the weekend, talking myself out of suicide during a John Kerry stump speech, when an Ad Man approached me in the back of the crowd.

"Those press tags?" he said.

"Yup," I said.

"Print or air?" he said.

"Print," I said, pantomime-typing.

He nodded. "So—the studied slovenliness, affected cigarette consumption, strained interpersonal relationships, sure-you're-the-next-I. F. Stoned-and-pissed-because-nobody-notices kind of print? Or are you just a geek for somebody's news desk?"

I stared at him. "The first kind," I said.

"Joe," he said, extending a hand.

March 9, 2004, *New York Press*.

"Matt," I said, shaking it.

He pointed, indicating the stage. "What is this, a presidential candidate?" he said.

"Yeah," I said. "John Kerry."

"Who?"

I took a deep breath and translated.

"You know," I said, "Massachusetts breeding, hunt club jackets in informal settings, whatever-gets-you-through-the-night ideology, occasional bouts of quizzical hesitancy. Off-the-cuff Red Sox allusions."

He nodded. "Right," he said. "I've seen that. Can't say I find it too exciting."

"No?"

He shook his head. "Nah. See, I'm in retail advertising. Wal-Mart, Kmart, Target, those guys. A little food and beverage stuff. Politics, I never saw much in it. The pay is good, but who's your client? Seriously, who's your client? A bunch of primitives. Win or lose, they go out of business in six months. And Jesus, look at these posters! Who designed them—the fucking Girl Scouts?"

"I don't think they were Girl Scouts," I said. "I think it was Hill & Knowlton."

He rolled his eyes. "Like I said, Girl Scouts. And another thing—I mean, I don't want to be picky, but look at the candidate! They couldn't do better than that? Look at his *face!*"

"But," I protested, "that's his face. That's what he was born with."

"Bullshit," he said, shaking his head. "Seriously, if he had a better face, we'd be interested. But it's just too long, too serious, too 1880-chimney-sweep. It doesn't say to me, 'I retain a comfortable disposable income and I'm really enjoying this Heineken.'" He paused. "Actually, how much do you think it would cost—to get him to walk around with a bottle of Heineken?"

"I don't think he'd be interested," I said.

"You see what I mean? It's a dead business, politics," he said, shaking his head sadly. "I mean, you can put beer in anything, even the news. What makes this different?" He frowned. "It's too bad, because that's where all the money is now—product placement. All my clients are after me about it. It's that goddamn TiVo. It's changing everything."

At this point the Ad Man entered into a long lecture about the intricacies of his business. By the time he was done, I was ready to give money to the Ad Council of America. Me, the person who once thought seriously about fire-bombing the offices of Burson-Marsteller. In the discussion, the Ad Man reverted to his professional state. That is, he was extremely persuasive. Because what he was telling me was that new customer-friendly TV technology designed to blot out commercials was already forcing the hand of the industry. Denied space for advertising, the business was going to be forced to move on to a new canvas: reality.

"Look," he said. "TiVo right now is a relatively small percentage of the market. We're talking about 2 million people across America. But in a very short time, and everybody knows this, it's going to be at least half of America. And then where will we be? No one's going to voluntarily watch commercials, except for people like me. And I only do it because the production values are so much better. And we'll have no choice but to focus exclusively on getting the products in the programs. That's already happening, but it's going to get a hell of a lot worse even by next year.

"You watch. By December, the defendants on Court TV will be wearing Seikos. Girl falls in a well: fireman rescuing her on CNN is wearing a Seiko. U.S. invades Syria: troops distribute TastyKakes in Damascus. And don't even think about laughing. That's already happening. It's just going to get worse."

"You don't seem too upset about it," I said.

He shrugged. "Shit, I don't get upset about anything. It doesn't matter to me one way or the other. But I'll tell you one thing—this whole thing is actually a quantum leap forward for the business. Eliminating TV advertising will make my job a hell of a lot easier. I'll have a fleet of yachts within three years. I won't even sail them. I'll just dump 'em in the backyard, just so that people like you can stare at them. No offense."

"None taken," I said.

"You see," he said. "The thing is, a placed ad is a lot more effective than the booked ad. I'll give you an example. Name me a magazine."

I shrugged. *"Muhammad Speaks,"* I said.

He frowned. "Come on," he said. "That's just not called for. We're friends here. Name me a real magazine."

I thought about it. "Okay," I said. *"Teen Muhammad Speaks."*

"Much better," he said. "Okay, so you want to sell your Libby Lu Muslim teen princess fantasy package. If you put it in the book, you get one result. But if you get an article with a picture of Mary Kate X and Ashley Shabazz wearing Libby Lu princess tiaras, that's—shit, I'd say one hundred times more effective. And that's a conservative estimate. You've locked up your Muslim teenager demographic. That's worth a year of book ads."

"Huh," I said.

"Someday they're going to look back at this time and just laugh at how unsophisticated we were," he went on. "The shit we're pulling now is going to look as dumb as socialist realism. Remember that big controversy about those assholes in the White House who were putting anti-drug messages in shows like *Friends* and *E.R.?* Or that stuff about CBS digitally painting ads onto the background landscapes of news programming? People are going to look back at that and just laugh their heads off."

"Why?" I said. "How can you make it worse than that?"

"Because look at the content," he said. "You're still placing ads *in* something. The trick is to place ads in ads. *Friends, E.R.,* the news . . . the plots are all wrong. You've got all this horrible stuff in there: love interests, curing someone with mesothelioma, elections. There's too much distraction here. You've got to make the entire drama of existence the choice of the next product. Now, some of the new vehicles out there are getting it nearly right. Take this new magazine called *Cargo* that's just coming out. Have you seen it?"

"No," I said.

"It's a shopping lad mag. *Seventeen* for grown men, if you can still call them that. It's ads surrounded by ads, with ads placed in the ads. It's fucking beautiful. I'll give you an example of content. They have this feature in there that's called, 'Honey, does this make me look gay?' Now, a reasonable person would deduce that, if you made it to page 72 of *Cargo*, that question is already moot. But, fortunately, people aren't reasonable. So you get this great thing where it's a whole book full of ads that the guy flips through, only to come to the 'content,' which is basically, 'Buy this or you're a fucking queer.' It doesn't get much better than that. That's where TV is going. Hell, that's where politics are going. Buy or you're queer. Buy or you're queer.

"We've got to move product," he went on. "This shit"—he waved a hand in Kerry's direction—"just takes up too much time. We need people focused. And they will be. As soon as those old ads are out of the way—they will be."

Memories of John
Negroponte was a Great Boss

Editors' note: New York Press *proudly publishes this exclusive excerpt from the new book by David Twatt, the former senior diplomatic attache to Iraq. From the summer of 2004 straight through to the last bloody days of the U.S. withdrawal in November 2005, Twatt served as the senior aide to the late U.S. ambassador to Iraq, John Negroponte. His book,* They Kicked Our Asses: An Iraq Diary, *offers a painstaking account of the extraordinary, but ultimately fruitless, efforts by U.S. diplomats to bring democracy and freedom to the Iraqi people. In the excerpt below, Twatt describes his relationship with Negroponte.*

John arrived in Baghdad in the first days after the June 30 transfer in 2004 and was immediately briefed on the security issues, which were already central to our mission and would remain so throughout our stay. From the very first moment, I could see that John had a calming influence on the mission. Many of us were young and untested and had been struggling with the situation foisted upon us, and suddenly here was John, a veteran diplomat who had seen much and seemed equal to the task. His confidence was infectious.

I explained to him the situation. Rebel Mahdi militias loyal to Muqtada al-Sadr occupied Fallujah, Kufa, and much of Najaf. A second militia of indeterminate origin, mostly "tallish guys," according to British commanders, had seized much of Umm Qasr. There was periodic street fighting in Baghdad,

April 20, 2004, *New York Press.*

and we were coping with the recent abductions of three Danish mimes; as a result of those kidnappings, Mimes Without Borders was threatening to cease operations in Iraq unless we provided additional security guarantees.

John listened intently, not saying a word. At times his professional focus was so intense that it almost seemed like he wasn't listening. When the briefing was over, he frowned for a moment, lost in thought, then stood up. "It sounds like we're going to be busy," he said, "but let's go knock one back first."

That was like John. Throughout our entire ordeal, no matter how rough things got, embassy morale always remained at the forefront of his concerns. There could be a full-fledged shooting war breaking out in the triangle, but John would still remember your birthday, would still ask about your kids' soccer games back home. That was just the way he was. The staff loved him.

We went to the "Polo Lounge," which was what the marines nicknamed the bar in the embassy. It was encased on all sides in twelve-inch depleted-uranium plating, but the staff had done a good job of making it seem festive. There was a plastic palm tree and one of those spinning balls you see at dance clubs. John ordered Manhattans and, gazing wistfully at a tropical seacoast print on the wall, told story after story about his time in Honduras.

"The United Nations gig was okay, but a diplomat ought to be in the field," he said, patting me on the back. He took a deep breath. "David, my friend," he said, "you just can't imagine how great it is to be on the front again."

We drank round after round, hitting it off surprisingly well. He told me his war stories from the Reagan years; I told him about my 3.4 GPA from Arizona State, my wife Sheryl, my Ford Windstar. When we were quite drunk, John leaned over to me and whispered, "Come on, David run back. Let's you and me take this embassy out for a spin. Let's get ourselves a panel truck and round up a bunch of nuns."

"Nuns, Mr. Ambassador?"

"Of course," he said. "David, you may not have noticed, but we have a serious situation here. And it all starts with the nuns. We've got to get them before it's too late. There's no telling what they might leak to the press. Before we know it, this place will be crawling with reporters—the bastards."

"Sir," I said. "The press is already here. The whole war is on television. And sir, there are no nuns here. We're in a Muslim country."

"Bullshit," he said. "Call General Sanchez. He knows where the nuns are. Call him now, he'll be awake. We pay him enough, he ought to be."

Thus began what for John would be a very painful transitional period of his tenure in Iraq. One morning in that first month, a U.S. supply convoy was ambushed outside of Balad and the bodies of two dozen servicemen were paraded on the streets, their heads ultimately lodged on sticks. The AFP photo was carried all around the world.

"Look at this!" John shouted, when I came into his office the next day. "Front page of the *New York Times*! Those goddamned nuns are leaking everything! Get Azcona in here!"

We summoned Chalabi, who after showing great promise early on had proved a disappointment to our office. Privately, many of the staffers had urged him to insist upon a more pragmatic policy line in his meetings with John, but instead he took the easy way out and merely indulged John's every naive or misguided conception of the situation. He had even taken to wearing a pencil mustache and epaulettes.

"Señor Azcona!" John shouted. "I thought you assured me that your people were going to take care of those 'unwanted elements.' "

"Don't worry, Señor Negroponte," Chalabi said, "my men assure me that everything is under control."

I had to hand it to Chalabi. He picked up Spanish pretty fast.

"Well, that's good," John said. "We'll get 'em yet. As long as the people still love us."

"Sí, señor, the people still love you."

A few days later Chalabi called up in the middle of the night to say he had a present. His "Battalion 316," the covert Iraqi police unit John had had the agency guys train, had finally accomplished its mission. We drove out to an abandoned warehouse on the outskirts of Baghdad. Inside were the bodies of twenty Iraqi men, lined up side by side, all with bullet holes in their heads. They had monobrows and bushy mustaches, but they were all dressed in identical

black-and-white Catholic habits. They looked suspiciously like the Shia workers
we had supplied Chalabi to handle the domestic service duties in his mansion.

"We found them, Señor Negroponte," Chalabi said. "The nuns. You were
right. They were telling all sorts of lies."

John was thrilled almost to tears. "Good work, Jose. I knew I could trust
you. Now they know we're not fucking around!"

"Sir," I said. "These aren't Catholic nuns. They're Iraqi men. Look, sir,
they even have mustaches."

"Of course, of course," he said, patting my shoulder. There was shelling in
the distance; it was getting closer every day. Still gazing with relief at the bodies, he whispered to me.

"Listen, David, you'll have to keep this under wraps. If the word gets out
that we're killing nuns over here, we'll never hear the end of it."

I sighed. "Yes, sir."

"And David, take these out and bury them in the jungle somewhere."

I did as I was told. I respected the strength of John's convictions, but even
then—even then—I began to have my doubts that our policies in Iraq would
succeed.

*In next week's installment: Negroponte offers the entire Mahdi militia a free lobster
dinner—and it refuses!*

I Confess

Abu Ghraib Was the Time of My Life

—OFFICIAL TRANSCRIPT—

U.S. DOJ PRISONER INTERROGATION
Recorded by: SACs Richard Carter, Janis Hrblitz; witnessing civilian personnel
G. Harris et al. (OGAs)
Prisoner: PFC Matthew Taibbi (372nd Military Police Unit)
Location: Hanscom AFB, Belmont, MA

Date: June 31, 2004 (debriefing prior to congressional testimony)
Agent Carter questioning.

Q: Have a seat, private.

TAIBBI: Sure, I'll have a seat. I'll do anything you guys want. You guys look *bad ass!*

Q: Let's just get down to it. We're going to show you some pictures. . . .

TAIBBI: That was the first thing I said to myself, when I got here. Don't mess with these people! Hell, I didn't even mind wearing the hood. I'm thinking, it's probably better for me that I can't see! Who knows what you're going to do to me!

Q: Private, just to set things straight for the record, we didn't put a hood on you. You put that on yourself. And it wasn't a hood, it was your own pillowcase. If you remember, we had to forcibly remove it from your head.

TAIBBI: Oh, I remember. Sent shivers up my spine. No messing with you guys!

Q: (sighing) All right, private, let's move on. Now, for the record, is this you in this photo?

TAIBBI: Just like my momma made me!

Q: Now, what is it that you have the prisoner doing in this picture?

TAIBBI: (pausing, laughing) C'mon, guys, are you serious?

Q: Oh, we're serious.

TAIBBI: Well, what does it look like we're doing? We're putting the guy on the ground and making him lick whipped cream off a goat's balls! Sheesh! And I thought you guys were smart!

Q: Private—

TAIBBI: I mean—hey, you guys aren't going to do that to me, are you? Because I know you could. You could bring a goat in here right now, and what could I do? Scary guys like you!

Q: Private, get a hold of yourself.

TAIBBI: Oh, please don't hit me like that!

Q: Private, no one's hitting you.

TAIBBI: Oh. I thought you were going to hit me. I would have hit me.

Q: (sighing) Now, what about this picture?

TAIBBI: (nostalgic) Oh, that. There we're sodomizing the prisoner with a chemical lighting unit.

Q: Why?

TAIBBI: Why? What do you mean, *why?*

Q: We mean, why?

TAIBBI: Look, it's the same thing I told *Le Monde.* What would you do in that situation? Seven thousand miles from home, all these guys behind bars—shit, when are you ever going to get a chance again to sodomize a guy with a chemical lighting unit? I mean, I'm thirty-four years old already. Carpe diem, dude!

Q: What do you mean, it's the same thing you told *Le Monde?*

TAIBBI: Just now. When you guys gave me my phone call.

Q: You called *Le Monde?*

TAIBBI: I was going to call my mother, but then I thought to myself, hell, I can talk to my mother later! Then I thought about calling a lawyer, but I ended up ditching that idea, too. So I called *Le Monde.*

Q: Jesus! What did you tell them?

TAIBBI: Oh, all kinds of stuff. They were like, "Are those photos for real?" And I was like, shit, that wasn't the half of it! We did stuff that would have broken the camera if you tried to take a picture of it. It was fucking sweet! I told them this one story about a guy, just an ordinary guy, he was actually one of the quieter ones—anyway, we took him and shoved his head completely up a horse's ass. Just to see if it would fit! You'd be amazed, but it did.

Q: Um—

TAIBBI: And then they were like, did you do this on your own, or was there clearance from a superior? And I was like, a superior? Hell, we had carte blanche from the president himself! A written presidential order!

Q: Wait—is that true?

TAIBBI: Come on. Of course it wasn't. You guys know that. But that's what they wanted to hear, right?

Q: Private, do you mean to tell us that you shoved a prisoner's head up a horse's ass, systematically tortured others, allowed yourself to be photographed in these acts, and then, after you got caught, called a French newspaper and told them you were acting on the orders of the president of the United States?

TAIBBI: Sure!

Q: Jesus.

TAIBBI: What? What did I do?

Q: Private, about your testimony tomorrow . . .

TAIBBI: Oh, that's going to be sweet. I'm psyched. Is it going to be on the Spike channel? *Stripperella* rocks!

Q: Private, they're going to ask you some very sensitive questions. . . .

TAIBBI: Don't worry. I won't tell them about the other stuff.

Q: What other stuff?

TAIBBI: My lips are sealed. You can count on ol' Matt.

Q: Private, goddammit, what other stuff?

TAIBBI: You know. All those weapons of mass destruction we found. That'll be our little secret.

Q: What weapons of mass destruction?

TAIBBI: Under the prison. You know.

Q: No, we don't know.

TAIBBI: Sure. Under the prison. We were taking a prisoner down there to burn his testicles with a hot fork, and we were looking around for a quiet room, when all of a sudden we pull open this door and there's this space under there that's as big as an airplane hangar. All filled with these creepy steel drums. Had all these inscriptions on 'em. So we got one of the prisoners who speaks English down there, and had him translate it for us. Turns out it was an—anthr—shit, I can't remember.

Q: Anthrax?

TAIBBI: That's it. Turns out this stuff is totally deadly. Kills people in hundreds if it gets out. We read all about it on the Internet. So we figure, if we let this stuff lie around, someone's going to get hurt. So we did the right thing.

Q: What was that?

TAIBBI: Well, we drove it out in trucks to this little area of the desert about ten miles upwind of this little shitbag village where's there's nothing but a children's hospital and some other stuff. Then we put it into this crater and piled all of our unspent ordnance on top of it. Then we drove about three miles away and started firing mortar rounds at it. Took us a while to get a hit, because it had been so long since we'd done that in basic. But when we finally did—boom! Shit went up in this huge cloud. We sent one of the translators out there to check it out later. Said there was nothing left, no trace. Funny thing, the guy died a few days later.

Q: You destroyed *all* of the anthrax?

TAIBBI: Not all of it. We kept one drum. See, we figured this was a matter of national security. Congress had to know. So we scooped out little bits of it into army envelopes and sent one apiece to every member of the Senate and the House. We didn't want to get the press involved, but we figured our leaders could take care of it real quiet-like without scaring the public.

Q: You just sent it in envelopes? Did you enclose a report or anything?

TAIBBI: (smacks forehead) *Damn.* We forgot that part. No, we just scooped a little of the stuff in each one and sent it out.

Q: Private?

TAIBBI: Yes?

Q: I think it's time for you to put that hood back on.

Donkey. Elephant. Chicken.
The Green Party Sells Out

Well, thank God the Green Party came to its senses last week and nominated David Cobb to run for the presidency, ending that whole ugly Ralph Nader episode. I was afraid I might have to make an actual decision before this upcoming election—but now I can safely be a gutless worm and throw my vote away to a gang of ferrety, querulous, self-flagellating intellectuals who learned politics from the 1961 Mets.

What a relief! Now, when I have to explain my electoral choices at Upper West Side cocktail parties in 2005, I can have it *both ways!* I did—and I didn't! It's perfect!

For those of you who didn't follow this story, Cobb snatched the Green Party nomination away from Nader last week largely through his embrace of the so-called safe states strategy, known affectionately in political circles as the "crack suicide squad" approach to campaigning. In this scenario, Mr. Cobb agrees in advance to refrain from campaigning in any state where the

July 6, 2004, *New York Press.*

Greens might have a chance to affect the outcome of the Bush-Kerry race. Bravely, however, he condescends to campaign balls-out in any state where a vote for the Greens doesn't matter. This is the kind of political warfare that would have made the Mensheviks proud: whistle-stop tours full of rowdy Greens singing "Kum Ba Yah" and "Give Peace a Chance" in front of crowds of two dozen in Cambridge and Portland and Seattle.

There is simply no way to explain the Green Party's decision to nominate Cobb except as a formal admission/cementing of its national role as a quixotic affectation for the spineless intellectuals of the Starbucks-and-SUV set. This is the kind of politics you get when you raise a generation of people who don't understand the difference between brand identification and ideological conviction. Much the same way that Burger King and McDonald's are scrambling to figure out a way that you can be on the Atkins diet and still spend your money at their vile, ass-inflating restaurants, Cobb and his party basically figured out a way that *Nation* subscribers can wear Green this fall and still keep their friends. They have turned politics into a shoe and a handbag, a conquered market demographic.

Vote Green—elect Kerry! Lose weight—drink Lo-Carb Coca-Cola! It's the same thing, on many different levels. Because both decisions really boil down to the same insane compromise: trying to fit an instinct to reject corporate consumer culture into the ruling paradigm of corporate consumer culture.

Logic dictates: if you want to lose weight, the way to do that is not to drink the *right kind* of Coca-Cola. The way to do it is to *not drink Coca-Cola*. It doesn't take a genius to figure this out, but it is apparently beyond the grasp of most Greens.

Similarly, if you don't believe in things like corporate personhood, if you are against the war in Iraq, if you are against the scourge of corporate money in politics, if you are in favor of a reduction in military spending, if you want to abolish the WTO and NAFTA, if you want to end the export of arms, if you want to break up media monopolies, if you want to get Channel 1 out of public schools, if you want to end the targeting of children by corporate advertisers— if you believe any of these things, or more to the point, if they are embedded in your party platform, then you can't vote for either the Republicans or the Democrats, because they're united against you all the way down the line.

I understand the logic of the Greens' decision. I don't agree with the "anybody but Bush" idea, but I will admit that it is a rationally defensible position, one that makes sense on some primitive level. What does not make sense here is why the burden of "anybody but Bush" should fall on the Green Party. The burden really rests with the Democrats. If they want to end the Green Party problem, then those votes are there for the taking. All the Democrats have to do is renounce the WTO and NAFTA, create a universal health care system, and slash the defense budget, putting the proceeds into education and health care. Among other things.

But the Democrats won't do that; they're too addicted to corporate money. They're money junkies. And as anyone who's had any experience with junkies will tell you, junkies cannot be trusted. They'll say anything you want them to say about going straight, but at the critical moment, they'll still steal your television and shoot it right into their arms.

The only way to deal with a junkie is to change your phone number or, if you ever find him in your house, chain him to a radiator. If you're feeling generous, you might consider bringing him hot chocolate and chicken broth during the three days he spends freaking out and writhing on your floor. But the one thing you can't do is keep giving him that one last chance. That only guarantees that he will come back again very soon, covered with mysterious bruises and needing 200 bucks to pay for—tchya, right—a hepatitis shot.

Shit, just look at what's happened since the last election. The junkies got kicked out of office, which ought to have been a wake-up call, and what did they do? They went out and almost unanimously voted for the Patriot Act, the No Child Left Behind Act, and two wars.

And now here they come, four years later, and they say: "We need all your votes *right now* or we're fucked." Am I the only one laughing?

That said, I also understand the Democrats' point of view. I used to take a lot of drugs, too. And when you take a lot of drugs, absolutely nothing matters except getting off. In the quest for drugs, any kind of behavior is excusable. You will be standing with a nice fat gram firmly in your fist and you'll still stare your best friend right in the eyes and swear to him that you couldn't find anything, either. And the funny thing is that later, when he finds out that you've been smacked out watching *Starship Troopers* for three days, he won't even be mad. He'll *laugh*. Because he would've done the same thing to you.

That's junkie morality. That's why, from the Democrats' point of view, it makes perfect sense to nominate a gazillionaire missile-humping aristocrat who'll have more corporate logos pasted on him than a NASCAR driver when he gets into office. What's the difference? *We got off!* Why is everybody complaining?

But this line of reasoning doesn't make sense for the Green Party. If you're going to suck a cock in a train-station lavatory, you ought to at least get something for it. But the Greens are going to roll over for John Kerry, and in the best-case scenario all they're going to get for it is another insane trade agreement, more troops in Iraq, more corporate handouts, and another my-dog-ate-my-homework health care fiasco.

Yes, Bush is a moron and a monster, and it would be better if he were not around. But America's political problems are bigger than Bush. The real problem in American politics is the rule of calculation and money over principle, and until this problem is fixed, the Bushes of the world will always be with us.

The Greens used to offer a solution. They've now become part of the problem.

Bin Laden Speaks Out

On the Citicorp Building, Spidey 2, *and Those Persistent*
Marisa Tomei Rumors

Editors' note: Through surrogates in Austria, Portugal, Karachi, and other locations, the Press *has been negotiating the terms of this exclusive interview*

August 10, 2004, *New York Press.*

*with Osama bin Laden since March of this year. Among other things, we
had to send a reporter who was comfortable filing from a remote location,
and also with whom—how should we put this?—we were willing to, shall
we say, part.*

*In a cave along the Pakistani-Afghani border, Matt Taibbi recently sat down
with the man who brought 9/11 to the United States, and the long scary beard
back to the Middle East.*

TAIBBI: Good morning. Thanks for sitting down with me.

BIN LADEN: No problem. Did you bring the latest issue of *Essence?*

TAIBBI: Right here.

BIN LADEN: Thanks.

TAIBBI: That's okay. So, did you really have plans to blow up the Citicorp building?

BIN LADEN: Refresh my memory.

TAIBBI: The Citicorp building. In New York. There were new reports
you planned to blow it up.

BIN LADEN: (squinting) I'm trying to get a picture.

TAIBBI: The big white one in the Fifties. Looks like a giant tee marker.

BIN LADEN: Oh, right. Well, probably we were, yes. But nothing on the
front burner.

TAIBBI: Is there a particular reason that the United States announced a
terror alert about it and about several other locations this week?

BIN LADEN: Not that I know of. But I tend not to spend a lot of time worrying about where people like your Mr. Ridge get their information.

TAIBBI: You don't even want to speculate?

BIN LADEN: I couldn't possibly guess. Perhaps he has headaches and his
neighbor Sam's German shepherd talks to him at night.

TAIBBI: (laughing) I hadn't thought of that one.

BIN LADEN: Neither had I, until just now. But I like it. Maybe I'll use it in
my next speech.

TAIBBI: Are you planning a major act of terror in the United States in
the near future?

BIN LADEN: That depends. Honestly, we haven't decided who we want as
your president yet. Both have pluses and minuses.

TAIBBI: How's that?

BIN LADEN: Bush we can count on to go stumbling around the planet with his dick in his hand, giving us a whole bunch of troops to shoot at. He'll divide the entire world and turn this whole thing into a referendum not just on us, but on the United States. On the other hand, I just love that Kerry. We have a guard here who does a great impersonation.

TAIBBI: Can you do one?

BIN LADEN: I try, but it comes out sounding like Katharine Hepburn. I do a pretty good Michael Madsen, though.

TAIBBI: Did you like *Kill Bill*?

BIN LADEN: I'm thinking more of *Species*. Hell of a movie. You got some great-looking broads over there.

TAIBBI: Since we're on the subject of movies, what did you think of *Fahrenheit 9/11*?

BIN LADEN: You people are a strange nation. You think everything in the world belongs to you. If there's oil in Saudi Arabia, it's yours and we're just watching it for you. Then we do something like blow up the World Trade Center, and a few years later you show all these ghastly pictures and make it seem like the whole thing was George Bush's fault. You can't even let other people take *credit* for something. It's like a sickness with you.

TAIBBI: What is it about Americans that makes you so bent on killing us?

BIN LADEN: I . . . I hate you for your freedom.

TAIBBI: Really?

BIN LADEN: (laughs) No, I'm just fucking with you. Mainly we hate you because you support Israel and because you maintain army bases in the Arabian peninsula. But also—six dollars for a cup of coffee? What the hell is wrong with you people?

TAIBBI: Well, we're not asking you to pay it.

BIN LADEN: Not yet.

TAIBBI: Right. (flipping through notebook) Okay. Since 9/11, how has your life changed? Do people come up to you on the street now and say, "Hey, aren't you Osama bin Laden?"

BIN LADEN: No. What they say is, "Sir, we found this one sneaking around in sector four. Should we kill him?" That kind of thing.

TAIBBI: What's the best thing about being the scourge of Western civilization?

BIN LADEN: The food. The prosthetic limbs. Getting high and making scary videotapes to send to Al Jazeera. Inventing one's own fucked-up

moral calculus and forcing others to live by it. Weaving a tangled con-
spiratorial web. The skiing. The caves full of stinky man-smell. Playing
your lieutenants against each other to solidify your position. Rooting
out leakers and torturing them in front of the men. The feeling of being close to God and doing the right thing. All of these things and
more. But the absolute best thing is not having to be just another bour-
geois real estate dealer with a big nose in Saudi Arabia, in a family full
of them. I needed to have something of my own. I didn't want to have
to go through life hearing people say, "Which one?" when the name *bin
Laden* was mentioned.

TAIBBI: Do you ever think to yourself, "I don't need this pressure. Maybe
I should just give all of this up and teach high school?"

BIN LADEN: All the time. But I think that once you've been involved in
something like this, you'll always be looking for that adrenaline rush. I
don't think I could give up being a terrorist now. Among other things, it
would force me to confront the enormity of my moral choices. Once
you start killing large numbers of people, you pretty much can't stop.

TAIBBI: Isn't this conflict between the West and radical Islam just an extension of the same religious crusades that have been going on for
about the past 1,000 years?

BIN LADEN: That's the way we see it.

TAIBBI: Isn't that . . . silly?

BIN LADEN: I'm sorry? My English.

TAIBBI: Silly. Uh . . . comical, without being noble.

BIN LADEN: Umm . . .

TAIBBI: Like Pauly Shore.

BIN LADEN: Oh. Yes, of course it is silly.

TAIBBI: Then why do it?

BIN LADEN: Because the world is silly. It must be dominated by silly people. And I am a very silly person.

TAIBBI: Is George Bush silly?

BIN LADEN: Sometimes I lie awake at night and worry that he is sillier
than I am.

TAIBBI: Isn't that a good thing, from your point of view?

BIN LADEN: I don't know. Probably.

TAIBBI: Did you have anything to do with Bucky Dent in 1978?

BIN LADEN: No. That was Baader-Meinhof.

A Closer Look at John Kerry's Acceptance Speech

John Kerry had to give the speech of his life—and he did.
—Mark Shields, PBS political analyst, minutes after Kerry's acceptance
speech in Boston

After listening to John Kerry's acceptance address last week, I did a little experiment. I decided to remove everything that was bullshit and see what was left. I invite *New York Press* readers to follow me on this journey, step by step.

I admit to using the widest possible interpretation of *bullshit*. Bullshit can be outright lies, bullshit can be calculating come-ons, and bullshit can be self-aggrandizing self-mythology, which is more commonly known in this country as *self-aggrandizing bullshit*.

I acted on all of these varieties of bullshit, but I also went a little further.

I edited out phony religiosity (*pious bullshit*) and pointless political platitudes of the sort that could be used by any politician in any situation, including Hitler (i.e., "We're the optimists": *meaningless bullshit*). I also chopped out all gratuitous flag-waving (*patriotic bullshit*), all forced and hollow tough-talking (*saber-rattling bullshit*), and all draping of the clearly unworthy self in the ill-fitting cloak of the great figures of history (*name-dropping bullshit*).

Further down the line were the intellectual crimes. Lies went out right away, but I also cut out things that were not lies exactly, but mere words. Also banished were the many species of literary fraud—from facile generalizations to redundancies to such crass, hypersentimental, factory-generated clichés as "Trees [are] the cathedrals of nature." There were also many shades of disingenuousness to deal with, most of which came into play when Kerry levied attacks against George Bush—but more on that later.

I wasn't sure where to start, so I decided to first go after what one might call *typical campaign bullshit*, which includes such standbys as callow patriotism, syrupy talk about love of our vast and beautiful country, and Hallmark-y

---

August 10, 2004, *New York Press.*

references to the flag and the wonder and might of our armed services. Also targeted here were those nauseating constants of modern campaign speeches, the bald paeans to focus-group words like *hope, the future, freedom, change, truth, pride, values,* and *heroes.*

A typical victim of this stage of the elimination progress was a line like "I felt goose bumps as I got off a military train and heard the army band strike up 'Stars and Stripes Forever,'" which actually could have been struck on three or four grounds—there were two army references, a flag plug, and a fake memory of a fake emotion. I-can't-believe-somebody-actually-wrote-this lines like "I learned the pride of our freedom" were similarly double- or triple-eliminated.

In some cases, this set of cuts blitzed out whole paragraphs, as in the case of the diffidently delivered, "We have it in our power to change the world again. But only if we're true to our ideals and that starts by telling the truth to the American people. That is my first pledge to you tonight. As president, I will restore trust and credibility to the White House."

Cut around the edges here, and this is just a straight focus-group word list: *power, change, truth, ideals, truth, pledge, trust, credibility.* It can all go in the bin.

At times Kerry's determination to ram buzzwords down the audience's throat caused his speech to dissemble into near-total incoherence. Just look at passages like the following:

> For four years, we've heard a lot of talk about values. But values spoken without actions taken are just slogans. Values are not just words. They're what we live by. They're about the causes we champion and the people we fight for. And it is time for those who talk about family values to start valuing families.

This sounds like it makes sense at first reading, but upon closer examination it's actually maddening gibberish. A rough translation would begin like this: "It is meaningless to merely say one has values without backing it up, but yet we say—we have values. Values are real. You know what I mean. Let's talk about causes you champion [which causes?] and people you fight for [which people?]."

Then, having arrived at this whatever-values-float-your-boat point of the passage, Kerry uses the old "to make America better, we must first better America" technique to simply flip values over on its back like a turtle and watch as its legs flail around in the air: "And it is time for those who talk about family values to start valuing families."

An accurate translation would go like this:

> Some people don't have values. That's wrong. Values are real. Values are whatever you think they are. And it is high time for you to watch as I turn this turtle over on its back.

In some cases Kerry's overreliance on fuzzy, grammatically promiscuous words like "about" to mask the list-like nature of his rhetoric was so obvious, it was embarrassing. Some passages read like army color-blindness tests, which may in fact be where Kerry stole the idea from: if you squinted hard enough to avoid seeing the connecting words, you could make out the underlying message.

Take this passage, which is Kerry-ese for the human sentence *elections, choices, choices, values, policies, programs, principle*:

> My fellow citizens, elections are about choices. And choices are about values. In the end, it's not just policies and programs that matter; the president who sits at that desk must be guided by principle.

Again, this sounds like it makes sense. But when you think about it, what is he really saying? "The president ought to have principles." After 200-plus years, we still need someone to step up to a podium to tell us that? Are we fucking *children*, or what?

By my count Kerry had about 175 words' worth of references to his religious beliefs, which accounted for roughly 3.5 percent of the speech. I struck all of them on the grounds that I simply do not believe that Kerry is a religious man. Kerry is probably religious in the way that a person who has to be reminded to invite God to a ball is religious. I will eat my own foot if it ever comes out that he really "humbly prays," as he said he does in his speech.

By comparison, I believe that George Bush sincerely believes he believes in God. When Bush talks about Jesus, even die-hard Jesus people buy it. I know I buy it, because it scares the shit out of me. But when Kerry talks about God, even James Carville probably thinks his makeup is wrong or his lines need a little tweaking. Take this passage:

> But faith has given me values and hope to live by, from Vietnam to this day, from Sunday to Sunday.

Kerry's so nervous about the word *faith* that he has to sprint from its fleeting use straight into the focus-group safe haven of *values* and *hope,* and from there straight to a place where he really feels comfortable—Vietnam, a.k.a. the war George Bush didn't fight in.

As for the Vietnam business, there is something embarrassing and insulting about Kerry's insistence on bringing up his war service at every opportunity. It's embarrassing because it's painful to watch a man so shamelessly prostitute his most meaningful life experiences. And it's insulting because the sheer volume of Vietnam references in Kerry's addresses strongly implies that Kerry or his handlers believe that America's undecided voters are incorrigible dolts who are ready to defect to the Republicans at the drop of a hat if they don't hear at least nine times a day that John Kerry Served in Vietnam.

Kerry's self-mythologizing in this area might be excusable if he didn't insist on referring constantly to Vietnam without offering a judgment, an opinion, or even some information about that war. Kerry talks about Vietnam as though it were a territory on a distant planet, where the only human beings were his buddies on a swift boat, and the only salient fact about the place is that he was once there.

Kerry does not ask America to apologize to Vietnam, but he does ask America to let Vietnam help him get elected. This is a lie of omission (Kerry's actual views about the righteousness of the war have been well-documented).

It is also an impressive show of spinelessness and an enormous insult to the Vietnamese people, who are being used to make an insecure Democrat look tough one more time.

All of which makes his Patton-esque grandstanding ("My name is John Kerry, and I'm reporting for duty!") and his mawkish Band-of-Brothers hugs-and-medals act all the more transparent and meaningless. Kerry reminds voters that he served and fought seven times in his speech. He makes another half-dozen or so references to his military background—and at no time does he ever say anything more specific than "I fought" and "war is hell." The verbal gymnastics that Kerry performed in order to avoid saying anything definitive about his Vietnam experience can be viewed in this passage:

> I know what it's like to write letters home telling your family that everything's all right when you're not sure that's true.

Here Kerry is hinting at the kinds of letters that soldiers in Vietnam wrote home at the time, letters that not only told their families they were safe, but also that they were doing the right thing. "When you're not sure that's true" is the giveaway. No soldier at war is ever "not sure" that his situation is unsafe—he *knows* it isn't safe, and that he may not be all right.

But "not sure" is exactly how a lot of Vietnam soldiers, Kerry included, felt about the war mission itself. Kerry wrote this passage in such a way that you can take it the other way, too, if you feel like it. This is Mobius-strip rhetoric, which reads, "I'm not sure I'm coming home" and "I'm not sure I'm doing the right thing" on the same side of a one-sided strip, and is as plain an example as you will ever see of a politician talking out of both sides of his mouth.

Kerry's name-dropping was not particularly egregious by campaign standards—seven solemn references to great figures past—but I struck nearly all of them.

Kerry's first reference was to writer Thomas Wolfe. Kerry didn't mention

Wolfe's name, saying only, "A great American novelist wrote that you can't go home again." This seems harmless enough, except that in the course of the last year, while following Kerry, I noticed on numerous occasions that he was reluctant to say aloud the names of writers or intellectuals.

A typical example is a line written by a famous poet that he uses in his stump speech. The line was also used by Ted Kennedy in his eulogy to his brother Robert: "'Some men see things as they are and ask why. I dream things that never were and ask, why not?'"

Kerry uses that line a lot, but he always introduces it by saying, "He [Ted Kennedy] quoted the poet who said. . . ." When I asked a Kerry spokesman why Kerry didn't just say the poet's name out loud, he told me that the average voter might be confused by the mention of too many academic references. (The same spokesman also told me the line belonged to Carl Sandburg. It was actually written by George Bernard Shaw.)

If voters are going to be confused by too many references, why mention that the line was recited by Ted Kennedy at a funeral for Bobby Kennedy? The answer, of course, is that John Kerry is happy to have his name associated with the Kennedys in voters' minds, but reluctant to admit to being the sort of person who reads George Bernard Shaw—a European in a sweater!

That's why, in his acceptance speech, Kerry proudly says "John Kennedy" out loud but turns Thomas Wolfe into "a great American novelist." (Almost the same as "a great American," except for the novelist part. If you think this is accidental, you haven't watched enough American politics.)

If you were to write a history book with only the speeches of presidential candidates as source material, you might conclude that the only great thinkers in history were American presidents. I defy any journalist out there to show me a candidate not named Dennis Kucinich who would dare to publicly mention, let alone honor, a great foreigner, a Gandhi or a Tolstoy or a Mozart. I have had campaign spokesmen admit to me that they don't do this because they think the average Joe can't identify with such people (although one Kerry spokesman once humorously protested, "[Kerry] was saying something about Gandhi to Maureen Dowd the other day").

It is always difficult, when you look closely at the speech of a Democratic Party candidate, to determine what is a lie and what are mere words. I think the most obvious lies in John Kerry's case are his pledges about health care and trade. Take this passage:

> And when I'm president, America will stop being the only advanced nation in the world which fails to understand that health care is not a privilege for the wealthy, the connected, and the elected—it is a right for all Americans.

If you honestly think that Americans will have easier access to health care under John Kerry, raise your hand. At best, Kerry's federal reinsurance plan sounds like a hugely complex legislative fiasco that will die in committee sometime around Lebron James's thirtieth birthday. At worst, it sounds like a means of funneling enormous amounts of taxpayer money to insurers and employers without guaranteeing that the cost benefits will be passed on to the consumer.

Every Democratic politician in the past thirty years has made promises about health care, and none of them has ever amounted to anything. And you're crazy if you think that John Kerry, one of the easiest marks in the history of the party for corporate influence, will be the one to break that pattern.

Then there are lines like this:

> We value an America that exports products, not jobs. . . .

Kerry voted for NAFTA, GATT, the WTO, and permanent Most Favored Nation status for China. His solution for stopping job exports revolves around tax penalties for companies that open mailbox headquarters in foreign tax havens. That is not even a fig leaf of labor credibility. It is more like a daisy petal. You have whole industries moving to slave-wage territories like

China and Indonesia, but Kerry wants to keep Tyco from having an extra corporate address in Bermuda. Look out, Eugene Debs!

Something that would qualify as *mere words* is a line like the following:

> What does it mean when Deborah Kromins from Philadelphia, Pennsylvania,
> works and saves all her life only to find out that her pension has disappeared
> into thin air and the executive who looted it has bailed out on a golden para
> chute?

What does it mean? I imagine it means *sucks to be her*. Beyond that, who
knows? It's nice that Kerry makes the point, but does anyone really think that
he's going to stop golden parachutes or the looting of pension funds? Maybe
when it's done illegally, as in the case of Enron, but this hideous immoral practice is actually legal in this country. Will you hold your breath waiting for
Kerry to change that?

Kerry's speech was basically divided up into three sections.

First was the introductory part, an autobiographical section, in which
prospective voters learned that Kerry the child had a model airplane, a baseball mitt, and a bicycle, and found the world "full of wonders and mysteries."
His father was a member of the Greatest Generation and he learned at a
young age that communism was different, and that the Stars and Stripes were
good. Then the 1960s happened, and that taught him to value change and
cherish a hope for the future. After the 1960s, he looked back and realized
what a debt he owed to his parents, who incidentally were members of the
Greatest Generation. Then he went into the Senate and put 100,000 cops on
the street before deciding to run for president.

Next came a long policy statement that doubled as an indictment of the
Bush presidency. Not all of this was bullshit. There are a number of pledges
in here that he would certainly honor. There would be some kind of middle-
class tax cut under Kerry, and some of the higher-end Bush tax cuts would be

eliminated. We can feel confident that his vice president will not have secret meetings with polluters. He can be counted on not to increase the size of the military, double the Special Forces, and spend more on weapons systems. He won't privatize Social Security. And he won't allow American troops to fight under foreign command.

The rest of it, about the economy and health care, is basically balder and dash and I chucked it in the bin.

Finally, once his policies were laid out, Kerry moved on to his "big idea," another idiotic prerequisite of these proceedings. Bush I had kindness and gentleness; Bush II had compassion; Kerry went with "optimism." I don't know why anyone ever does anything but vomit when politicians lay things like this on us. "We're the party of optimism." As opposed to what? Despair? Psychic agony? I don't know what the hell any of this means, and so tossed that stuff, too.

Close to the end, Kerry rallied for one final flourish. Clearly pointing a finger at Bush, he denounced the practice of politicians "wrapping themselves in the flag" and questioning the patriotism of "Americans who offer a better direction." Then he charged those politicians to remember that America is about (he lapsed into a list) *idea, freedom, purpose, democracy, challenge, heart, soul,* and *patriotism*. Recovering himself, he then brazenly stole Howard Dean's shtick of pointing to a flag and hurling handfuls of patriotic paint at the audience ("We call her Old Glory . . . it was shot through and through and tattered, but it never ceased to wave in the wind . . . that flag is the most powerful symbol of who we are. . . .") before screaming out that that flag belongs to *everybody*, not just to Republicans.

Of course, if you were paying attention to the previous "Red, White and Blue states" part of Kerry's speech, you knew that in the Sister Sledge–themed party this year, the Democrats believe they are everybody.

In other words, the Republicans think the flag belongs only to them, but we think it belongs to everybody—and everybody is us.

Kerry closed his speech with a remarkable passage.

It is time to reach for the next dream. It is time to look to the next horizon. For America, the hope is there. The sun is rising. Our best days are still to come.

If you can fight your way through all the stale clichés—through those dreams you reach for, across the horizon, past the rising sun—just look at that one sentence: "For America, the hope is there." Just look at the way the passive *is* leaves the fake *hope* lying like a dead fish on the sun-baked deck of this wrecked address. Then ask yourself how someone as seemingly intelligent as Mark Shields could moments later call this the speech of John Kerry's life.

It's not fair to expect brilliance from politicians. It's not fair to expect them to be charismatic, or to electrify the hall with their speaking skills. It's not even realistic to expect them to tell you what they actually think about things.

But it is fair to demand that they at least make an honest attempt to tell us something about something. Give us some kind of plan; explain something to us. John Kerry has had a front-row seat to the inner workings of the highest levels of the U.S. government for nearly twenty years. He knows more about how the world actually works than all but a handful of people in this country. He has something to tell us.

But what does he do? He climbs up a mountain of clichés, shouts "Think Positive!" from the summit, and then calmly skis down into a sea of champagne and confetti with a toy M-16 draped over his shoulder. That is a gross insult, both to our intelligence and to our natural human desire to have some kind of active role in the management of our own affairs—and we all ought to be mighty pissed about it.

Don't get me wrong. Kerry said nothing in this speech, but nothing is still a vast improvement over the other guy. Maybe that's what he was thinking. Just don't tell me this is a great speech. It isn't. It's crap and an affront to human thought. This incredibly cynical politics of mechanized pandering and condescension poisons all of us. And the worst thing is, John Kerry is smart enough to know this—and he doesn't care. Not as long as he's still in this thing, anyway.

When I was done cutting, there were only two lines left.

> I was born in Colorado.
> America can do better.

Amen.

8

BUSH LIKE ME
Through the Looking-Glass into the
Other America

This article also appeared in shorter form in Rolling Stone, *and covers a period of about seven weeks that I spent volunteering for the Bush campaign in Orlando, Florida.*

I spent many years longing to go to Africa, because of what that continent offered in its wilderness and great diversity of free-living animals.
—from *Gorillas in the Mist*

With all due respect to the late Ms. Fossey, studying gorillas is relatively easy. It is not difficult to get out of bed in the morning when you know you are going to be spending the day with the noblest and most beautiful animals in God's kingdom.

I believe her enthusiasm for Africa would have been tempered significantly if the Rwandan lowlands had been inhabited by Republicans.

I never felt any longing to go to Orlando, Florida. What I felt, in traveling south to volunteer for the campaign of George W. Bush, was an obligation.

Let me explain by first saying something about the critics of our president.

September 2004, *Rolling Stone.*

A great many of them like to laugh at George Bush for not reading books and for being uninterested in visiting other countries. But a lot of those same people are guilty of the opposite offense. They *prefer* to read books and to travel abroad than to actually get to know their own country face to face.

I've met a lot of people in New York who would visit a temple at Machu Picchu long before they would deign to enter a Southern Baptist church—and I'm sure I couldn't even count the number of people I know who've read Eric Alterman's book more than once without even bothering to seek out and talk to someone who really believes in the Liberal Media Conspiracy.

There is a big difference between knowing what you think, and just plain knowing. And citizens on both sides of our great political argument are much more interested in the former than the latter.

This is one of the reasons I volunteered for the Bush campaign. I wanted to know.

And knowing isn't easy. When it comes to George W. Bush, it is a lot harder than knowing what you think. The president's critics do a terrific job of mocking his mental deficiencies, punching holes in his policies, and dismissing his supporters as hapless morons, but they do not do a very good job of explaining the nature of his support. Just as the racist believes that all black people look alike, there are people out there who would explain George Bush by saying that all idiots vote alike.

The few dissident commentators who do try to explain the Bush phenomenon seldom do more than reach for the nearest Marx-inspired academic cliché. They will tell you, for instance, that Republicans are a vast intellectual underclass cynically manipulated by the rich through a mesmerizing cocktail of yahoo enthusiasms, xenophobic fears, and ancient superstitions—and those same people will insist, if forced to offer an opinion on the subject, that one should feel sorry for most of them.

These are the typical explanations that emanate from the liberal left when asked to describe the Republican opposition. *They're idiots. They're dupes. They're the inarticulate victims of economic security.* And maybe these things are all true—but it doesn't change the fact that they're all the condescending, cowardly characterizations of a group of people who would rather look down at the next guy than risk looking him in the eye.

This is wrong. As a professional misanthrope, I believe that if you are going to hate a person, you ought to do it properly. You should go and live in his shoes for a while, and see at the end of it how much you hate yourself. If you've done a good job of it, you can then go back to your old, intolerant life with perfect justice.

This was what I was doing down in Florida. The anthropology was only the part I was getting paid for. The real challenge was in becoming the best Republican I could be. It was something I felt I owed to my prejudices—a fair trial.

Hombre Secreto

Republicans are everywhere, but everywhere is not a good place to look for them. For my purposes I wanted to try to catch them in their ideal habitat—not necessarily the place where they lived in the greatest numbers, but the most Republican *place,* the place where they felt happiest.

That was why I chose Orlando. For me it is hell on earth, the worst city on the planet, a place that I correctly guessed would quickly make me long for Kinshasa or Volokolamsk. But for Republicans it is ideal: a scorching hot paved inland archipelago of garish shopping malls and stadium-sized steel-and-glass Baptist churches, with no nonhuman life apart from the lizards and the caged animals at the theme parks, and an entire economy organized around monstrous temples to fake experience.

Forget about metaphorical holy sites like Disneyworld and Universal Studios: Orlando now also offers a recreated Bethlehem theme park called the Holy Land Experience, which costs about as much to enter as a water park does and is a stunning likeness of old Judea—apart, of course, from the miles of chain-link fence and the "No Trespassing" sign to keep out the homeless.

I arrived in early June 2004, not bothering to find an apartment. I simply moved into a cheap hotel, called the local Republican offices, and offered to volunteer. They told me to come on by. So I went, arriving early on a Tuesday morning at their small strip mall office on the east side, not knowing what to expect.

My cover story was a travesty, an idiotic tissue of halfhearted lies. I said I was a New York City schoolteacher named Tom Hamill, down in Orlando to spend a summer with a girlfriend who was originally from the area, and wanting to fill my free time with service to the president. It was the best thing I could come up with to explain my northern accent, my lack of local connections, and all that free time.

The story's only saving grace was that the truth was so much more unbelievable. Republicans are paranoid enough to expect a mole from the Kerry campaign, but I was a thousand times worse than that—a dissolute, drug-abusing anarchist who keeps a copy of Vo Nguyen Giap's diaries in his trunk, roots for Russia at the Olympics, and once published an article entitled "God Can Suck My Dick." I was, in short, the most offensive individual who could conceivably be planted in the campaign of George W. Bush. In the many down times I would have on this trip, this was the one cheering thought I kept coming back to.

I had assumed, coming in, that I would be entering a large campaign operation. Orlando, after all, is the critical city along a stretch of interstate called the "I-4 corridor," a swath of central Florida running from Daytona Beach to Tampa. Home to 3.7 million of Florida's 9.3 million registered voters, it has the bulk of the state's undecided voters, and is therefore the key to winning Florida's twenty-seven electoral votes. And we all know how important those are.

I expected a teeming, ultramodern, NORAD-style Bush campaign headquarters, where I would have to work my way up a giant totem pole from worker bee status. But in fact what I found was . . . nothing at all.

For all intents and purposes, there *was* no campaign for George Bush in Orlando in early June. All there was was one paid staffer, a central Florida field director named Vienna Avelares, and a corner of a table at the local Orange County Republican Executive Committee. That was it: a person and a few phones. I was shocked. If the Republicans were building an electoral Death Star somewhere, it sure as hell wasn't in Florida.

The situation was completely disarming. It was so *human*. Vienna, a gregarious Puerto Rican single mother who insisted on introducing herself as "Vienna—like the sausage," seemed desperately in need of help. I had planned on doing a good job anyway, but after meeting her I had a genuine desire to help her out and get things going. She put me to work on a phone survey, and within a day or so I was watching things for her around the office during her increasingly frequent absences.

After just a week of coming in every day like this, I became, along with a young blond Sean Hannity fan named Ben Adrian who also volunteered at that time, one of the most important Bush people in all of central Florida. Within a few weeks after that, we would both be given keys to the office and offered full-time jobs, so hard did we work for our president.

The cover story was no longer a problem. Now the task was to find a way to help George Bush win.

Here I want to make a general observation about the social aspect of working for Bush. It's very different working for a Democratic candidate. Corny as this sounds, it is much more egalitarian and brotherly than the vibe of Democratic campaigns.

Almost every Democratic campaign I've seen has let itself be seduced by the *Primary Colors* paradigm—the hip clique full of mildly sexually gregarious twentysomethings who have been working on their memoirs since high school, dreaming of that chance to crack saucy jokes on *The Jimmy Kimmel Show*, and wearing hip sport jackets at sit-ins full of adoring college students.

If you've ever spent time with the Trish Enrights and Joe Trippis of the world, you know that the operative vibe of the Democratic insider is wisecracking cool. It is not a reach to say that the ideological vision that mainstream Democratic politics has offered America since Clinton has been the super-cool high school, the party of the popular kids. For all the talk about the Democrats being the party of inclusion, it really doesn't feel that way from the inside.

That's not true of all Democrats, of course. For instance, the campaign of Dennis Kucinich was very different. For the most part these were people who were collectively motivated by something other than ambition, and just being part of that campaign meant you were in a besieged minority, with the whole world out there laughing at you. And because of that, the feeling in that campaign, at least from what I saw, was much kinder and more accepting than in the others. Kucinich supporters stuck up for each other, treated each other in a brotherly way, because they had to. There is a certain feeling that is generated among a group of people when they strongly believe in something that others laugh at.

You get that same besieged fraternal feeling in a Republican campaign office. There is none of that *M*A*S*H* ensemble-cast witticizing one-upsmanship you get in the typical Democratic office full of young liberal arts grads. Nobody wears T-shirts that mean something, and nobody looks like an extra from the Czech set of *XXX*. As I would later find out, most Republicans hate "cool," particularly the older women ("They all think they're so *cool* and *artistic*," griped one woman as she watched Fox coverage of Democratic delegates arriving in Boston). Many of the parent-volunteers I met are especially bitter because they think that *cool* is what liberals use to lure their children away from their early convictions. Which they might very well be right about, of course.

I recognized the DCZ (decoolified zone) of the Bush offices as being strikingly like those sanctuary corner tables in public school cafeterias I used to sit at because no one was going to give you shit about your haircut there. That is what the Bush campaign is like. If you come in, so long as you're a Republican and you swear by the flag, it doesn't matter how square you are, how friendless you are, how uneducated you are, how long ago you lost your children's attention, and, most important how openly Christian you are. Not only is no one going to laugh at you, but they're actually going to like you.

In my first month on the campaign, I did not meet many people who came into the office with the serious intention of working hard for the president. I did, however, meet a great many very lonely people who came in because they knew the Bush offices were the one place where they could share certain deeply held ideas without being ridiculed. Part of my job, I soon came to understand, was to be encouraging and supportive when people like Tampa Deputy Sheriff Ben Mills came in to share their weird adolescent visions of the future American utopia.

"Cloning is just around the corner," said the deputy. "And once we have cloning, we won't have controversies like Iraq."

"Oh, yeah?" I said. "How's that?"

" 'Cause then, if we had to raise an army to go fight in these places, we could just grow all the forces we need. We need 5,000, we grow 5,000. We need 20,000, they grow 20,000. They grow at an accelerated rate. And people wouldn't be upset about their casualties, because it wouldn't be like their sons and daughters was being shot."

"I never thought of that," I said honestly.

"Plus we'd save a hell of a lot on benefits and medical expenses. 'Cause you know if they got wounded. . . ."

"You could just shoot them," I said.

"Exactly—pow! Just shoot 'em dead right in the ground."

"Hmm," I said. "But wouldn't they feel it? I mean, they might not like being treated like that."

"Well, that gets back to the programming, genetics," he said. "You'd have to program 'em right. Plus you got to train 'em from birth to serve their countries. Be obedient. I know that's kind of a communistic idea, but you know, it's kinda necessary."

"Well, no arguing that," I said.

"We'd just have a big breeding farm in Colorado," he said. " 'Course, it'd be a security problem if they got out, you know, if you had rogue clones running around. You'd have to have a special security force to maintain 'em."

"That's where folks like us would come in," I said.

"Exactly," he said.

Folks like us. That's what the Republican Party is all about. A special brotherhood in a world of mutants. It feels great from the inside. The only problem is—what happens to everybody else?

The Vermin Factor

The Orange County Republican Executive Committee office, which doubled as a small Bush-Cheney outpost, was manned by a cantankerous retired plumber from Philadelphia named Dave Copeland. He would sit behind a desk and for four hours a day watch Fox News and scream into the phone every time it rang. A perfect way for a retired bog monster to live out his golden years.

I am sure that every prominent Republican in Orlando is already terrified at the mention of Copeland's name in print, because they know the kinds of things that come out of his mouth. I'm not going to get into too many specifics, but imagine an unreconstructed Archie Bunker happily alone in his row house, having scared Meathead and Gloria into Belgian citizenship.

I'll give Dave credit for one thing. He never liked me, not from the first moment. He had a better nose than the rest of the Orlando Republicans. Our quarrels were numerous and diverse, but the principal issue dividing us was garbage.

Dave didn't like me or anyone else using his garbage pail, despite the fact that it was the only one in the office. A few times, after I brought a fast-food lunch back to my desk, I threw the packaging in his pail, and he nearly had an aneurysm each time. In one of my last days there, I bought a large Diet Coke from a restaurant across the street. I was just about to lift my lips to the straw for the first time when Dave exploded.

"You're not going to throw that soda in the *trash* when you're done, are you?"

"I guess not," I said, thinking: *Of course not. I'll just shove it up my ass.*

He went on. "You throw things in the trash here, the ants get in. The ants get in. Once they get in the trash there, you can't ever get 'em out."

I laughed and imagined the bumper sticker:

BUSH-CHENEY '04
This time, the ants won't get in

Forget about race, the environment, the economy, or any other issue. You can sum up the fundamental difference between Republicans and Democrats with one word: *vermin*.

Democrats are afraid of manmade or mechanical things: toxic waste, bombs, ECHELON, television, Wal-Mart, the Pentagon, stone tablets inscribed with the Ten Commandments, the stock market.

Republican fears are all biological. A recurring theme in almost every area of their belief systems is contagion of their virgin, protected world by living vermin greedy for rape of their treasure.

Republicans are weirdly not afraid of sprawl or the shopping malls that swallow their old neighborhoods, but they *are* afraid of the Mexicans who clean the kitchens in those new food courts. They have a disproportionately sized bug up their asses about PETA (they try to release lab chimps! Didn't those faggots see *Outbreak?*), and when a mountain lion roams into a Colorado suburb and gets shot, you automatically know whose side of that issue they're going to come down on.

In the pantheon of vermin, one group loomed larger and fouler than the rest. It didn't take long to figure out which group that was, even though they were seldom mentioned by name.

Because you knew who state party officials were talking about at a big July 21 meeting in Orlando when they told a huge crowd of horrified white volunteers that the pro-Kerry group ACT was hiring "felons" as canvassers. And I knew who one of my volunteers was talking about when he said he was afraid "people who are inclined to receive welfare" might complain about the election results if Bush were to win. Or who that sheriff's deputy, Ben Mills, was talking about when he complained about crack dealers who "breathe air that real people could be using."

But even if that's too difficult for you, all you have to do to figure this one out is look around a Bush-Cheney campaign office—and see, besides ants, what happens to be missing.

To judge by Orlando alone, the overwhelming majority of Bush volunteers belong to a specific demographic group. They are white, married, middle-aged-to-elderly women. By late July, our volunteer rotation was a nearly un-broken string of Bobbi Fleckman glasses, saggy necks, and loose-fitting Dress Barn slacks. If sexually retired white women were stricken from the voter rolls, Republicans would never win another election in this country.

Young, college-age people, a staple of all Democratic campaigns I've ever seen (even Joe Lieberman's "Liebermaniacs" were kids), were almost completely absent from our offices. Apart from my ponytailed office cohort Ben Adrian, no young person was regularly involved with the campaign. The situation was so extreme that even as a thirty-four-year-old with thinning hair, I was regularly complimented by the local Republican higher-ups for providing a "youth presence" to the campaign.

But if young people were rare, the, er, African American situation was flat-out hilarious. You know that Chris Rock joke about Native Americans? "When was the last time you saw *two* Indians?" That's what this was like.

I did see one young black man in the office in my very first week on the job. It was a bizarre circumstance that was much commented upon afterward and doubtless will be legend for some time to come. An older Republican candidate for county commissioner named M——— came in to chat . . . with a friend.

M——— is a frightening-looking person. She looks like a Latina Harvey Keitel in drag. Dyed beet-red hair, cartoon robin's-egg-blue eyeliner seemingly applied with a ladle. I came back from a trip to get milkshakes for the office to find her sitting at a table with a strapping, intense-looking young black man in a Sean John shirt who kept glancing around the office and tapping out

his excess energy through a rapidly oscillating foot on the ground. M——
was chatting with Vienna and another constant of the office, the cheery Republican Party of Florida operative Rhyan Metzler; it all seemed friendly.

They were talking about something or other when the mystery paramour suddenly pointed at a picture on the wall.

A *Do the Right Thing* aside about the wall in that office. It has fifty-three portraits of great Americans on it. Two, Alan Keyes and Condi Rice, are black. Mystery man was not looking at those.

"That Christine Whitman?" he said.

"Yes," Metzler said.

"I hate that bitch," he said. "If I ever see her, I'm going to hit her in the face with a brick."

As Anton Chekhov would have said: an angel of silence flew over the room. Metzler cautiously asked the man why he felt that way. He answered with a long speech about Whitman "changing all the laws," and then he added mysteriously that "because of her, I did a five instead of a three."

Everybody tried to laugh it off, but the tension level had clearly elevated. The conversation quickly wound up and M——, who was trying to talk about a precinct walk she had coming up, suddenly stood up to go. Vienna said something to Angry Man about how she hoped he would vote for Bush.

"I can't vote!" he said. "I can't vote! I'm a convicted felon!"

"No kidding," I said. "What did you go up for?"

"Armed robbery," he said.

"Well, you know, everyone makes a mistake once," M—— said quickly.

"No, I did it a bunch of times," he quipped.

"Yes, that's an—er, a terrible law, that they can't vote," said Vienna, quickly scooping up her laptop and moving it across the room.

"Heh, heh," Metzler said. "I hope it wasn't all on the same night."

"I plead the fifth," the man said, then walked outside to light a cigarette.

I followed him out and introduced myself. He said his name was Lamont and that he was from Newark. We started talking, but then M—— came out and led him to her car. Apparently, they were going to go on a precinct walk together. I would later see the two standing together at a Fourth of July event at downtown Lake Eola.

"I wonder what that's all about?" I said a few minutes later to Metzler, who along with Vienna had come out for a smoke.

"I don't know and I don't want to," Rhyan said, laughing. "The less I know, the more I like it."

"I didn't know what to say," Vienna said. "It's not that I don't agree with that law, but I didn't want to get him upset. . . ."

"Hell, I'll take that law," said Rhyan. "It keeps the Democrats from voting."

"Still, it's strange that he was with her," I said. "Not exactly the best PR for a Republican candidate."

"Maybe it's a jungle fever thing," Vienna offered.

"Yeah," said Rhyan, chuckling. "It's like that song: ain't nothing better than head from a thug."

After that incident, about six weeks passed without a black person so much as stumbling into the office by accident. Cars owned by African Americans do not break down outside of Republican offices, and their drivers do not come in to ask to use the phone. It takes effort to bring black people into the Bush tent—and effort was what I gave.

In mid-July a girlfriend came down from New York to visit me. I recruited her to help me with an idea I'd had for at least temporarily diversifying my office environment. We decided that she would pose as a reporter for *Vibe* magazine, call our offices, and ask whoever answered the phone if she could interview "your black volunteers."

The idea was that I would be in the office at the time, and would be around to listen in on the panicked office conversation as we scrambled to come up with a black Bush supporter for "Penny" the *Vibe* reporter to talk to.

On Tuesday, July 13, "Penny" got young Ben Adrian on the phone. Ben has a future as the next generation's Ron Ziegler. In the space of a five-minute conversation he came up with every conceivable verbal iteration of the concept "We don't have any black volunteers" without actually saying it. For example:

PENNY: All right. I just have a question. How involved are African American youths in the Bush campaign down here?
BEN: Well, you know . . .
PENNY: I mean, how many volunteers do you have?
BEN: Uh, personally—uh, I haven't been—we're actually starting coalitions for Bush. That is one of our coalitions, the Black Republicans for Bush.

At one point, he tried to sell Penny on some other kinds of minorities, noting that the boss, Vienna, was "actually a Hispanic-American herself."

BEN: Specifically you're looking for the, uh, African American volunteer, not just any kind of minority?
PENNY: (viciously) Yes. Well, I work for *Vibe*, so we're focusing on black youth involvement in presidential campaigns.
BEN: Oh, okay.

"Penny" stuck to her guns and scheduled an appointment for later in the week. When Ben hung up the phone, I was alone in the office alone with him and an older, white-haired volunteer named Don Madden. Don was in charge of three things in the office: bad jokes ("In an earthquake, just jump in the air and wait for it to end!"), updating the volunteer list, and being really friendly to anything that was female and under fifty years old. When Ben broke the news about *Vibe*, Don presciently smelled a liberal media plot:

DON: It's a drive-by, come on.
BEN: She said she's down, you know, and going to talk to all the campaigns in the area.
BEN: It would be interesting if she did something positive. What she's probably looking for is nothing. Zero. Null-set. That was gonna be the big splash.
TAIBBI: Right.
DON: So if we have somebody to talk to her, it would be interesting to see if that got in.

BEN: Yeah, she was like, "I've been talking to the ACT folks, and it seems like they're doing quite a lot with the . . ."
DON: It's the Job Corps.
TAIBBI: What's the Job Corps?
DON: They're paying those people.
TAIBBI: Oh, really?
DON: Yeah. The ACT guys, they're all paid.

But of course, since we weren't paying our black people like the pro-Democrat organizations—no welfare state here—we had to get them to come out of the goodness of their own hearts. But how, and who?

The irony of that particular situation was that before the *Vibe* call, Don, Ben, and I had been organizing a list of 6,500 local Bush volunteers. So we were literally sitting atop a mountain of volunteers when Don searched his memory to remember if there were any black people in the bunch. Eventually he came up with a black professor out at the University of Central Florida (a half-hour outside Orlando) and a friend of the professor's whose name he couldn't remember. "He probably knows some people out there," he said. He ended up going to look for the name in the trunk of his car, but couldn't find it. I nearly blew my cover laughing at that moment: *the black guy must be in the trunk. I'll go find him!*

Poor Ben didn't get any help from any superiors with this one. When I told Vienna that *Vibe* wanted to interview our black volunteers, she said, "Do we have any black volunteers?" and then quickly changed the subject. She didn't give a shit. Metzler was the only salary-collecting Republican willing to help. He gave Ben the name of one Johnny Hunter, the chairman of the Federation of Black Republicans for the State of Florida.

Poor Mr. Hunter. An elderly man from Sarasota, he was apparently quite busy fulfilling these kinds of requests. Trotting him out for *Vibe,* of course, was as absurd as sending Bella Abzug to talk to *Seventeen*—but Hunter didn't care. In fact, he seemed resigned to his role, which was showing up on cue wherever he was asked to:

HUNTER: Yeah, I just move around. You know, I was in Fort Lauderdale and Miami this past week and I'll be going to. . . . I got a call up in Gainesville, they ready to take their club establishment to the next level. I just move around the state.
PENNY: You move around the state. Got it. Okay, Mr. Hunter . . .
HUNTER: But I'm headquartered in Sarasota.
PENNY: Okay. . . . You're headquartered in Sarasota.
HUNTER: Because, being chairman, that's where I live at.
PENNY: Okay.
HUNTER: Because I live in Sarasota.
PENNY: Got it.
HUNTER: And I'm chairman of the Federation of Black Republicans for the Republican Party of the State of Florida.
PENNY: So you must be a very busy man right now.
HUNTER: So wherever they need me, that's where I be rolling to.

Finally Ben came through. He managed to convince a thirty-seven-year-old Promise Keeper Christian named Lorin Jones, a phlegmatic fellow who was recovering from two brushes with congestive heart failure, to come in for an interview.

We scheduled it, but Penny never showed up. I wanted to be there for what I knew would be an excruciatingly awkward situation; the lone black volunteer, dragged into the office to show off to the media, surrounded by a bunch of nervously small-talking white Republicans who would keep checking their watches every five minutes waiting for the no-show journalist.

Exactly this situation materialized. The bespectacled Lorin sat surrounded by me, Ben, Don, and an older county Republican bigwig named Geri Buchanan, and treated his anxious clock-watching crowd to a lesson in the vagaries of black urban existence:

"My Dad's an alcoholic," he said. "He cared about the bottle more than he loved us. But what my Mom did was she worked, she was there in the after-noon, she wanted to see what we were doing in school. . . ."

"Gee," mumbled Ben. (He actually used the word *gee*.) "I can't imagine the strength. . . . I'd like to meet her."

"I know what it's like to have a parent who'll put a belt on my butt," Lorin continued.

Nervous silence, nods.

Soon after "Penny" called to cancel, citing car trouble. Lorin hung in there for a few minutes. Don Madden came over to chat; the two of them apparently went to neighboring schools in California. Don's school, Don said, was great at basketball, but he said, winking, to Lorin: "You were probably the only guys who could have beaten us."

Lorin laughed uncomfortably. "We were okay," he said. "We were pretty good. Our college was pretty good at basketball."

Then Rhyan Metzler came over to say hi. They knew each other. Rhyan asked if Lorin was planning on coming in to do phone banking. Lorin answered that he wasn't, that he was busy setting up a book supplies giveaway charity event in his neighborhood on behalf of the Republicans (this was true). Rhyan laughed.

"Oh, come on," he said. "I know how you people don't like to work."

Lorin, who was halfway out the door, stopped at this. His smile disappeared. For a moment, he was genuinely pissed off. "*We* don't like to work?" he said. "That's all I do, is work to make you white Republicans look good."

Rhyan, a jovial, funny guy whom I normally liked quite a bit, did not notice that Lorin was really angry. He said nothing and simply slapped Lorin on the back, laughed, and helped him out the door.

"Good old Lorin," he said, going back to his office.

Vienna, making a rare appearance at her office, also chimed in after Lorin left. The two of them didn't like each other, having once publicly disagreed at a community meeting.

"I don't like that guy," she said. Then she explained. "After that meeting, we really got into it. We were really shouting. He called me a spic. And so I said to him, hey, I may be a spic, but at least I wasn't brought to this country as a slave. I was *born* here."

Man, I thought. We're just one big happy family.

Racism is a tricky word. One doesn't want to use it casually. It means different things to different people, and some of the things that it means to some people clearly do not apply to the vast majority of Republicans. Most of them are probably not lying awake at night praying that their daughters will run away to the Keys for a bungalow weekend with Baron Davis, but they're not burning crosses or wearing sheets, either. Activist, hood-and-noose racism in the party mainstream is clearly a thing of the past.

But what do you call it when you know you're *supported* by real bigots and racists, and you quietly let it happen? I ran across this quite a lot, even in relatively cosmopolitan Orlando. When I manned a voter-registration table at a gun show in town—gun shows being Bush territory—our booth was just a few feet away from a woman who was selling, like hotcakes, etchings of Confederate General Nathan Forrest (her classic quote: "People are so narrow-minded. They think that just because he founded the KKK, he was a racist"). And a little ways across the hall, there was a guy selling bumper stickers with confederate flags that read, "IF I'D KNOWN THIS WOULD HAPPEN, I WOULD HAVE PICKED MY OWN COTTON."

When I bought one of those and showed it to Metzler, we both burst out laughing. "Hell, I'm glad I'm a *socially liberal* Republican," he whispered.

It's all a big joke. Mainstream Republicans know that those people are a part of their base—and they don't give a shit. They think it's funny.

One time at the office I was sitting with Todd Sykes, who replaced Vienna as the Bush-Cheney Central Florida field coordinator over the summer, and the abovementioned uber-volunteer Don Madden. Todd was talking about how we needed to get out to Bithlo, Florida, to do voter registration. We needed to go to Bithlo, Todd explained, because it was a backwoods place that ran its own figure eight school bus races—again, clearly Bush territory.

And when he mentioned a nearby community that was also "kind of cool, because it's rural with some rich people in it," Don interrupted.

"The Klan is still there," he said.

"Oh, yeah?" Todd said.

"I know they have some Klan leaders out there," Don said.

"Well, that's probably Bush country, then, don't you think?" I said, laughing.

"Yeah," Don laughed. "Absolutely."

One time, I told Todd that I'd been doing a survey call when a woman told me that she loved President Bush because he was against gay rights (I actually had such a call). I asked Todd: "Should I correct her? I mean, the president is against gay marriage, not gay rights, right?"

Todd thought about that, then leaned over and whispered. "No, don't correct her," he said.

If there's bigotry in the Bush campaign, that's mostly what it sounds like—nothing. Silence at the right time.

There may be nothing at all that's racist about not having black volunteers, and nothing any Democratic pol could ever get righteous about when it comes to turning one's head to win the votes of wrong-headed morons. But there's something a little strange about going out of your way to troll for votes in prehistoric Confederate backwaters, when you won't even *visit* a black neighborhood—not even when you have an invitation, and not even when there are votes to be won there.

I ended up getting to know Lorin Jones fairly well. He was an odd, sincere person who interested me largely because he was by far the most dedicated, effective, and intellectually honest Republican volunteer the party had in the area, and yet the campaign more or less completely ignored him.

Lorin came into the office several times after the *Vibe* fiasco. He was organizing an event in which our volunteers would solicit donations of bookbags and school supplies to be given away in black neighborhoods. A devout Christian, Lorin supported Bush not only because of the social/religious issues, but also because he sincerely believed that state financial aid had had a corrosive effect on the black community, and that communities should support themselves through charity. He was the living incarnation of the "Thousand Points of Light" idea. He ought to have been a poster child for Republican values.

"In my neighborhood, you can go up to anybody, and ask where the black Republican lives," he said. "And they'll lead you right to my house. But they respect me because of what I've done."

And I saw this. At a function I would later attend in his neighborhood, I met several people who had been converted to Bush by Lorin. He was working round the clock for the president, but the campaign wasn't showing him any love. They were trying to turn him into another Johnny Hunter.

"All they want me to do is start clubs," he said. "Tallahassee keeps calling and bugging me to start black clubs. And I hate that, because I think that puts us all in boxes. I think we should be going out into the community more."

Lorin firmly believed that Republicans could win 20 percent of the black vote—not the usual 10 percent—if they were smart about it. His plan made perfect sense. All they had to do, he said, was visit black churches and hand out fact sheets showing the Republican and Democratic stances on social and religious issues.

"You wouldn't even have to campaign," he said. "You'd get an extra 10 percent right there."

I must have heard him put forward that plan a half-dozen times in our offices, but no one did anything but smile and nod.

Some of the Republicans, however, were willing to help Lorin—sort of. A smallish contingent of five YRs (Young Republicans) met Lorin in front of an Office Depot in a white suburban neighborhood one Saturday to man a booth soliciting school supply donations. They worked cheerfully throughout the afternoon, giving away hot dogs to donors, and helped Lorin get a good amount of stuff. The whole thing was clean, cheery, and upbeat, and reminded me of a frat event or a pep rally, which was probably not a coincidence.

But when it came time a few days later to actually give away the stuff in Lorin's West Orlando neighborhood, none of the YRs showed up. I was the only white Republican who made it. It was a remarkable event. Well over 200 people, mostly single mothers and their children, showed up at a funeral home called Gail and Wynn's to receive the bookbags and notebooks Lorin had gathered to give away in one of the reception rooms.

Not having the money to rent another venue, he'd asked friends to let him hold it here. Kids walked right into the darkened room with their parents in tow, took bags, and walked right past the stand where the coffins usually rested and then from there down the somber corridor. No one seemed to care. In that neighborhood, a funeral home is just another room.

I helped distribute bags to the children. "Vote for Bush," I managed to whisper a few times.

That day Lorin confided to me that this might be his last go-around with the Republicans. "I think this might be it," he said. "I think I might be done with these people."

A Left Behind Dinner

The stress of the assignment caused a lot of strange behaviors, none of which I could control very well. At times I would just get exhausted, and I would slump in my chair in the morning at the inevitable sight, through the glass door, of the very first flabby-kneed housewife ambling from her Ford Aerostar toward our office in search of Dubya bumper stickers. . . . And at other times I would seem to be fine and perky during the day, a diligent Republican operative buzzing with confidence from the afternoon Hannity broadcast, only to wake up screaming later that same night after long nightmares about vampires or my mother. It was strange.

At first I thought this was a result of the stress of living a double life, but after a while I began to suspect that this was just a by-product of campaign work in general, and that my own particular situation was just an aggravating factor. Among other things, I noticed that my counterpart Ben was also beginning to crack under the strain. Once this week, I caught him staring off into space in the morning, an uncharacteristically thoughtful look frozen on his face, after he made a "W Rocks" survey call.

"Hey," I said. "How's it going?"

"Great," he said.

"Really?"

"Yeah," he said. "You know that special feeling you get when you make that first phone call in the morning, and your voice is all sharp and crisp. . . ."

There was no question mark; his voice just trailed off. He wasn't even talking to me, really. He went silent.

A week or so before that he'd started to complain about sleep problems. He was only getting a few hours of sleep a night. He'd come in with dark circles around his eyes and his Ray Bolger scarecrow-hair humorlessly knotted behind his head and mumble something about not getting that "real deep sleep" until five in the morning. I'd recommend Ambien or, in a too-loud voice, offer some other dilettante medical advice—just to break up the boredom, you know, for the pleasure of hearing myself speak:

"Maybe you need some exercise," I'd say cheerfully. "Of course, at your age, you shouldn't have any problems. Now, normally, men sleep less as they get older. My father, for instance, he gets up at three-thirty every morning, walks around the house in his underwear. . . ."

"Yeah, uh-huh," he'd say, ignoring me, and go back to the phones.

"You should maybe play a little more tennis. Or try Nyquil," I'd say, smiling.

"Yeah," he'd say, suddenly looking forward to his phone call and wishing he hadn't said anything.

Such were the dynamics of our work relationship.

There were the days when I'd wake up just feeling *bitchy*. Not mad enough to blow my cover, but mad enough to not be able to control the urge to needle everyone around me with pointless, passive-aggressive questioning. Once, for instance, I came in and within about three minutes honed right in on Dave Copeland, the poor old rummy in charge of the OCREC office:

"Hey, Dave, I've got a question for you," I said. "Yesterday this guy called up and asked what the difference was between a conservative and a neocon-servative. What is it, do you know?"

Dave frowned and shrugged. He didn't know. It was too early for this bull-shit.

"Yeah," I said. "I didn't know how to answer that, either."

"Did he have an, an, uh," Dave said, feigning interest, "an explanation of it, or. . . ?"

"No, no, he just was curious, said he saw something on television, wanted to know what the difference was, thought maybe we knew."

Just then Paul Moy, a small, quiet, fortysomething volunteer with a mustache who organized his schedule around the occasional yard work he apparently did for a living, jumped in with an answer. In a weird way Paul was a stand-up guy who tried to have backbone. He recognized this question as a test that needed to be taken. If he was going to have beliefs, he was going to define them.

"A neo," he offered, "is like a real hard conservative."

"A real hard conservative, eh?" I said.

"A conservative can like fluctuate a little bit," he said. "I mean, you can be a conservative and almost support, you know what I'm saying, almost be . . . mid. You know what I'm saying, kind of relative to. . . ?"

"Right!" I said.

"A neo," he continued, "is all the way to the extreme, gone right."

"So," I said, not letting it go, "does that mean a neoconservative is for no taxes at all, and no government spending?"

Paul thought about that.

"Yeah," he said. "Anything that's like, liberal, they're totally the opposite."

We went back to the phones. After about an hour I tried to start another conversation.

"That was interesting, Paul," I said, hanging up. "That woman I just talked to asked me what the president's *gay policy* is. What is it, I wonder?"

Silence. Finally, in the background, Dave Copeland piped up.

"I don't know," he said. "He's never said anything."

"No?" I said.

"He's never said anything about gays," Dave said, this time with finality.

"Huh," I said.

This kind of thing kept me mentally busy for about two and a half hours, but there's only so much needling you can do before it becomes conspicuous, and finally I had to shut up.

In a vacuum of mental initiative, the usual business of the OCREC office gushed back into its regular crevices. Dave turned up the volume on Fox News, which oscillated unpleasantly between low-level editorial attacks on John and Teresa Heinz and urgent reports about the latest still missing pregnant white woman, Lori Hacking. Commentator after commentator came on to speculate that the stress of living a lie had caused Mark Hacking to go "completely berserk" and kill his wife in a "rage attack." In between reports from the Fleet Center in Boston, there were periodic live updates from the landfill where a tipster had indicated police should search for Lori Hacking's body.

A still shot of the face of Mark Hacking—a demented, shorter, balder version of Mark McGwire—kept drifting across the screen during voice-overs. They have to keep throwing villains at you, fresh ones to go with the regulars. They also like to create scary new popular buzzwords like *Amber alert* and *weapons of mass destruction* and *hanging chad* that can be depended upon to purposefully bounce around in your cranium. Today's term was *cadaver dogs*.

I went back to the phones. An energetic-sounding middle-aged woman explained to me why she didn't like Kerry. "I'm just really worried that he's going to take us in a *communistic* direction," she said.

I looked at the sheet. That answer fell under the category of "I am concerned about John Kerry proposing to raise taxes as the economy is growing." I checked the appropriate box.

"Right on, ma'am," I said. "I'm with you all the way."

"Well, I'm glad somebody has sense," she said.

I hung up and relaxed for a moment, resting my head in my hands. In the background I could hear Dave talking to Bill Peters, the cranky old racist who "owned half" of OCREC's nonfunctioning computer and wouldn't give anyone, not even campaign staff, the password. Dave and Bill were fast buddies who liked to plan their drinking bouts about four days ahead of time. Their conversations inevitably revolved around various ethnic and ideological vermin who were muddying things up somewhere out there in the unclean world.

"Well, now the Muslims are upset about what we're doing in their country," Dave was saying.

"Uh-huh," Peters said.

"They're—they're not content to just sit around doing whatever it is they're doing," he said.

Neither are you, I thought. Just then the door opened. Husband and wife, each about fifty-five-years-old, both going on about three bills. The husband's gut was about a foot and a half over his waistline, and the wife had heads of lettuce for knees. I had seen this act enough times before to know that before speaking they would slowly make their way all the way into the center of the office, looking leisurely in all directions along the way, before finally stopping to announce themselves. I cut them off at the halfway point.

"We don't have any," I said.

"Hi. We're looking for—huh?" the husband said.

"Yard signs," I said. "Bumper stickers. We don't have any."

They sagged, like animals taking a bullet. "Well!" the woman said. "When are you—"

"About two weeks," I said. "We just ran out. We'll have them in two weeks."

"Well, I'll be damned," the husband said.

As I knew they wouldn't, they didn't move, still standing there, bloblike, with their arms out at their sides, refusing to let go of the dream. Wife's face contorted in an angry frown.

"I can't *believe* this," she said. "My neighbors all have those Kerry signs up, and it makes me so mad! You have to get signs for us right away! Y'all have to get on the ball!"

"Yes, ma'am. Two weeks," I said, getting up and heading right past them for the door. Time for a lunch break. As I left they remained in place. They would be starting on Dave any second now, I thought.

There is no place to eat in Orlando that isn't a chain. Even the things that don't look like chains, like cutesy salad bars, are chains. Your choices range between fatty corporate and somewhat healthier corporate. I opted for a nearby Subway clone called Sobik's that made tasteless but edible vegetable subs. While in line, I picked up a magazine (the complimentary used magazine rack is a Sobik's feature): *Newsweek* had a cover story on "The New Infidelity." It was about the phenomenon of married women empowering themselves by sleeping around with people like health club instructors. I read:

"'He tells me my skin is soft and that my hair smells good. I know it sounds stupid, but that stuff matters. It makes me feel sexy again,' says a thirty-nine-year-old married woman of her five-year boyfriend."

Hollywood-based personal trainer Mike Torchia, who estimates that he's had affairs with "about forty women," chimed in.

"It's natural to want to have sex with your trainer," Torchia told the magazine. "Remember that training is very hands-on. I'm touching them, motivating them, encouraging them, listening to them, relieving their stress and channeling their energy in a more positive way."

I munched my bland sub. In the corner of the restaurant a puffy-looking professional woman about my age was reading intently from the new Candace Bushnell book, *Trading Up*.

I went outside and dialed the cell phone of my girlfriend in New York. No answer. I went back to the office. The previous fat couple was long gone, but there was a new one of almost identical dimensions in their place. They were standing, arms at their sides in the same fashion as the other couple, right in front of Dave, who was on the phone. When I came in, they whipped around.

"Hi," the husband said. "We just came to pick up a few yard signs and bumper stickers!"

I sighed, and this time answered politely. It was going to be a long day.

Three hours and about thirty more yard-sign requests later I was just holding on, morning belligerence a distant memory, waiting for the day to end. A new recruit was talking in my ear. Her name was Susie Thompson and she was an opinionated fundamentalist Christian mother of five. She had grand-children, but I'll give her credit; she looked almost good for her age, with long dark hair, a slim waist, and a frankly oversized chest that almost made her look like a shoplifter. She was originally from West Virginia, where I imagine she lit up the interior of a few parked pickup trucks in her day. Thirty years later, though, she was manning the phones for George Bush and sounding off bitterly on humanity's declining morals and the agents of the ever-advancing international liberal conspiracy.

"I had someone from the Green Party come to my house the other day," she said. "And he said, 'Would you mind telling me who you're voting for?' And I said, 'No, I'm proud, I'm voting for Bush-Cheney.' And he's like, 'Can you tell me why?' And I'm like, 'I'll give you two reasons. *Morality* and *strength*.' And he had his little legal pad out, and he's like, 'Oh, okay.' Didn't write anything down and just left. How's he gonna argue against any of that?"

I had been spacing out a little, staring out the window, and I missed what she'd said, so I just threw out the first thing that came to mind. It didn't matter; it never matters in this crowd.

"I know what you mean," I said. "It's like, uh, with this gay marriage thing . . . they're going to try to say that we should *pander* to these people."

"No, no," Susie said. "Not me. I wish every single one of those Hollywood elitists who warned they would leave if Bush became president would just do what they said they'd do."

"They won't even do us that favor," said Ana Rautsch, another volunteer, who was sitting across the room.

"That's right," said Susie. "I wish they would just go."

The conversation went on like this for a while, passing the usual conversational signposts of the office: a discussion of the brilliance of Hannity's *Deliver Us from Evil*, some praise for that straight-talking anti-Democrat Democratic Senator Zell Miller (Miller is considered a real hero in these circles; for the right, he's the Run-DMC "Walk This Way" crossover bridge to the "saved" Democratic Party), more bemoaning of the absence of bumper stickers, some Teresa-bashing, etc.

Quietly excusing myself during the Hannity discussion, I went to the bathroom. When I got back to my chair, my eyes were watering and Susie was starting to talk about hell.

". . . children, Tom?" I heard, as I sat down.

"Huh?"

"Are you married, Tom?" Susie asked.

I squinted in apprehension, sensing a Jesus conversation on the way. These were the tensest acting moments for me. "Uh, no," I said. "I'm neither married, nor do I have children."

"My oldest," Susie began, "he has a three-year-old, and has been with the same girl for six years, and he *will not* marry her."

"Oh," I said, remembering to sound shocked. "That must really upset you."

"It *kills me*," she said.

"Does he not go to church?"

Don't wait for them to ask. Take the offensive.

"Oh, occasionally," she sighed. "He will tell you right off. . . . He encourages her to go, and to take their little daughter, and he tells you, he knows, he's walking on glass right now. He's hopeful that God doesn't come, or nothing happens to him before he rededicates his life. But he's definitely not living a life that either honors God, or is even pleasing to himself."

"You should give him those *Left Behind* books," I said solemnly.

I took a deep breath. Throwing *Left Behind* at her was like being a novice wizard and saying a magic spell for the first time; I wasn't sure it would actually work. It did:

"He won't read 'em," Susie answered seriously.

"He won't read them?" I cried, shocked.

"He won't read them," she repeated. "He doesn't . . . he doesn't like the way it makes him feel."

We talked for a little while longer, then Susie got up to go. Her daughter, whom she homeschools, was not used to being away from Mom for that long. On the way out, she gave me her pastor's name as a contact who might help me find volunteers. I told her I was actually looking for a church and might stop in that Sunday to see him in person.

At this news she gave me a funny look. Then she left.

A half-hour later, the phone in the office rang. It was Susie. She was inviting me to dinner with her family. It was the act of a good Christian. I must have sounded lonely. "I'm making fettucine Alfredo," she said.

I told her: I *love* fettucine Alfredo.

Left Behind. That raises a good question. Who gets left behind, exactly? Who among us gets to suck eggs all the way to earth when God snatches the pilots out of the plane?

In the book it's the nonbelievers, and God, of course, is making the decisions. But what about on earth, right now?

One of the great clichés of liberal criticism of the Christian right is the idea that these people are wrong-headed because they profess to know the will of God. H. L. Mencken put that one best, and perhaps first: "It is only the savage, whether of the African bush or the American gospel tent, who professes to know the will and intent of God exactly and completely."

These criticisms sound like they make sense. But I think they are a little off-base.

The problem not only with fundamentalist Christians, but with Republicans in general, is not that they act on blind faith, without thinking. The problem is that they are incorrigible doubters with an insatiable appetite for Evidence. What they get off on is not Believing, but in having their beliefs tested. That's why their conversations and their media are so completely dominated by implacable bogeymen: marrying gays, liberals, the ACLU, Sean Penn, Europeans, and so on. Their faith both in God and in their political convictions is too weak to survive without an unceasing string of real and imaginary confrontations with those people—and for those confrontations, they are constantly assembling evidence and facts to make their case.

But here's the twist. They are not looking for facts with which to defeat opponents. They are looking for facts that will *create* opponents. *Bill Clinton's* *education budget was $800 billion. American petroleum costs $9 a gallon to refine. Teresa Heinz supported a communist front called the National Lawyers Guild.* They can be correct facts, incorrect facts, irrelevant facts, it doesn't matter. The point is not to win the argument; the point is to make sure the argument never stops. Permanent war isn't a policy imposed from above; it's an emotional imperative that rises from the bottom.

Once you grasp this fact, you're a long way to understanding what the Hannitys and Limbaughs figured out long ago: these people will swallow anything you feed them, so long as it leaves them with a demon to wrestle with in their dreams.

Which brings me back to *Left Behind*. Who gets left behind? Nobody, that's who. How could they leave any of us behind? They couldn't live without us. Even their most intimate family meals would seem lonely if we were missing.

The vacationing New York schoolteacher Tom Hamill didn't say much at first at the Thompsons' dinner table. Speak when spoken to, help serve the fettucine, pass the white bread and margarine. Ask politely about Ricky's senior year at high school, twelve-year-old Missy's home-schooling, the bricklaying job Rob lost two years ago, or maybe it was five. Smile in placid agreement as Susie compares Massachusetts Democrats (like Tom's real-life mother) to al-Qaeda. A cozy family dinner in Anytown, U.S.A.

Dinner started about seven. John Kerry was set to accept the nomination at the Fleet Center in a few hours. Dinner Table wondered if the terrorists would strike.

"No, no," Susie said. "The criminals wouldn't attack their own kind."

"Hear, hear," I said.

(Just to be clear about something: she wasn't kidding.)

"What we have to worry about is New York," Rob said. "They'd stop at nothing to get the good guys. They know who the good guys are."

"We'd be lost without our president," Susie said.

I concentrated on my food. It was really difficult to know what to say. Grace was easy: just hang your head. But once they moved into politics and religion, I began to worry that my silence was becoming conspicuous. Susie was shooting me searching looks. I noticed Rob, the wiry gray-haired dad with the slow voice and the henpecked posture, was watching me whenever I chewed. Like he was checking to see if I would swallow. Finally the discussion switched to Ricky's high school; he had a couple of crazy teachers there, a mean lady and a guy with man-boobs. . . .

"We have a transvestite at our school," I whispered, suddenly inspired.

Jack and Ricky were still talking about the man-boobs teacher. "Whaddya mean, which one?" Ricky said to his dad. "You guys pointed him out while I was jogging the other night."

"We have a transvestite at our school," I repeated.

Only Susie heard me. "No!" she said.

"He was an albino," Rob said. "An—"

"No!" Susie repeated.

"An albino man, with boobs—" Jack said.

"No, no, no!" Susie screamed. "Did you HEAR what he said? He has a *transvestite* that works at his school!" She turned to me in horror. "Is he allowed to dress like a woman?"

Now I had everyone's attention.

"Oh, yeah," I said. "It's somebody, believe it or not, I did a little undergrad with for a year in New York. Totally normal guy, except that at some point, he started reading all kinds of . . ."

"Books!" Susie guessed.

"It's called possession," Rob said.

"Yeah, books," I said. "It started, he was reading Agatha Christie books at first, then he got really into detectives, he was reading Dashiell Hammett. Next thing you know, he's reading Nietzsche. You know, the German philosopher."

"The weirdo German!" Susie exclaimed.

"He started getting really crazy," I said. "He was doing like this . . . he had this weird *pirate laugh*. Like he'd walk up to you and go, 'Mwah-hah-ha!'"

Everyone was staring at me in shock. I laughed.

"And he comes up to me one day in the hall and he says to me, you know, 'Well, since there's no God, I might as well be gay!' "

"Oh, my *God*," Rob whispered.

"And he starts talking like this, and his appearance got more and more strange. . . . He started coming into work in drag, and wearing eyeliner. . . ."

"Oh, my God," Rob repeated.

"And his boyfriend would come and pick him up at school. . . ," I went on.

"Oh!" Susie shrieked, scrunching her nose, as though smelling rotting cheese.

"But *that's* okay with them," I said.

"Yeah, that's okay," Rob said. "All you have to do, to understand how things really are, is go back in time. Make it safe, say fifty years. And everything that was bad and evil back then, make it good. And everything that was good, make it bad. Then you're totally politically corr—"

"The thing is, I'm the one who gets in trouble," I said. "Like there was this one little girl. I caught her listening to 50 Cent, you know, the rapper, and I started telling her about the torments of hell, and how she'd pay in eternity and all of that. And the principal comes up to me and he's like, 'Stop, you're scaring the children!' "

"Oh, yeah," Susie snorted.

"And I'm like, 'I'm *scaring* her? Are you crazy? This girl is already seven years old. She needs to know about these things!' "

"I get an e-mail every single day," Susie said, "with a little mini-sermon, it's called prayermanager.com. They e-mail me, and the one yesterday or the day before talked about how we now have two whole generations that are not churchgoers. In the old days, people went to church even if they didn't believe, even if they were just embarrassed not to go. . . . But now, you have whole generations growing up, and they don't even know who Jesus is!"

"But they know who Puff Daddy is," I snorted.

"Absolutely," she said. "I know who he is, for crying out loud."

Young Billy shot a look at Ricky. Both of them suddenly seemed to lose interest in their food.

"We have kids now, because they know you're a Christian, they go out of their way to make your life miserable," I said. "I know this one guy. They'll take his Bible from his classroom, and snort cocaine off it right in front of him!"

Susie put her hands over her heart.

"And what?" I said. "They'll get suspended for a week, but they're right back in there."

The table fell silent. Ricky, the high schooler, quietly slipped away. Billy followed soon after, taking little Petey. The next generation of Christians probably does a little too much outside reading. Little Missy was the last to leave. Soon the only ones left were me, Mom, and Dad, and a nearly empty bowl of fettucine. Forty minutes in, my fork was still scraping the plate.

"Now *this* is good fettucine," I said.

A Close Shave

Toward the end of my stay in Florida, I started to get very sloppy with my cover. I was like Jeffrey Dahmer in his last days before capture, too far gone to keep a job, literally stumbling over the bodies in his apartment.

I stopped shaving regularly (Republicans are well-groomed). I forgot myself a couple of times and used my real name in public. Then out of boredom I started sticking fake lists of names into our real pile of voter phone lists, and nearly got caught doing it twice: one volunteer actually shrieked in protest when I handed her a list containing the names not of ordinary Floridians but of the Manson family (although the field director, Todd Sykes, digested all nineteen names of the 9/11 hijackers without complaint).

But the closest call of all came when I left town for a weekend to visit friends in Washington, D.C., and found myself in line at the airport on the way back behind none other than Florida Senator Bob Graham.

Graham didn't remember it, but we'd met twice the year before, while

I was covering the campaign in New Hampshire and then later in New York. We chatted pleasantly for a few minutes; he seemed happy to talk. He told me about his forthcoming book, *Intelligence Matters,* due to be released in September. Then he let me in on what I could expect from his upcoming speech at the Democratic convention—at the time, only three days away. Once we were in the plane, we found our respective seats, and I went about the tedious business of getting back into Tom Hamill's character.

As we deplaned I ran into the senator again. He had forgotten my name and asked it again. I told him, whispering—Matt Taibbi. Then he started in about his book.

"I don't mean to be immodest, but you should really read it," he said. "I think it says a lot about what went wrong."

"Don't worry about being immodest," I said. "You're a U.S. senator, for God's sake."

"Right," he said, laughing. Then he went to give me his card. As he did so, he asked: "Do you have a card. . . . I'm sorry, what was your name again?"

And just then, who popped out of the plane, back from his own vacation, but Jason Hoyt, head of the Orange County Young Republicans—a twentysomething Doug Niedermeyer lookalike in miniature, who knew me by another name. I stared back at Graham in terror.

"Uh, I'm Tom," I said, extending my hand. "Tom Hamill."

Graham peered at me quizzically. That didn't sound like the same name I'd just given him. "Oh," he said. "And who do you write for again, Tom?"

Hoyt by then was standing right next to me.

"Write?" I answered. "I don't write, senator. I'd like to learn, though. Admire those people!"

Graham scrunched his nose, confused. Then Hoyt piped in.

"Hey, Tom, did you tell him you work for Bush-Cheney?"

I laughed and looked back at Graham in plain agony. "Hah-hah, Bush-Cheney!" I said. "He's just kidding, senator."

"Tom Hamill," Graham said. "Wasn't there another reporter named Tom Hamill?"

"You're thinking of Mark Hamill," I quipped. "And he's not a reporter, but an actor. . . . Well, goodbye, senator!"

"Will I see you at the event tomorrow?" Graham asked, still very confused. "With the press pool?"

He meant a John Kerry speech at Cape Kennedy. "Nope!" I said. "Because I'm not a reporter. Good-bye!"

"Bye!" he said, rooted to the spot.

I took Hoyt by the arm and ducked away.

"What was that about?" he said.

"Nothing. Let's get out of here," I said. "Nice guy, that Graham, but a liberal bastard."

It was close—too close. A week or so later, I got word that the Secret Service needed my social security number, to clear me for access during a presidential visit. A false statement to the SS would have been a crime; the choice was now to break the law, or leave.

So I left. By mid-August, I was back in New York.

Surrounded

The police barriers were everywhere. There were about thirty of us and about thirty thousand of them. The cops had us in a little pen, about twenty yards in diameter, in the middle of 28th Street. The police themselves formed a wall just beyond the pen, and just behind them was a teeming mass of bad facial hair and "Buck Fush" T-shirts, screaming for our blood.

I look up at the sign I'm carrying, which I was given at the start of the protest. It is by far the worst one that anyone in our group has to carry. It reads:

REPARATIONS TO BLACKS!
We already take half of people's money by force and redistribute it,
what's the big deal?

Amazing, I think to myself. I knew there were a lot of black people in New York, but I never noticed that there were so many large, male black people.

For the fourth or fifth time I look behind me in search of a police-guarded exit. As I do, I notice three extremely cute protester chicks in tank tops looking my way. I smile back, instinctively, then remember where I am. No man is ever less of a threat to get laid than he is when he takes part in a right-wing counterdemonstration in the middle of New York City.

The girls are standing next to a young Viggo Mortensen lookalike who is holding up a "No Blood for Oil" sign. I lean over the barricade and shout:

"Hey, you! Get a haircut!"

The kid spots me and his eyes instantly pop wide open in anger. "Fuck you, you ugly motherfucker!" he shouts.

Shit, I think. He's right. I am kind of ugly. "Um," I shout back. "U-S-A! U-S-A!"

"Go back to Texas!" the kid shouts.

"Actually," I say, in a friendly tone, "I grew up in Boston." He stares back at me, confused. Then another chant from my side of the fence begins: "Stop hating your parents! Stop hating your parents!"

That's actually a good one. I look back at Viggo and give him a shrug. "Stop hating your parents!" I shout. "Stop hating your parents!"

He frowns. I may be ugly, but he *does* hate his parents. Welcome to American politics, 101.

It is September 2, the last night of the Republican convention. I'm out of Florida but still not out of the cold. My president is due to give a speech and I've hit the streets in support, with a group of right-wing counterdemonstrators called Protest Warrior.

Protest Warrior is the Stuttering John of the Republican right. They are like a walking undead memo from the desk of Donald Segretti, an organized group of ratfuckers who show up at every anti-war or "leftist" protest to wave venomous placards at the hippies and nail down twenty progovernment seconds for every two-minute local news account. You can join them online at www.protestwarrior. com, which is what Tom Hamill did, and then at some point you will be sent a "mission dossier" instructing you to appear at such and such a time and place, ready to cause a scene.

The leaders of Protest Warrior claim that they are self-sufficient and funded entirely by donations and the sale of paraphernalia. I don't believe it, but whatever. Suffice it to say that their placards all have a clean, professional-design look to them. Virtually every Protest Warrior sign is a direct parody of goofy lefty protest slogans ("Except for slavery, fascism, Nazism, and communism, WAR NEVER SOLVED ANYTHING"; "SAY NO TO WAR—unless a Democrat is president"). This isn't an accident, just like it isn't an accident that Protest Warrior never has more than a handful of people show up to carry these signs.

What they are parodizing isn't so much the ideology of the anti-Bush protesters as it is the concept of protest itself. They don't have their own slogans because they don't *want* their own slogans; *no slogans* is the message. Protest Warrior hates people who take to the streets and sing "Give Peace a Chance" when they should just be sitting on their asses at home and quietly voting to bomb foreign states and build more prisons like all the rest of the grown-ups.

That's why they hate us. They hate us because every time 100,000 smug, sexually viable East Coast kids take to the streets instead of sitting at home like they do, it says to them something about what's inadequate about their lives. That's why the tone of Republican radio and right-wing protests is never idealistic. The underlying emotion is always wounded pride. Don't like my shitty life? Love it or leave it, pal. Love it or leave it.

I was exhausted by the whole scene by the time the convention rolled around. I had gone down to Florida with an open mind, and I did change my views about a few things. Like I'm no longer sure about the New York feminist who wears a "Keep Your Laws Off My Body" T-shirt and then tells Christians in Georgia how to run their schools. And at least most Republicans have a plan for raising children beyond "Everyone's equal, everyone does his own thing, everything works out." That's something that starts to seem striking after a while: how much, from this point of view, the East Coast liberal ethos looks like a celebration of indulgent selfishness as a way of life.

But it gets tiring being a Republican. It's the motivation that's the hard part, finding a reason to get up in the morning.

Even the Nazis had an exciting Big Idea. They wanted to take over the world. But rank-and-file Republicans don't want the world. They want the world to go away and leave them alone. If it must stay, let it speak English and not call during *Survivor*. That's a hell of a thing to hope for, especially since it's never going to happen.

No wonder they're so angry. Even Hitler had a chance.

Well, That Was Fun
Huge, ineffectual protests make me proud
to be a white middle-class coward

Hey, you assholes: The 1960s are over!

I'm not talking about your white-guy fros, muttonchops, and beads. I'm not talking about your Che T-shirts or that wan, concerned, young-Joanie-Baez look on the faces of half of your women. I'm not even talking about skinny young potheads carrying wood puppets and joyously dancing in Druid circles during a march to protest a bloody war.

I'm not harping on any of that. I could, but I won't. Because the protests of the last week in New York were more than a silly, off-key exercise in irrelevant chest-puffing. It was a colossal waste of political energy by a group of people with no sense of history, mission, or tactics, a group of people so atomized and inured to its own powerlessness that it no longer even considers seeking anything beyond a fleeting helping of that worthless and disgusting media currency known as *play*.

I don't want anyone to get the wrong idea. I admire young people with political passion, and am enormously heartened by the sheer numbers of people who time after time turn out to protest this idiot president of ours. But at

---

September 7, 2004, *New York Press.*

the same time, I think it is time that some responsible person in the progressive movement recognizes that we have a serious problem on our hands.

We are raising a group of people whose only ideas about protest and opposition come from televised images of forty years ago, when large public demonstrations could shake the foundations of society. There has been no organized effort of any kind to recognize that we now live in a completely different era, operating according to a completely different political dynamic. What worked then not only doesn't work now, but it also doesn't even make superficial *sense* now.

Let's just start with a simple, seemingly inconsequential facet of the protests: appearance. If you read the bulletins by United for Peace and Justice ahead of the protests, you knew that the marchers were encouraged to "show their creativity" and dress outlandishly. The marchers complied, turning Seventh Avenue into a lake of midriffs, billabong, bandannas, and "Buck Fush" T-shirts. There were facial studs and funny hair and man-sandals and papier-mâché masks and plenty of chicks in their skivvies all jousting to be the next young Heather Taylor inspiring the next Jimi Hendrix to write the next "Foxy Lady."

And the *New York Post* and Fox were standing on the sidelines greedily recording all of this unbowed individuality for posterity, understanding instinctively that each successive T-shirt and goatee was just more fresh red meat for mean Middle America looking for good news from the front.

Back in the 1960s, dressing crazy and letting your hair down really *were* a form of defiance. It was a giant, raised middle finger to a ruling class that until that point had insisted on a kind of suffocating, static conformity in all things—in sexual mores, in professional ambitions, in life goals and expectations, and even in dress and speech.

Publicly refusing to wear your hair like an Omega-house towel-boy wasn't just a meaningless gesture then. It was an important step in refusing later to go to war, join the corporate workforce, and commit yourself to the long, soulless life of political amnesia and periodic consumer drama that was the inflexible expectation of the time.

That conformist expectation still exists, and the same corporate class still imposes it. But conformity looks a lot different now than it did then. Outlandish dress is now for sale in a thousand flavors, and absolutely no one is threatened by it: not your parents, not the government, not even our most prehistoric brand of fundamentalist Christianity. The vision of hundreds of thousands of people dressed in every color of the rainbow and marching their diverse selves past Madison Square Garden is, on the contrary, a great relief to the other side—because it means that the opposition is composed of individuals, not a Force in Concert.

In the conformist atmosphere of the late 1950s and early 1960s, the individual was a threat. Like communist Russia, the system then was so weak that it was actually threatened by a single person standing up and saying, "This is bullshit!"

That is not the case anymore. This current American juggernaut is the mightiest empire the world has ever seen, and it is absolutely immune to the individual. Short of violent crime, it has assimilated the individual's every conceivable political action into mainstream commercial activity. It fears only one thing: organization.

That's why the one thing that would have really shaken Middle America last week wasn't "creativity." It was something else: uniforms. Three hundred thousand people banging bongos and dressed like extras in an Oliver Stone movie scare no one in America. But 300,000 people in slacks and white button-down shirts, marching mute and angry in the direction of Your Town, would have instantly necessitated a new cabinet-level domestic security agency.

Why? Because 300,000 people who are capable of showing the unity and discipline to dress alike are also capable of doing more than just march. Which is important, because marching, as we have seen in the last few years, has been rendered basically useless. Before the war, Washington and New York saw the largest protests this country has seen since the 1960s—and this not only did not stop the war, but it also didn't even motivate the *opposition* political party to nominate an anti-war candidate.

There was a time when mass protests were enough to cause Johnson to give up the Oval Office and cause Richard Nixon to spend his nights staring out his window in panic. No more. We have a different media now, different and more sophisticated law-enforcement techniques, and, most importantly, a different brand of protestor.

Protests can now be ignored because our media have learned how to dismiss them, because our police know how to contain them, and because our leaders now know that once a protest is peacefully held and concluded, the protestors simply go home and sit on their asses until the next protest or the next election. They are not going to go home and bomb draft offices, take over campuses, and riot in the streets. Instead, although there are many earnest, involved political activists among them, the majority will simply go back to their lives, surf the Net, and wait for the ballot. Which to our leaders means that, in most cases, if you allow a protest to happen. . . nothing happens.

The people who run this country are not afraid of much when it comes to the population, but there are a few things that do worry them. They are afraid we will stop working, afraid we will stop buying, and afraid we will break things. Interruption of commerce and any rattling of the cage of profit—that is where this system is vulnerable. That means boycotts and strikes at the very least, and these things require vision, discipline, and organization.

The 1960s were a historical anomaly. It was an era when political power could also be an acid party, a felicitous situation in which *fun* also happened to be a *threat*. We still listen to that old fun on the radio, we buy it reconstituted in clothing stores, we watch it in countless movies and documentaries. Society has kept the "fun" alive, or at least a dubious facsimile of it.

But no one anywhere is teaching us about how to be a threat. That is something we have to learn all over again for ourselves, from scratch, with new rules. The 1960s are gone. The Republican Convention isn't the only party that's over.

WIMBLEHACK 2004

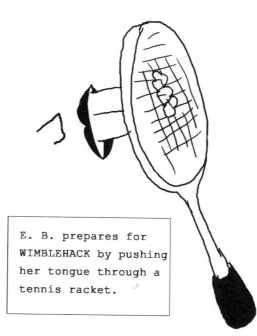

E. B. prepares for
WIMBLEHACK by pushing
her tongue through a
tennis racket.

9

WIMBLEHACK!

Round 1: The Competition Begins

These last few weeks of the presidential election campaign season are turning out to be not a whole lot different than the last peaceful hours before a prostatectomy. That is, a brief moment of fatalistic calm before something painful and unavoidable, something you were dreading when it was far off, but something that is easier to face now that you know it will all soon be over.

The end is in sight. That much we should be thankful for. But that's about all we have to be thankful for, as this Bush-Kerry fiasco is turning out to be one of the greatest and most prolonged insults to human dignity the world has ever seen.

It is hard to imagine anything more meaningless, underhanded, vapid, shameless, pointlessly vicious, embarrassing, uninspiring, degrading, and even unentertaining than this billion-dollar daily exchange of sneering teenage accusations between the Bush and Kerry camps. And it is hard to imagine anything more galling than the unspoken media subtext of the election—the idea that this slime-fest somehow represents an important moment, a landmark memory, in our own lives. The implication that we're such losers that we would actually want to watch this crap twenty-four hours a day for fifteen or sixteen months is almost more appalling than the behavior of the candidates themselves.

Though we're tempted to blame the politicians, it's time to dig deeper. It's time to blame the press corps that daily brings us this unrelenting symphony of horseshit and never comes within 1,000 miles of an apology for any of it. And it's time to blame the press not only as a class of people, but also as individuals. We must brand anyone who puts his or her name or face on credulous campaign coverage an eternal Enemy of the State. Hopefully, over time, this will have a deterrent effect.

To begin this important process of collective healing, we must find that first person to mark with our scorn. That is why we are launching the First Quadrennial Election Hack Invitational—a tournament, to be held between now and the week after the election, to answer the question "Who is the worst campaign journalist in America?"

The rules are very simple. We have chosen thirty-two of the country's leading campaign reporters, mostly from the world of print, and bracketed them into pairs. Each week, the pairs will square off against one another. Whoever writes worse, advances. It's that simple.

The tournament progresses until the week after the election, when the writer of the worst and most slavish and dishonest election postmortem among the two remaining contestants will receive an Illustrious Mystery Prize from the tournament committee.

To determine a winner in each matchup, the contenders' articles will be examined by a three-person panel of drug-addicted judges culled from the editorial ranks of the *New York Press*. Our decisions are completely subjective and cannot be appealed. In fact, one of our rules is that any appeal from a contestant, whether in private or in public, results in automatic advancement through to the next round.

That does not mean that we are unsympathetic to the plight of reporters who are "just doing their jobs." For those many reporters out there who, for whatever reason, are covering the campaign against their will—who wince with shame as they write phrases like "Democratic nominee John Kerry went on the offensive today . . ."—we offer several outs.

First, reporters may get out of the tournament through a simple monetary bribe, paid to the editors. The sum is not fixed, but dependent upon the reporter's economic circumstances. A Joe Klein, for instance, would pay more than a Ron Fournier.

Reporters may also be excused if they agree to submit to our offices a videotaped confession of wrongdoing. Extra credit will be given to reporters who openly beg for their lives—again, on the tape.

Reporters who do not file during any given week of tournament competition do not advance. This is not a logistical loophole in the tourney, but has an ideological basis. The best way to be a better journalist, especially when it comes to the campaign, is to not practice journalism. Therefore, any reporter who does not file is to be rewarded.

Competition commenced last week, when each of the thirty-two contestants in the tournament was mailed an official notification, printed on the reverse side of a photo of the fangs and underbelly of a Cameroon red baboon tarantula. The Cameroon red baboon tarantula is the official symbol of the New York Press First Quadrennial Election Hack Invitational.

The seedings and bracketings are self-explanatory. Let the games begin!

KAREN TUMULTY (1), *TIME*
Def.
ADAM NAGOURNEY, *NEW YORK TIMES*

New York Times reporters in a tournament of election hacks are like Spaniards at Roland Garros. There are a hell of a lot of them, and if the first one doesn't beat you, the second or third usually does. They wear you down. That's why only the real bruisers, the Borgs and the Lendls and the Musters, can be counted on to blast their way through the draw on the slow clay of the election season. When it comes to bad journalism, stamina is the midwife of greatness.

Karen Tumulty is Lendl in his prime. Mortals don't stand a chance against her. She is the standard-bearer for a new breed of campaign journalist: the reporter who is incapable of comprehending the election as anything other than a horse race. She appears quite honestly not to understand that it might have some other significance. In the old days, reporters used to lapse into poll-watching and political sportswriting on the campaign trail when they got tired or lazy. Thanks to shameless hacks like Tumulty, the sportswriting has actually replaced issue politics as the only meaningful story of the race.

Tumulty's articles are all the same; they are all about momentum, who has it and why. Every piece is essentially a reaction dealt in response to some new poll, often commissioned by *Time* and limited to a few dozen mysterious respondents (a recent widely cited *Time* poll showing Bush ahead had just 857 respondents). The deck to a typical Tumulty piece reads something like this: "A new poll shows Kerry trailing Bush by nine points in four key battleground states. *Time* looks at why the Kerry campaign was fucked from the start—and what it must do now to convince us it takes our poll numbers seriously."

Tumulty's most delicious moments of happiness come when she can report on those panicked reactions by the candidates—as she did here on a recent panel appearance on CNN:

> What we're seeing is a lot more aggressiveness out of the Kerry campaign and they're continuing to drive this message. They have lost the timidity that a lot of Democrats were criticizing them for. And of course the Bush campaign is ready for it and they're going to hit back just as hard.

Aggressiveness . . . timidity . . . ready for it . . . hit back just as hard. . . . Is she talking about a football game, or an election? This is as full-of-shit and meaningless as political journalism gets.

That said, it was hard to vote against Adam Nagourney in this one. In two successive recent articles, the September 15 "Democrats Seek Louder Voice from Edwards" and the September 18 Sunday front-pager, "Bush Opens Lead

Despite Unease Voiced in Survey," Nagourney did his best Tumulty imitation, chasing polls in the latter and wondering aloud about Edwards's lack of aggressiveness in the former.

In fact, in the Edwards piece, Nagourney hit what had to be a new low in WWF-style campaign journalism when he wrote, "[Several Democrats] said they were concerned that Mr. Edwards, like Mr. Lieberman, would duck when it came down to the vice presidential debate next month." He left out the logical next sentence: "Spokesmen for Edwards said the senator was not planning to duck, but rather to bob and weave."

This matchup was basically a tie. In this tourney, though, we give points to reporters who look like pre-op versions of Dave Barry, yet still go on TV every chance they get. The mannish Tumulty therefore advances; Nagourney goes back to Seville.

BILL SAMMON, *WASHINGTON TIMES*
Def.
WALTER SHAPIRO, *USA TODAY*

Sammon, a semifinal loser in the qualifiers, secured a late entry into the tournament when the *Boston Globe*'s Glen Johnson withdrew at the last minute with a torn meniscus. And the tournament's "lucky loser" makes the best of it, routing the stolid Shapiro in three punishing sets. He could be this year's Ivo Karlovic, or maybe even its Wayne Arthurs.

Sammon seized control of the match early when he made headlines by quoting Karl Rove, in the run-up to the debate, as saying of Kerry: "He will be the best debater the president has ever faced." Every other journalist on the campaign trail groaned audibly at the sight of this quote, understanding immediately that Rove had chosen the one reporter on the planet who would not add the caveat, "which is exactly the same goddamn thing he says before every debate."

It didn't take long for the rest of the press corps to dig up Rove's nearly identical 2000 quotes about Gore: "The word's best [debater]." "[Gore] is a very accomplished debater . . . and has sort of carried them to a high art form." Or, about Bush versus Gore: "Our debate strategy can be summed up in one word: survive." Or even, after Bush had won the first two debates against Gore, the hilarious "He's a smart man, he's an able politician, he's a fantastic debater. He's not going to have three bad debates in a row."

Sammon, of course, left that stuff out, completely deadpanning Rove's "best debater ever" pitch. Out of all the Washington beat writers, Sammon is the only one who can always be counted on to deep-throat, to the root, whatever foul, mud-streaked accusation the Bush camp happens to be throwing out the window that day. Just look at the headlines to Sammon stories from the last month:

"Bush Camp Rips Kerry Rhetoric" (9/29)
"Bush Attacks Kerry's Flip-Flops" (9/28)
"Bush Slams Kerry over 'Brave' Iraqi" (9/25)
"White House Rips Rather for Report, His Advice" (9/17)
"Kerry's Evolving Stance on Iraq Derided by Bush" (9/17)
"Bush Slams Kerry's Stand on Iraq War Cost" (9/11)
"White House Accuses Kerry of 'Coordinating' Guard Attacks"
(9/10)

Don't be fooled into thinking that Sammon doesn't have range. Not all of his articles are about Bush/the White House/Karl Rove ripping, attacking, slamming, deriding, or otherwise accusing some deserving enemy. This summer, Sammon also published articles on the diverse themes of "Bush raps . . . ," "Bush hits . . . ," "Bush mocks . . . ," "White House scolds . . . ," "Bush ads rip . . . ," "Bush camp hits back . . . ," and, last but not least, the deftly alliterative "Cheney . . . chides. . . ."

This is nice work if you can get it. One can only hope that Sammon can find a job in the next world holding a spittoon for Idi Amin.

Shapiro, meanwhile, quietly publishes his Kerry trail diary, *One Car Caravan*, and nobody wants to interview him about it because there's no dirt in it. He drops out; lucky loser Bill "Superstretch" Sammon advances.

CAL THOMAS, *CHICAGO TRIBUNE*
Def.
THOMAS FRIEDMAN, *NEW YORK TIMES*

Thomas, whose last column ("The Media's Trust Problem," September 29) gushingly opened with a quote from Rupert Murdoch, walks right over the unprepared Friedman. The latter, just returning from a book-writing sabbatical, was clearly not ready for live action. His first "comeback" column ("Iraq: Politics or Policy?," October 3) was suspiciously low-key, and completely free of deranged metaphors. There is a whiff here of a dog who has just eaten a pair of your shoes upstairs greeting you obediently at the door; Friedman's upcoming book must be a doozy. We'll have to wait to find out, though. He exits, Thomas still alive.

ROBERT NOVAK (8), *CHICAGO SUN-TIMES*
Def.
DAVID GERGEN, *U.S. NEWS & WORLD REPORT*

Viewers of MSNBC were witness to an extremely disturbing scene during that network's coverage of the Republican convention. It involved Gergen, and you wouldn't have noticed it unless . . . well, unless you happen to spend a lot of time doing LexisNexis searches on the rhetorical habits of conservative columnists.

A few years ago, after Bush's post-9/11 State of the Union speech sparked a wave of Winston Churchill references in the periodical media, I started keeping track of Churchill-humping among American pundits. I found that Gergen, the former Reagan communications aide, was far and away the national hack most pathologically determined to quote Churchill at every conceivable opportunity. He's referenced Churchill in his *U.S. News* columns roughly two dozen times; it's a habit so ingrained that regular Gergen readers don't even blink anymore when he begins an article previewing the Bush-Kerry debates as follows: "On May 10, 1940, as Britain trembled at Hitler's sweep across Europe, the king summoned a new prime minister to power . . ." (August 30, "Time to Face the Real Issues").

And it doesn't stop in his print work. Even when Gergen goes on television, you can almost see him drifting away mentally during the broadcast, like he's having trouble paying attention over the sound of the bombs falling on the London streets above.

The only figure in American media who even comes close to Gergen in his Churchill-worship is Chris Matthews. So when he and Gergen are together on the set, sparks fly.

Thus, on August 30, Gergen appeared on a special RNC *Hardball* with *Newsweek* monster Howard Fineman and the defiant and mostly unwelcome Ron Reagan. And Matthews and Gergen, the chummy Churchill fans, spent much of the show engaged in what can only be called flirting. Two moments in particular stand out. In the first, the pair engages in a little four-hands Churchill piano:

GERGEN: Well, but yes and no. One of your great political heroes, Winston Churchill, as you'll recall, he switched parties twice.
MATTHEWS: And he said?
GERGEN: Well, he—he . . .
MATTHEWS: He said, "Anybody can rat. It takes somebody special to re-rat."

But the real kicker came here:

MATTHEWS: You know, when Ron showed up, even though he's not a Democrat, it was such a big deal at the Democratic convention. Now we got Ron—we got Zell Miller. Is this the way it goes in politics now, a switch?
GERGEN: Everybody's a switch-hitter these days. . . .
(crosstalk)
MATTHEWS: . . . more than that way!
(laughter)
GERGEN: We may not want to go there too far, right?

MATTHEWS: We're already too far!
(laughter)

As the Russians would say: "We leave without commentary."

Nonetheless, Novak advances. He advances because of that dreary purse-lipped sadist's face of his. (You've seen that face before: the prison warden meets high school vice principal of your nightmares, shitting on your wife's back.) He advances because his outing of Valerie Plame is suddenly being upheld as a free-press issue. He advances because he recently told an audience of Penn State students that he is only able to stand James Carville because "CNN pays me a lot of money."

But here's the worst thing about Novak. Six years ago, Novak's column was the favored destination of anonymous leakers from the office of special prosecutor Ken Starr. They gave him such nuggets as the revelation that it was their "educated guess" that Hillary Clinton would be named as an unindicted co-conspirator in the Hubbell case ("Clinton's Woes Far from Over," November 26, 1998). At the time, Novak had no problem being the submissive love-slave of an overzealous independent prosecutor seeking, in a clearly inappropriate manner, to try his case in public.

Now Novak is going to sit back and let people like William Safire blast special prosecutor Patrick Fitzgerald for going too far in hammering Novak for his sources in the Plame case. Live by the leak—die by the leak, you fucking dog.

JILL ZUCKMAN, *CHICAGO TRIBUNE*
Def.
JILL LAWRENCE (5), *USA TODAY*

This was a tough one. Lawrence, author of some of the most notoriously lowbrow horse-race pieces this campaign season, came out last week with what appeared to be another doozy—the September 22 "The Election Is Turning into a Duel of Manly Men." There were many objectionable things in this article, but the worst was probably its legitimizing use of the phrase "Toughness Gap"—a recent invention by vile *Newsweek* scoundrel Jonathan Alter that may be the media's most purely adolescent campaign analysis since 1987's "Wimp Factor."

That said, Lawrence's 2,200-word piece so exhaustively catalogs all of the candidates' pathetic and shameless attempts to look tough (Kerry praising "Lambert field" in Wisconsin; Bush campaigning on his opposition to child safety locks on handguns) that it almost sounds like she's sincerely deriding them.

But, no. In the end, she is really criticizing only Kerry, whose tough-guy act, unlike Bush's, is unconvincing. Bush, she eventually concludes, is more of a real regular tough guy. "As useful as it might be politically, Bush's passion for outdoor activity is not exaggerated for campaign season," she writes. Lawrence conveniently ignores Bush's tendency to actually invade foreign countries and goad terrorists to attack as a means of looking tough, surely a more extreme form of posturing.

Zuckman, the squirrelly bitch who once complained about me, Matt Taibbi, to *Washington Post* media policeman Howard Kurtz for shooting video of the political press, seems to have pioneered a new he-said/she-said campaign journal technique with her self-serious Floridian colleague at the *Trib*, Mark Silva. In it, Zuckman follows Kerry while Silva follows Bush, and every other day or so they file a single-bylined piece in which they alternate paragraphs full of the day's accusations and counteraccusations from the two camps.

While this makes one hate the candidates more than usual, at the writing level it creates a sort of touching, Prince-and-Rosie-Gaines "Nothing Compares 2 You" effect. Who knows, the Silva-Zuckman byline might be this year's romantic smash hit, the campaign's very own *You've Got Mail*.

New York Press says, give 'em a chance. Don't smother love in the cradle. Zuckman advances; Lawrence hands the ball to Al Neuharth and walks off the mound.

BILL HOFFMANN AND HEATHER GILMORE, *NEW YORK POST*
Def.
PIA CATTON, *NEW YORK SUN*

The *Post* and the *Sun* both did well to make sure the public was served by a crusading free press investigation of John Kerry's mysteriously lustrous, apparently painted-on, pre-debate tan. But only the *Sun*'s Catton did the job correctly, quoting a former stripper as a tanning authority in her story. If there were more passages like the following in campaign journalism, voter turnout would certainly rise:

> If the tan is something you notice, you've gone too far. You should never look at someone and think: "Wow, that man is tan," said Jessica "Kayla" Conrad, a former stripper and author of the self-help book *Dance Naked: A Guide to Unleashing Your Inner Hottie.*

That's the only way we're going to save American democracy: by turning the race for the presidency into a full-blown porn circus. Civic-minded, the *Sun* drops out. Hoffmann and Gilmore, their article just the usual *Post* bleating and gloating, advance.

NEDRA PICKLER, AP
Def.
RON FOURNIER, AP

Are you ready for some football?

Excerpts here from two articles: Nedra Pickler's September 29 preview of the first debate ("Bush, Kerry Hope to Win Voters in Debate"), and ESPN's Scouts, Inc., preview of last Sunday's Bengals-Steelers game.

> PICKLER: Kerry may try to knock Bush off stride, but the president is famous for staying on message, keeping to his political point no matter what.

SCOUTS, INC.: Giving RB Rudi Johnson 20-plus carries takes some pressure off Palmer and helps keep an aggressive Pittsburgh front seven on its heels. . . . However, establishing an effective running game won't be easy working against a Pittsburgh defense that is giving up 3.1 yards a carry.
PICKLER: Kerry needs to hold back enough to give Bush the opportunity and time to create errors.
SCOUTS, INC.: Pittsburgh has the front seven to slow Cincinnati's ground attack and force Palmer into some obvious throwing situations . . . and the result should be some costly mistakes that the Steelers turn into turnovers.
PICKLER: Kerry needs to make people envision him as president, says Alan Schroeder, a presidential debate expert. . . . 'He has to diminish George W. Bush without being personally mean about it,' Schroeder says, even as he tries to 'dispel the negative stereotypes that have been created about him.'
SCOUTS, INC.: Cincinnati's offensive linemen can't lunge at their blocks because the defender lined up over their head may not be attacking up-field. They'll struggle to recover in time to pick up the blitz if they fire out of their stances too aggressively.
PICKLER: The senator criticizes Bush's Iraq policies in every speech, and he will try to drive home his argument that the war is going badly and Bush doesn't understand or know what to do about it.
SCOUTS, INC.: Look for Pittsburgh to spread the Bengals' run defense with some multireceiver sets and then pound the ball inside with RBs Duce Staley and Jerome Bettis to exploit this weakness.

The format isn't exactly the same—Pickler doesn't have headers in her piece that read like "When Kerry Has the Ball"—but it's pretty close. Meanwhile, Fournier's post-debate analysis ("Nation Hears Tough Questions, Pre-Tested Answers," October 1), which strongly suggested that Kerry was the winner, was one of the most picked-up pieces in the country, and probably had a significant effect on national debate perceptions.

It's hard to tell whether this was a good thing or not, but it's certainly less interesting than seeing if Pickler continues her *NFL Today* routine for another week. She therefore advances; Fournier is voted off the island.

HOWARD FINEMAN (4), *NEWSWEEK*
Def.
PHILIP GOUREVITCH, *NEW YORKER*

It's tempting to shove Gourevitch into the next round solely on the basis of his use of the word *totemically* in a recent campaign piece ("Bushspeak," September 13), but that's probably not fair. The poor guy has struggled all year to win the campaign trail's media modifier battle, ravaging whole stacks of thesauruses in an attempt to launch his catch-descriptions into pop usage—to no avail.

He missed out on *feisty, testy, angry,* and *pugnacious* with Howard Dean; he missed out on *cadaverous, lantern-jawed, droopy,* and *long-faced Easter Island mask* with Kerry. His desperation to get in on the action was particularly evident when he tried to dolphin-surf on the edge of the Easter Island craze—started by Dennis Miller, I think, who called Kerry an "Easter Island statue in a power tie." Alas, his effort was characteristically long-winded, and didn't stick: "A long, angular face [that] has something of the abstraction of a tribal mask."

The closest he ever came to launching an adjective phenomenon was his innovative February 2 use of *stentorian* to describe Kerry. A few of the bus reporters tried that one out for a while, then discarded it. Still, he keeps trying, recently pasting the description "simian modeling" on the face of George Bush.

But Gourevitch must lose to Fineman, who is a real beast in these proceedings. The *Newsweek* fiend is the patron saint of media hypocrites. His usual punditry cycle begins with a piece that bemoans the lowbrow nature of the campaign, then moves on to a feature aggressively and joyously selling the "Vince McMahon presents" campaign storyline ("the blood sport that is politics," as he puts it), then moves back to the angelic, "Gosh, what about the issues?" piece.

Typical Fineman: on September 20, *Newsweek*'s cover story was a thing called "Slime Time Live," in which Fineman explicitly blames unregulated money (he doesn't mention the media) for the back-alley pissing-match

character of the campaign. "And here it is: it's slime time in the most vituper-
ative presidential campaign since the divisive days of Richard Nixon—which,
not coincidentally, was the last time the country was so riven by war, culture
and fear, and the last time our politics was so inundated by a flood of unregulated cash."

A week or so later, he's on a TV panel, complaining that the Rathergate
business is going to distract the media from the job it really wants to do—
reporting the issues: "I think it's going to make it difficult for the media, the
big media, the national media," he said, "to write and produce and put out
there some of the stories that they might want to be doing about George
Bush's presidency."

Right, the serious pieces the media want to do about the substance of
Bush's presidency. Like when Fineman wrote: "But Bush will be a hard man
to beat if the race boils down to which preschool-trained rich kid can play
regular guy on the road." Or when he lauded: "Heavier artillery is on the way.
Last week the president and Mrs. Bush quietly taped a long interview with
Dr. Phil, the psychologist made famous by Oprah Winfrey."

Or when he discouraged lowbrow attack campaigning by saying on TV,
just before the first debate: "Kerry has to be the aggressor. And even
though Kerry's favorable numbers are low, even though he is not well-liked
by the American people, the Kerry people seem to feel they have no choice
but to send their man out into the middle of the ring swinging." Fineman
would later say of the first debate: "This is the eighth round of a championship fight of ten rounds."

This is the media dynamic nobody talks about. When the candidates don't
bash the shit out of each other, people like Fineman say they need to be more
aggressive. Even the *New York Times* will run a front-page story, wondering why,
say, John Edwards isn't on the attack. Because in the absence of this kind of behavior the press will be left to cover policy differences, turning the election into
a "battle of position papers," as one reporter once put it to me derisively.

No matter how much they say otherwise, reporters love the celebrity rock
'em–sock 'em stuff, and are the chief drivers of it; it sells magazines and

leaves their evenings free. You think Howard Fineman wants to spend his nights reading the text of the Clear Skies Act? As if!

ELISABETH BUMILLER (3), *NEW YORK TIMES*
Def.
DEBORAH ORIN, *NEW YORK POST*

It's always a little surprising to remember that the *New York Post* has a "Washington bureau chief" filing ostensibly factual stories from the Hill about the movements of the president and other real, breathing government officials. The effect of reading these touchingly earnest impersonations of credible journalism is a little like watching Koko the gorilla play with a kitten or punch the "buttons" on a toy telephone. My God, you think. It's so human!

But sooner or later Koko plugs her ears with her own turds again, and she's back to being just another lovable ape. The same goes for Deborah Orin, whose tepid reports in recent weeks might have had you worried until you saw her classic Murdochian lede from September 24:

> Clintonista-turned-John-Kerry-strategist Joe Lockhart's account of his role in Memogate boils down to this: I did not have National Guard conversations with that man, Mr. Burkett.

The *Post* should teach its national political writers to sing these ledes in German accents while leaning on pianos in fuzzy lingerie. The future Reich will be in much better hands if we have our nightclub acts well trained in advance.

As for Bumiller. . . . Let's make one general observation about campaign reporting. For the traveling press regulars, even the ones working for an overstaffed organization like the *Times*, it is a given that there are going to be slow days when you're just going to be forced to pull 850 words out of your ass. If you have a sense of humor, that piece is going to be funny. If you are a sensitive, reflective person, accidentally employed as a journalist, the piece is going to be full of cogent observations gleaned over time from your privileged spot at the summit of the American political process.

If you're Elisabeth Bumiller, that piece is going to be the September 20 "In Any Language, Two Candidates Are a World Apart"—comparing the Spanish accents of the two candidates. She writes:

> [W]hile Mr. Bush has for years tossed a few sentences of Spanish with a West Texas accent into his speeches—the Spanish wire service Agencia EFE has noted that the president speaks the language poorly "but with great confidence"—last week Mr. Kerry spoke an entire and very careful paragraph of Spanish, much practiced beforehand, in the neutral accent of Spanish-language television anchors.

Two questions. One, if Bumiller needed to cite EFE as an authority on Bush's accent, on whose authority does she compare Kerry to a Telemundo anchor? Second, who gives a shit? This is typical *Times* reporting: six writers on each campaign plane, each reaching for 900 words of Big Picture every time one of the candidates touches his nose. Meanwhile, the actual country passes undetected 30,000 feet below.

BRIAN MOONEY, *BOSTON GLOBE*
Def.
MICHAEL KRANISH, *BOSTON GLOBE*

Any reporter who files a "nation bitterly divided" or a "most fiercely contested election in history" piece is going to advance automatically. When 100 million people don't vote, the nation is not bitterly divided. The nation mostly doesn't give a shit.

One can only hope that in the future, the fairness rule will be revived to give nonvoters equal time in campaign coverage: ten seconds of silence for every ten seconds of Candy Crowley talking.

In this battle of soon-to-be-famouser *Globe* Kerry biographers, Mooney advances because he filed a "country that is horribly divided" piece from Iowa a few weeks ago ("US Political Divide Mirrored in Iowa," September 17). Iowa, it seems, is at the center of a "furious struggle for votes." Kranish, meanwhile, filed a piece about Republicans courting Catholics. *Globe* bitterly divided; Mooney moves on.

DANA MILBANK, *WASHINGTON POST*
Def.
E. J. DIONNE, *WASHINGTON POST*

There is a kind of mythology about the "Boys on the Bus" crowd that dates back to about the time that the campaign media became self-aware and dared to overtly recognize its own powerful role in the electoral process. That was a golden-age stretch of about ten years beginning with Theodore White's *The Making of the President, 1960,* continuing on through Joe McGinniss's *The Selling of the President* and ending in an exclamation point with *Fear and Loathing* and, of course, *The Boys on the Bus.*

To this day—and increasingly, it seems, with each successive election—the campaign press loves to celebrate the great media moments of lore that helped turn the tide in presidential elections. It loves remembering Muskie's tears, Gary Hart's "Monkey Business" picture, the Duke behind the wheel of a tank. To a man, the campaign press is positively nostalgic when it recalls these moments. Its members never get tired of reminding readers that the fates of great public figures often hinge upon these crystallized, accidental moments, and their references to these object lessons are always attended by rhetorical trumpet calls: "In a stunning public meltdown reminiscent of Ed Muskie's New Hampshire breakdown. . . ."

The subtext of all of this, of course, is a rolling campaign of self-congratulation, reminding both politicians and the public that media images and perceptions are the final arbiters of political power. Ultimately that's a lot of what this prolonged campaign season is about—a relentless, surprisingly humorless reinforcement of the dreary idea that we can be told who's winning, who will win, and why, before the polls open.

We have one person to blame for this: Richard Nixon. The signature moment in this mythology, the one that really birthed the organized study of

political imageering, was the Nixon-Kennedy debate. Every American knows
that radio audiences thought Nixon won, but TV audiences subjected to
Nixon's sweaty upper lip thought Kennedy won. To this day the media celebrate this as a righteous moment in American political history. And it gets away
with lauding it as treasured legend, and not as a sad signpost marking the first
major defeat of substance at the hands of image, largely because the hated
Nixon turned out to be a paranoid lunatic who needed to be dragged kicking
and screaming from the White House. Thus "Nixon's lip" references are usually offered not in shame, but with pride.

On successive days last weekend, the *Post* ran media mythology–heavy articles that attempted to place Bush's debate scowl in the context of the great
gaffes in campaign history. The difference between Dionne's Saturday piece
("Giving Democrats Reason to Smile") and Milbank's Sunday piece ("Reaction Shots May Tell Tale of Debate") was that Milbank's autoerotic glee
reached all the way back to Nixon, while Dionne's only reached back as far as
Gore. Writes Dionne:

> The Bush Scowl is destined take its place with the Gore Sigh and the Dean
> Scream.

Writes Milbank:

> Body language can be more descriptive than actual language in presidential de-
> bates. No line from the 1960 debate was as memorable as Richard M. Nixon's
> perspiration. And President George H. W. Bush's glance at his wristwatch dur-
> ing the 1992 debate has endured beyond that night's words.

The Milbank passage is where you spot the lie. He uses the word *memorable*
about Nixon's perspiration to mean intrinsically memorable, the wristwatch
line to mean that the glance was intrinsically enduring. But if the press hadn't
reminded us about it 500,000 times since it happened, would any of us even remember Bush I looking at his wristwatch? No way. In fact, if the media hadn't
ever made a big deal of it, and yet you still caught a close relative talking about

the wristwatch moment eight, ten, and twelve years after the fact, you'd have that relative forcibly committed. That's how insane this stuff is. But we usually let it pass.

Not here, though; Milbank advances, Dionne limps out.

JODI WILGOREN (6), *NEW YORK TIMES*
Def.
ANN COULTER

It's tempting to advance Wilgoren solely on the basis of the fact that she weighs 500 pounds and has the face of Ernest Borgnine, but—

Well—

Actually, yes, let's do that.

As for Ann Coulter, what is there to say? Like her predecessor, Joseph Stalin, she has her funny moments.

Shamu steams on; Little Treason Annie bows out.

GEORGE WILL (7), *NEWSWEEK*
Def.
ANDREW MIGA, *BOSTON HERALD*

Will advances, but not because he recently wrote a campaign piece that whined in a predictable way about George Soros's contributions to ACT ("As Goes Ohio . . .," October 3). He advances because he recently wrote a column calling "SportCenterese" the "lingua franca of ESPN Nation" ("25 Years of ESPN," September 7). It was yet another Will column that opened with Will sitting in the stands at a baseball game.

Is there no way to convince the UN to intervene to stop this man?

Miga, meanwhile, deserves some credit for being one of the rare campaign reporters to remain immune to Stockholm syndrome over a long period of time. A lonely figure as one of the few openly anti-Kerry regulars on the Kerry plane, he hasn't let up on Kerry at all. His was one of the only post-debate pieces that headlined Bush's performance in a positive way

("I'll Stay the Course: Bush Stays Firm vs. Kerry Attacks," October 1). At least he didn't file from the first-base line.

JAMES BENNET, *NEW YORK TIMES*
Def.
JOE KLEIN, *TIME*

With all due respect to a man who was nearly a victim of a kidnapping in Israel last May, a pair of James Bennet's articles from the past week perfectly demonstrates what happens when a reporter is forced to keep writing about a subject even after he concludes there really isn't anything to say.

Bennet's pre-debate piece ("In Debate on Foreign Policy, Wide Gulf or Splitting Hairs?" September 30) was a rational, obvious, and largely bullshit-free piece of analysis. In it, he sought to debunk one of the myths about the election—as he put it, the "axiom of the two presidential campaigns that their candidates offer a stark choice about America's role in the world."

And he did a decent (if not particularly comprehensive) job of it, pointing out that in many of the key issues that would be covered in the debate—what to do about Iraq, what kind of relationship to have with China, the level of support for Ariel Sharon, policy on the Gaza Strip, and more—the two candidates "differ only slightly, if at all."

Fast-forward a day. Bennet's assignment is a post-debate analysis. He can't do another "Much Ado About Nothing" story, because he did it yesterday. So what does he come up with? One of the all-time out-of-my-ass campaign whoppers: "Bush Talks About Heart; Kerry Focuses on the Brain" (sidebar, October 1).

Unable to repeat his assertion that there were no meaningful differences, a desperate Bennet scrambles in this shamefully overwritten piece to draw plausible contrasts between the candidates. In the headline it was Heart vs. Mind (an earlier version of the story, which ran online, had "Hope vs. Fear" in the headline).

Buried in the text were more "differences." Bush was "all topic sentence," while Kerry was "all paragraph and dependent clause." He talked about the contrast between "sunshine and the shadow," between "morning in America, and mourning in America." In closing, he talked about another set of contrasts, "between the actual debate everyone had witnessed and the campaigns' versions of it, and between the tactical world of ceaseless political positioning and the needs of a country fearful of terrorism, anxious about jobs and health care, and hoping for answers."

At times it almost appeared that Bennet had been ordered to write about contrasts and was rebelling against the assignment by overdoing it. Take a look at this passage:

> Mr. Bush . . . mocked comments Mr. Kerry had made about voting for financing the war before voting against it.
>
> "That's not a message a commander in chief gives," he said.
>
> Mr. Kerry shot back: "I made a mistake in how I talked about the war, but the president made a mistake in invading Iraq. Which is worse?" Grimacing, Mr. Bush reached for his pen.
>
> It seemed fitting that this clash of contrasts took place on the campus of the University of Miami, where sun-toasted students in bikinis and flip-flops strolled today across emerald grass past police barricades and scanning machines. For the debate, the entire campus was fenced.

Why is this "fitting"? What do Bush's and Kerry's hissy comments have to do with "sun-toasted students" and "emerald grass"? And what do any of these things—the Bush-Kerry exchange, the emerald grass—have to do with "contrasts"? What the hell is he talking about?

When writers don't have anything real to write, they lapse into Las Vegas–act versions of John Updike in order to fill space. Probably because their audience can so reliably be counted on to mistake it for literary instinct, *Times* writers in particular are frequently guilty of Updike-itis. And nobody at the *Times* is more consistently guilty of it than Bennet. Take this passage from his "heart and mind" piece:

Steps away from the debate hall—across a road and a parking lot—unfolded a very different scene, as thousands of journalists and scores of campaign aides, party officials and congressmen analyzed, declaimed and chuckled in a froth of commentary, reportage and badinage.

Someday I hope to run into Joe Lockhart and say to him, "Hey, do you remember me? We met in Miami, after the first debate, when you were declaiming in a froth of badinage."

Klein, meanwhile, has been Updike-free for months. He did describe the press–White House divide over the National Intelligence Estimate as a "taffy pull," but that actually made sense. He drops out; Bennet surges.

BOB WOODWARD, *WASHINGTON POST*
Def.
CALVIN WOODWARD, AP

Battle of the Woodies. Calvin has been the AP's self-appointed campaign factchecker lately, running a number of finger-wagging stories in which he corrects the factual assertions of the candidates. Bob, meanwhile, has not been publishing, but has instead been humping his latest opus, *Plan of Attack,* in speaking appearances.

Woodward continues to seem ashamed of his activist-journalism legacy as the reporter who toppled a Republican president. His investigative efforts since *All the President's Men,* and especially lately, seem determined to seek relentlessly a centrist politics, to be gently corrective rather than crusading and muckraking. . . . And sometimes he drifts into outright shameless hagiography of the ruling powers (i.e., *Bush at War*).

Unlike his counterpart Sy Hersh, who appears happily poised to keep pissing people off well into his nineties, Woodward seems very determined to remain a respectable figure to parties on all sides. Therefore he says, with pride, things like the following about *Plan of Attack*: "It's a book that looks both ways." Or: "You can look at that and say that's what we need in a president or you can look at that and say that's exactly what we don't need in a president."

Or that Bush in *Plan of Attack* either comes across as a "forceful, decisive leader" or "shows he does not know what he is doing," depending on your point of view.

Woodward achieves this balancing act in subtle ways. He does the actual reporting of just enough damning facts about the Bush presidency (like the revelation that Bush talked about "taking the gloves off" with Gitmo prisoners after 9/11), then turns around and flatters the same interview subjects he just skewered. Thus he will report really damaging things about Bush, then will turn right around and blow smoke up his ass on national television, doing things like telling Tim Russert (September 12, *Meet the Press*) that he sincerely believed Bush was willing to take the risk to go into Iraq, even if that made him a one-term president. When a professional doubter suddenly starts credulously buying the transparent posturing of politicians, you know something's up.

Or, Woodward will say things like the following:

> I mean, Bush essentially says, when you get into this question, how is history going to judge the Iraq War? And he makes the point, "Well, we don't know. We'll all be dead." And I think that's true.

No, that isn't true. It's stupid. It's the grasping nonanswer of a junior-high fuckup who didn't do his homework. And Woodward knows it. But he does this stuff to ensure that he still gets to sit in the Oval Office a few times a year.

This is too bad, because Bush is a much bigger target than Nixon, his crimes much more outrageous and egregious than Nixon's, and America's most famous muckraker is softballing him in the middle of an election season, just to make sure he stays on the White House Christmas card list.

If there's one criticism of the campaign press that has really held true all across the board throughout this race, it's this tendency to kid-glove politicians, make excuses for them, make them seem more legitimate than they really are. It is important for the public to remember that a campaign reporter who would call the campaign a bogus, shallow farce—who would say, for instance, that the campaign is a mindless exercise in mudslinging diversion held between a pair of toothy millionaires with nearly identical plans for the management of the country—is also saying that his own job is bogus. Therefore the opposite instinct is usually in evidence in campaign coverage. The race is described as something profound, a true clash of ideals, led by two worthy men of unfathomable depth of character.

Thus you will sometimes see a situation where Bush will get up on stage and stumble around for twenty minutes like a man who's been breathing out of a bag for a year—and when it comes time to actually describe the things he says, someone like Philip Gourevitch will call him a "master of the American vernacular."

He's looking for something that isn't there, just to reassure himself that something is there. They all do it. Even Bob Woodward. He advances; Calvin hits the links.

JONATHAN ALTER (2), *NEWSWEEK*
Def.
MARK HALPERIN, *ABC NEWS*

Actually this one is a walkover. Halperin and the rest of his cohorts manning ABC's *The Note*, a comprehensive daily summary of campaign coverage, have no business even being on the court with the likes of Jonathan Alter. A weird wormhole / oasis of humanity buried deep in the anus of Disney, *The Note* is the only running campaign diary that even comes close to expressing the proper disgust and loathing for the entire process. The intro writing (each summary begins with a small essay about what to expect that day) is often remarkably savage, as in the case of a pre-debate spiel last week:

Here's what to expect in the next 72 hours. . . . #15. Elisabeth Bumiller could find yet another Yale angle on the race, and apologetically get it into the paper. . . .

Solid. Or check out the *Note*'s pre-debate talking points about debate coverage—about thirty themes we could expect to see. Sample:

How about those wacky, restrictive, detailed campaign-negotiated rules that make this less a debate and more a joint appearance blah blah blah.
    The first debate historically has the largest audience blah blah blah.
    John Kerry must sound more bar room than Brahmin blah blah blah. . . .

The only outlet with enough sense to add all those blahs.

Alter, still surfing on his "Toughness Gap" piece, remains a contender. A recent piece, "Where Kerry Went Wrong" (September 27), achieved a milestone in the business. In it, Alter explicitly condemns Kerry and handler Bob Shrum for not pursuing name-calling as a political strategy. The pertinent passage:

[Shrum] once told me as much, and that name-calling wouldn't work in post-9/11 presidential politics.
    That was wishful thinking. Politics has always been a contact sport where the winning team is the one that pins the kick me sign on the other guy.

Nice. That's just really nice work.

Alter advances; Halperin & Co. go back to the Challenger circuit.

Next week: Eight more hacks will be eliminated in round 2 of the First *New York Press* Quadrennial Election Hack Invitational.

Round 2: The Gorm Turns

Until this year's Wimblehack, few American fans had heard of Gorm Voelver, political correspondent for the Danish news mag *Politiken*. In fact, we'd never heard of him, either. But when *Newsweek*'s Jonathan Alter had to pull out of competition this week due to his observance of Satanic Thanksgiving, somebody had to jump into the fire.

That somebody was Gorm Voelver.

Chosen on the strength of his name alone from a list of more than 1,700 foreign campaign-trail hopefuls, Voelver represents this tournament's best effort to give a non-American wild card a shot at the title. He is a symbol of America's status as the ultimate land of opportunity, and our embrace of him into the tourney graphically demonstrates this country's passion for fairness and entrepreneurial spirit. He is journalism's Rocky Balboa, if you will, its Italian Stallion. Or rather—its Italian Danish.

"You may not know what to expect from Gorm. Get ready to be surprised," said *Politiken* head coach Tøger Seidenfaden. "At *Politiken,* we expect all of our players to perform, and whenever Gorm steps on the field, I have complete confidence that he'll get the job done."

We'll see. In any case, Wimblehack, the tournament to determine America's—er, the world's—worst campaign journalist, is entering a crucial phase. The presidential-election story is going to become markedly more dramatic in the next few weeks for the simple reason that the news (and entertainment) networks are going to throw more journalists at it. In the American media landscape, drama is a quantitative rather than a qualitative commodity. A story with ten live trucks parked outside is more dramatic than a story with five live trucks parked outside. When election time draws near, we don't look more closely at what the candidates actually stand for, but we do add a lot more live trucks. So expect it to get noisier from now on, and tougher for our contestants to stand out.

The formula is the same. Journalists in each draw bracketed into pairs. Whoever writes worse advances. This week, we're through to the round of eight.

KAREN TUMULTY (1), *TIME*
Def.
BILL SAMMON, *WASHINGTON TIMES*

Here's a fun game that all of you out there who have no lives can play at any time. It's a little thing we at *New York Press* call the AFRICAN CAMPAIGN SAFARI.

Campaign reporters are a lot like high school kids. Three weeks into the school year, one of the popular girls comes in wearing baby-blue Ugg boots and a Juicy Couture sweatshirt. Two weeks later, half the girls in school are wearing baby-blue Ugg boots and Juicy Couture sweatshirts.

The exact same dynamic is at work on the campaign trail. One of the big guys will come up with some dumb thing or other, and next thing you know, two weeks later, it's spread to the rest of the plane: "Hey, let's start referring to the debates as smackdowns! Everybody's doing it!"

You'd like to think that's not the way it works, but it is. It's always the same thing. One week, out of the blue, somebody uses a line once. Next week, it gets used three times. By the third week, fifty or sixty times by fifty or sixty different reporters.

Usually you don't spot it until that third week, when you suddenly start seeing it everywhere. By the fifteenth time you see a "smackdown" in a debate lede (incidentally, even CBS MarketWatch had one recently), you start scratching your head, wondering: "Jesus, where the hell did this come from?" That's when you know it's time to play AFRICAN CAMPAIGN SAFARI. You've got to find the source of the Nile.

One of the more loathsome themes of the coverage of the second debate was the "You know, it's funny, but these debates are really like reality TV" angle. By the end of last week, half the reporters in the country were whipping that one out. It came completely out of the blue.

"This is reality television at its best—only this time, the outcome really matters," wrote Gail Pennington of the *St. Louis Post-Dispatch*.

"We may get a little bit of reality TV here, if you will. Reality TV meets politics," said CNN analyst Carlos Watson.

"These debates are the best reality TV around these days," cooed the *Duluth News-Tribune*.

There was Bill Goodykoontz of the *Arizona Republic* making the unintentionally ironic observation that the debates had the same "drama" as reality shows, writing, "This was real reality TV, with all the drama of a *Survivor* or *Apprentice* but with, obviously, much higher stakes."

Or how about this one, a classic two-fer by the *Philadelphia Inquirer's* Dan DeLuca: "Even if the duo turn in disappointing performances, the smackdowns make for compelling television for the simple reason that presidential debates are like reality TV shows that really matter, and they hold considerably more weight than, say, the baseball playoffs they'll be battling with for viewers tonight."

Incidentally, the *Oregonian* hit the same cliché two-bagger just a few days ago in its TV listings for this week, writing: "The third presidential debate is the final smackdown . . . ! This riveting reality TV show will feature all the bells and whistles: A live audience! A moderator!"

This had to be coming from somewhere. And if you go back through the record and search, you'll find that it all started in one prominent outlet: an October 4 *Time* magazine feature called "Inside the Debate Strategies," by one Karen Tumulty. Characteristically, Tumulty invokes the "reality TV" idea in the form of helpful horse-race advice to candidates, this time imploring them not to be thinkers, but the same kind of desperate, pandering dickheads who make good reality-show contestants. She writes:

> The biggest mistake any candidate can make is to think of these as debates at all. Reality TV is more like it. "People watch these things more like they are watching *Friends* than the way they watch the Harvard and Yale debate societies," says Chris Lehane, who was Gore's press secretary. "They're not watching to see who scores the points. They're watching to see who they connect with and feel comfortable with."

Let's get this straight. The biggest mistake a candidate can make is to not act like a reality show contestant? And this woman went to Harvard?

Bill Sammon nearly advanced automatically when one of his editors wrote one of those "Hey, love the tournament, I'm right there with you fellers" letters that also quietly let us know that "Bill is a really nice guy" who won awards when he worked for the *Stars and Stripes*. We don't go for that sort of thing around here. If you think the guy's nice, tell your wife.

Fortunately for Sammon, however, he hasn't filed since the last issue, so he's out. Tumulty, the African Queen, advances.

CAL THOMAS, *CHICAGO TRIBUNE*
Def.
ROBERT NOVAK (8), *CHICAGO SUN-TIMES*

This is a tough one. Do you go with the mean old bastard who writes, without kidding, "I am a Ken Mehlman fan"—or do you go with the loopy mystic with the gay-porn moustache who blasted Dick Cheney, of all people, for being soft on family values, and spent the weekend buddying up to one of the rising stars of the Christian nut-job set?

We're going with Cal Thomas, solely on the strength of this photo of him with Joni Eareckson Tada, his most recent guest on the Fox program, *After Hours with Cal Thomas*—a show, incidentally, that is showing signs lately of mounting a strong ratings challenge to the automatic rice-cooker infomercials on MNN. Eareckson Tada, a quadriplegic, is an honorary co-chair of the Presidential Prayer Team, an organization devoted to praying for the health and success of the Bush administration. This is a group that issues daily instructions to pray for such people as Secretary of Transportation Norman Mineta and Secretary of Commerce Don Evans. With his invite of Eareckson Tada, Thomas has now been plugged as mainstream-media friendly on the group's website—twice. On the show, incidentally, he and Eareckson Tada engaged in a mutual congratulation session over their identically recalcitrant views on stem cell research.

Meanwhile, in his literary endeavors, Thomas performed admirably, blasting Cheney after the debate for having the temerity to assert that a job was the best antidote to poverty. According to Thomas, heterosexual marriage is a better weapon against poverty than a job. "[S]table two-parent homes with a mother and father . . . constitute the best anti-poverty program," he wrote.

That's a nice line of reasoning. Maybe it ought to be developed: "Homosexuality: it takes food off the table."

Novak, meanwhile, fell and broke his hip after the first debate, but was back blasting away at Don Rumsfeld from his hospital bed two days later. The guy is really unstoppable. At the end of his life, he's going to be like the machine in the last frames of *The Terminator,* legs gone, flesh all burned off, crawling forth in the abandoned factory, spewing venom about government spending. One has to admire that.

He drops out; the pious Cal moves on.

JILL ZUCKMAN, *CHICAGO TRIBUNE*
Def.
HEATHER GILMORE AND BILL HOFFMANN, *NEW YORK POST*

This is a forfeit, as neither Gilmore nor Hoffmann has filed a campaign piece in the last two weeks. Moreover, one of the things Hoffmann did write was a piece about a freelance graphic designer who got scores of dates after surreptitiously inserting his phone number into a Crate & Barrel catalog photo ("Crate Pickup Line—Bachelor Sneaks # into Catalog," October 8). Hoffmann grittily describes designer Marc Horowitz's travels to meet his callers:

> Horowitz insists his three-month trip, which he hopes to videotape for a possible documentary, absolutely is not about trying to have a coast-to-coast sex marathon.

Now that's journalism.

Zuckman and her *Trib* colleagues, meanwhile, filed a piece over the weekend ("Battle Gets More Personal—and Urgent; Candidates Offer Debate Rebuttals on Campaign Trail," October 10) that twice quotes Bush's new dipshit stump line, "He can run, but he can't hide." Once, thank you, was more than enough.

Incidentally, out of nearly 1,000 campaign reporters, only one—Chris Suellentrop of *Slate*—bothered to look up the ancestry of "You can run, but you can't hide." The line has obviously been used in the White House before, most recently by Scott McClellan about modern-day terrorists, but more famously by Ronald Reagan about terrorists involved with the hijacking of the Italian cruise ship *Achille Lauro*. Reagan also described the Tripoli bombing campaign as "you can run but you can't hide" air strikes. Candidates recycle lines all the time, and journalists, obeying the generally Orwellian relationship of campaigns to both fact and the past, rarely call them on it. This is positive because it allows the campaign sham to be cyclical as well as depressing.

Jill "Two Times" Zuckman & Co. advance; *Post* eliminated.

HOWARD FINEMAN (4), *NEWSWEEK*
Def.
NEDRA PICKLER, AP

Adoring, subject-sanctioned profiles of the Important Campaign Journalist appear with numbing regularity in student/alumni magazines. For reasons that are probably obvious only to the people who went to those sorts of schools, they appear more often than not in Ivy League circulars—though there are exceptions. The feature will typically include a handsome photo of the hack in a regal, professional pose, over the implied caption: "In his exciting career as a swashbuckling toilet who eagerly receives the piss of powerful political interests, X never forgets his Yale roots."

Such an article appeared recently in *Beta Theta Pi,* the fraternity's quarterly magazine. Appropriately in its How I Spent My Summer Vacation issue ("What Did You Do This Summer?," summer 2004), the fraternity profiled its famous journalist brother, Howard Fineman (Colgate '70). The story featured a gigantic, illustrated version of a *Newsweek* cover in which the irrepressibly serious Aaron Brown–wannabe face of Howard Fineman appears over the headline "Howard Fineman."

Most of the article is just the inoffensively overwrought flattery of the amateur feature writer ("As a journalist, NBC News analyst and active family man, Fineman is 'on the go' a lot"; "His personality is disarming and his demeanor is relaxed, evidenced by his loosened tie and disheveled hair"). But late in the article, the writer gets Fineman to come out with this:

He once interviewed the president on his cell phone from his son's Little League game. "I know Bush is no dummy—he's a shrewd, effective leader," he said, referring to Bush's cool persona that allows for a seemingly effortless style. "I recognized him from my fraternity life," he said. "They're a different breed."

Fineman also reveals that he thought Bush once tried to give him the Delta Kappa Epsilon grip:

> "But I sure didn't give him the Beta grip," he adds. "Understanding the role of fraternity in American life is important and relevant. It has helped me to understand George W. Bush. I appreciate him more and understand him better because of my fraternity experience."

Yikes! Apparently Brother Fineman quite appreciates Brother Bush, because his performance on his behalf last week was really a thing of beauty. Not since O. J. Simpson stared into the cameras and invited the whole incredulous world to help him in his search for the "real killers" have we seen anything as brazen as Fineman attempting to blame media bias for Bush's plunge in the polls. In his post-first-debate cover-story wrap-up ("Ninety Minutes Later, a New Race," October 11), Fineman all but openly raged at Kerry, using straight-from-Karl-Rove's-mouth language throughout the piece.

In one sequence, he echoed the Bush campaign's windsurfing ads ("Republicans use Kerry's love of windsurfing as a metaphor for weakness of character. But in the midst of an increasingly unpopular war in Iraq, Kerry has tacked to the popular position. . . ."), and later went on to deconstruct Kerry's Iraq position at length, leaving Bush alone. Finally in the piece, he attributed on two occasions Bush's "loss" to the inattention of the media. Here's the first instance; note the inclusion of the peevish "which may be true":

> [Bush] harped on the notion that Kerry was a flip-flopper, which may be true but which the press corps—primed for news—had heard before.

Is Fineman suggesting that the media underreports Kerry's "flip-flops"? He goes on:

> After being blown about in the spin room, Republicans concluded that they had underestimated the press corps's eagerness to see a close race, and they worried that reporters had awarded points to Kerry because they approve of his now clear antagonism toward the war.

Later, in online commentary, Fineman repeated a watered-down version of the same idea, only this time it was his own opinion. "George Bush's real political enemy now isn't so much John Kerry as it is the flow of the news," he wrote. "Good things are happening in the war on terrorism—the voting in Afghanistan, for example—but they are all but unnoticed in the rising flood of stories from and about Iraq."

It should be noted that a year and a half ago, when responsible observers in every country but America were freaking out en masse about the impending war, Fineman was leading the charge here in America in the area of stupendously irrelevant bullshit puff pieces about our heroic president's intentions. Just before the invasion ("Bush and God," cover, March 10, 2003), this is the kind of hard-hitting, critical journalism Brother Fineman was writing:

> George W. Bush rises ahead of the dawn most days, when the loudest sound outside the White House is the dull, distant roar of F-16s patrolling the skies. Even before he brings his wife, Laura, a morning cup of coffee, he goes off to a quiet place to read alone. . . .

Surprising that Fineman didn't add that Bush's personality was disarming, his demeanor relaxed, as evidenced by his loosened tie. . . . You see how this kind of behavior gets passed on down the ranks.

Anyway, nothing like a professional flatterer, masquerading as a journalist, chiding his press colleagues for being too hard on the boss. As for Nedra Pickler, she didn't have one NFL moment all week. There weren't even any boxing metaphors in her post-second-debate wrap ("Bush Defends Iraq Invasion, Kerry Says Decision Made World More Dangerous," October 8).

Pickler goes down; Fineman, whom Bush has flirtatiously nicknamed "Fine," advances.

ELISABETH BUMILLER (3), *NEW YORK TIMES*
Def.
BRIAN MOONEY, *BOSTON GLOBE*

When trying to judge campaign coverage, we utilize what we call the Jayson Blair Test. You apply the Jayson Blair Test to determine whether or not a campaign piece ostensibly filed from some remote trail locale could actually have been written from New York, in the tenement apartment of a $15 one-legged hooker, with no props beyond a gram of coke, a television, and a Rolodex.

An on-the-road-with-Bush report Bumiller recently filed from Iowa ("Bush Calls Kerry's Policies a Danger for World Peace," October 5) was a classic Blair test piece. The byline is Bumiller's and the dateline is Clive, Iowa, which means she was physically in Clive at some point, but you'd never know it.

The first stage of the Blair test checks the quotes. Here, every source in the piece was either on the plane or sitting by a desk in Washington somewhere. Bumiller quotes Bush, Kerry spokesman Phil Singer, and Scott McClellan. There are no Iowans in sight. Moreover, the piece only refers to a concrete physical setting twice. One of those moments takes place in Air Force One ("Asked by reporters en route to Iowa on Air Force One whether the change in Wilkes-Barre was because of polls that show the race tightening, Mr. McClellan demurred"). The other reference is to a YMCA in Des Moines, which Bumiller describes mainly by saying it sure as hell wasn't the White House:

> Mr. Bush's first stop on Monday was in Des Moines, where he signed the tax legislation in a YMCA gymnasium. The setting was in striking contrast to the splendors of the White House East Room, where Mr. Bush normally holds his signing ceremonies for significant bills.

The YMCA, incidentally, was in the photo sent in by *Times* reporter Doug Mills. Now, obviously, Bumiller really was in Iowa, but there isn't a single element of the article that couldn't have been dug up by any determined junkie sitting in front of an Internet connection halfway around the world.

In contrast, Mooney wrote a piece on the Pennsylvania race ("Facing GOP Push, Pennsylvania Is a Must-Win for Kerry," October 3) that was filled with local detail and quoted over a dozen people, ordinary citizens and elected officials alike, who actually reside in the state. The article also features a detailed demographic breakdown of the state's voting patterns and attempts at several junctures to explain what is distinctive about the Pennsylvania election.

In fairness, Mooney and Bumiller were writing different sorts of articles. Mooney seems to have been in Pennsylvania working on his piece for more than a week, while Bumiller just did the standard one-day pump-and-dump of the plane-bound trail writer. But it says here that there is something very negative going on when it is possible for a paper like the *Times* to run the same campaign article hundreds of times, quoting the same thirty or so campaign characters, with only the dateline and the crowd photo changing. You're presenting the illusion that you're covering the whole country, but except for the background, the whole thing, day after day, could be done in a studio in Burbank—which is probably where we're headed.

Bumiller, who doesn't seem to mind this, advances; Mooney drops out.

JODI WILGOREN (6), *NEW YORK TIMES*
Def.
DANA MILBANK, *WASHINGTON POST*

Pundits and politicians are fond of referring to the campaign as a conversation between the candidates and the public. Kerry even puts that in his stump speech, beginning Town Halls and rallies by gesturing to the crowd and saying, "You and I are going to have a conversation." But is it really a conversation?

In fact, if you look at it closely, the campaign is mainly a conversation with itself. And if you look at the campaign as it exists in the media, it is entirely a conversation with itself. Virtually everyone who is allowed to tell us what to think of the candidates, their positions, and the state of our politics in general is an insider of some kind. In this movie, only the guild members—candidates, spokespeople, talking heads, pundits, and pollsters—get the speaking lines. The rest of the country is represented by crowd shots and poll numbers.

In order to understand why this is, you have to grasp an essential truth about our political journalism. What our political reporters do for a living is sell the campaign to the population, not speak for the people to the campaign. This is most vividly demonstrated in who actually gets to talk in campaign coverage.

In the last month, dating back to September 10, Wilgoren has had a byline on some sixteen campaign articles. In the course of that month she's quoted some fifty-six professional campaign creatures, with the vast majority of quotes coming from the candidates themselves and spokesmen like Joe Lockhart, Karen Hughes, Dan Bartlett, Mary Beth Cahill, and Scott McClellan. Also represented are a trio of pollsters (Andrew Kohut, Frank Luntz, and Peter Hart), a half-dozen or so talking heads (e.g., Brian Riedl of the Heritage Foundation and Thomas Mann of Brookings), and other assorted humanoid flotsam and jetsam commonly found in campaign circles (a "top Democrat . . . in a hotel bar," a "debate expert").

During that month, Wilgoren traveled all over the country, from Allentown to Washington to Toledo to New York to Miami to Wausau, Wisconsin, and to half a dozen other cities, a journey spanning about 10,000 miles. In that time, amidst all that cross talk between campaign types, she quotes exactly three real human beings. She gives two lines to a Florida citrus farmer named Karen McKenna, one word to a man named Steve who tells Kerry which name to sign on a photo ("Steve," he says)—and lastly, an end-of-the-article shout-out by an unnamed elderly woman with Alzheimer's disease, who croaked out at a Kerry rally the words "It's too late for me."

In total, she clocked more than 23,000 words of coverage.

Wilgoren advances; Milbank, who continues with his impressive run of "I, Dana Milbank, Can Barely Contain My Impatience with the Bush Administration" pieces ("Urging Fact-Checking, Cheney Got Site Wrong," October 7), drops out.

JAMES BENNET, *NEW YORK TIMES*
Def.
GEORGE WILL (7), *NEWSWEEK*

Unless revenues go up at this newspaper, we're going to have to go without Wimblehack for the next election. That, or we're going to have to make sure somehow that George Will is never matched up against James Bennet again. The costs are too prohibitive; in order to even follow the match, every spectator has to be given a Fowler's usage dictionary, a *Chicago Manual of Style*, the *Oxford Dictionary of Difficult Words*, *Gray's Anatomy*, Sheldon Novick's *Henry James: The Young Master*, the *Rabbit* series, *Ball Four*, and, for the protection of the eyes, a welding mask. That's just too much for any sports-loving family to deal with as it tries to watch the game. Which hand does little Jimmy use to hold the ice cream?

That said, this is an interesting contrast in modes of pretentiousness.

Will uses big words and pompous literary references to dress up what are basically the brutish and vulgar thinking patterns of a nonunion meatpacking plant owner. He is a pig in a lace hat.

What Bennet does, on the other hand, is eat up huge chunks of space by continually firing fat starbursts of desperate verbiage at weirdly commonplace scenes and conversations—trying in this way to pummel them into relevance. It is really a remarkable thing to watch.

Take Bennet's wrap of the second debate ("In a Disguised Gym, Softballs and Political Drama," October 9). Bennet's general argument in this piece was that there was a special "dynamic" to the debate that you missed if, unlike Bennet, you weren't there.

"Inside the hall, the scene was of a theater in the round," he wrote, adding that "viewers at home were denied the peek behind the political and news media curtain that voters here received."

Bennet goes on to describe some of those elements of the "dynamic" that were invisible to TV viewers:

> Those viewers did not see how the moderator, Charles Gibson of ABC, hammed it up with a colleague, Chris Wallace of Fox News, who was seated in one of the network boxes overlooking the hall.
>
> "Hi, Chris," Mr. Gibson hallooed, before the debate began, to the delight of the assembled voters. "Hello, Charlie," Mr. Wallace called back with a grin.

In the hands of a mere mortal, this scene is written as follows: "Charlie Gibson said hi to Chris Wallace." But in Bennet's hands, this "hallooing" was a bit of "theater in the round," part of a "drama that mixed calculated stagecraft and moments of genuine improvisation," only discernible to those who were there to hear Charlie Gibson say "hi" to Chris Wallace. However, one paragraph later, Bennet was arguing that "one can learn more about a candidate by watching from a great distance, on television."

Now, a sensible person here will ask: with which particular mental and physical attitude should I learn more about the candidates by watching from a great distance? Bennet has your answer: from "the Olympian detachment of the couch." (Only Bennet can turn a couch potato into Zeus.) And it's just as well that you watch from there, because meeting the candidates in person is overrated:

> . . . face-to-face encounters with candidates are often overrated. Town halls are one thing, but you can keep your catch-and-release handshake, your dandled baby, your pale-brew kaffeeklatsch.

My what? What the hell is he talking about—and why? Bennet has about three of these moments per article. And even though Will's campaign piece last week ("Why Democrats Fear Bush's Domestic Agenda," October 7) was probably more ideologically offensive, Bennet's run is too interesting to let go. We were in mythological Greece and sixteenth-century Saxony this week—where will we travel to next week? Let's find out: Bennet advances.

GORM VOELVER, *POLITIKEN*
Def.
BOB WOODWARD, *WASHINGTON POST*

Woodward didn't file, so he's disqualified. Which is too bad for Voelver, because he really didn't deserve to advance. His latest campaign piece ("Bush Har Brug for Hjaelp," October 5) was a taut, trenchant piece of writing of the sort we don't often see in America. "Den proever at saette modstanderen John Kerrys helterolle fra soldatertiden i et daarligt lys," he writes, adding: "Filmen starter med at fortaelle, at mens Vietnamkrigen rasede, blev George W. Bush hjemme i Texas for at beskytte staten mod horder af vietcong-terrorister."

Later, he recounts Bush's response:

> Bevaeg laeberne, som om mikrofonen ikke virker. Stil spoergsmaalet: "Vi har aldrig tidligere haft en praesident med et hesteansigt. Saa hvorfor nu?"

Note the subtle farm reference. A nice piece of work, but unfortunately he has to advance. King Woodward gone; the Italian Danish advances to the round of eight. See you next week!

Next week: Four hacks will be eliminated as things get tense in round 3 of the First *New York Press* Quadrennial Election Hack Invitational.

Round 3: The Herd Thins

Owners love it, fans are grateful for it, but the advertisers hate it. It's the scourge and the savior of all organized sports:

Parity.

Designing a system in which all the contestants have a nearly equal chance of winning—like today's NFL, for instance—guarantees spirited play and close competition. But it also deprives the sport of juggernaut teams and dominant stars. It's a trade-off that works fine for football, but has been a disaster, say, for women's tennis or the NBA, which hasn't been the same since the days when the Celtics and the Lakers were perennial locks for the finals.

Campaign journalism is a sport that thrives with a built-in caste system. This is a league that makes its own stars, and part of being a star is sitting at the right table at the cafeteria. It's hard to go far in a tournament like Wimblehack if you sit in the back of the plane, but if you're within breathing distance of the candidates, up front with all the other Heathers, you've got a decent shot. It takes years of mutual back-scratching up there to get that really sharp, pointy head you need to succeed on this surface.

That's why there are so few upsets in Wimblehack. Three of the four top seeds made it to the semifinals, and it's no surprise that those surviving seeds represent three of the pointiest heads in the business. The only surprise entrant into the Final Four is James Bennet of the *New York Times,* who continues to impress. Is he an up-and-comer, the next Federer? Or is he just another Miloslav Mecir—a junkballer who's always a few rounds too lucky?

We'll see. One would hope that luck will have nothing to do with the outcome, and it's hard to imagine it will, judging from this Final Four lineup. In any case, the action from the round of eight:

KAREN TUMULTY (1), *TIME*
Def.
CAL THOMAS, *CHICAGO TRIBUNE*

Tumulty, the only female impersonator left in the draw, advances this week for a number of reasons. Press readers may recall that in the first two rounds, Tumulty was characterized as a third-rate sportswriter, a serial poll-humper, an archpriestess of conventional wisdom, the unrepentant human embodiment of the lowest common denominator, the sworn enemy of all political substance, and, incidentally, ugly. Last week, Tumulty wrote to the *Press* to angrily complain, "Who are you calling ugly?" Under the subject line "Mannish?" she wrote a two-line letter:

> pre-op version of dave barry? let's see how YOU look when you are 48 and have had two babies.

We were about to send a hurtful, gratuitous response to this when we spotted an article in the Swedish daily *Svenska Dagbladet*, which quoted Stockholm-born actress and sizzling nude-scene star of *The Unbearable Lightness of Being* Lena Olin as saying, "Now that I'm 48 and have two children, I look just like Karen Tumulty." That was a humbling piece of information for us, so we just shut our mouths in shame, and didn't answer the letter at all. Not content with this victory, Tumulty, clearly concerned about the next round, wrote again the next day:

> i'm not writing this week for next week. does that mean i'll have to forfeit, or can you find something you hate from this week's cover on the ground game? the pressure is getting so intense. . . .

Now, in Wimblehack, you advance automatically when you send in faux-sarcastic letters of the "Not that I care, but . . ." genus in an abject attempt to find out ahead of time if you're going to be savaged in the next issue. Besides, is there anything funnier than a campaign-trail journalist asking for a sneak-peek verdict from a reporter before the publication date? Can you imagine what Tumulty's reaction would be if someone like David Wade or Stephanie Cutter meekly asked for a private preview, three days early, of one of Tumulty's patented "Kerry: Why Women Snicker" pieces? She'd laugh out a twenty-foot hole in the fuselage; it'd look like a scene from *Airport '77*.

Tumulty also advances because, over the course of a lengthy taxonomic survey of evil campaign clichés last week, the *Press* was completely flummoxed in its attempts to find one worthy of being called a "Tumulty." The reason for that is that they were all worthy of being called a Tumulty. Every campaign reporter has something he can call his own. George Will has his unnecessary alliteration, Howard Fineman his boxing/combat imagery, James Bennet the unexplored vestiges of the liner notes to *Beowulf*. Tumulty is the only reporter with the perfect all-court game. She uses labels like *liberal* more consistently and derisively than Karl Rove; she can't file a single piece that isn't wrapped around a poll; she is more prone than most to imbecilic generalizations like "Kerry's [positions are] more like a kaleidoscope than like a circle"; and she is really the only reporter on the trail who can be consistently counted on to croak out dire warnings to candidates about the consequences of listening to reason instead of pollsters ("The Kerry campaign at times resembles a floating five-ring circus of longtime Democratic operatives who have all sorts of views. . . . That worked fine when it was up against Howard Dean's homespun Vermont militia. Against Bush-Cheney '04, a disciplined hierarchy run by Karl Rove . . . it could be a recipe for a landslide").

Like Tumulty, other reporters avoid talking to ordinary people, usually preferring to talk to staffers and pollsters and talking heads. But Tumulty's *Time* campaign team is probably the first magazine to actually outsource the job of talking to ordinary voters. If you look at the byline of Tumulty pieces, they are usually absurdly long, with five or six reporters contributing to each 2,000-word piece (typical *Time* byline: "Karen Tumulty, With reporting by Perry Bacon Jr. on the road with Kerry; and Timothy J. Burger, James Carney, John F. Dickerson, and Michael Duffy/Washington"). A lot of the man-on-the-street stuff naturally comes from these supporting writers, leaving the big gun free to talk to the real people.

That happens in the business and is nothing new; a perk of being a bigtimer is that you use assistants to talk to the rabble. But in *Time* you will sometimes also see a polling agency in the article credits—for instance, Schulman, Ronca and Bucuvalas (SRBI), which frequently helps out in poll data.

Last week, I called Mark Schulman of SRBI, and asked him if his agency ever provided *Time* with quotes from respondents in addition to polling data. He said no, although this was possible ("provided we get permission from the respondent"). However, he did note that *Time* had recently asked his agency's help in recruiting "real people" for its reporters to talk to.

"They said, 'We want to talk to some real people,'" he told me.

"They said that?" I asked. "Just like that? 'We want to talk to real people?'"

"That's what they said," he replied. "I mean, it makes sense, because there's the number, but the numbers aren't the people, of course."

A striking thing for a pollster to say, one would think.

"So where do you go looking for real people?" I asked. "That can't be easy."

"Um, we just get them off the street," Schulman said. "Although in this case, we just sort of called around, asked people we knew, and they put us in touch with some women they knew in the Philadelphia area."

The recruiting Schulman was referring to was actually for a Nancy Gibbs piece ("What Do Women Want?" October 11), to which Tumulty contributed. This sounds like an up-and-coming trend to me: you get the pollster to find "the people," leaving the reporter more time to spend on the plane with the Louis Quatorze crowd. It saves time and money, right?

In any case, see WIMBLEHACK GLOSSARY to learn the final definition of a Tumulty. She is still seriously ugly and advances automatically, rendering Cal Thomas's desperate, Simon-and-Garfunkel-bashing attempt to advance ("The Third Debate," October 14) meaningless.

HOWARD FINEMAN (4), *NEWSWEEK*
Def.
JILL ZUCKMAN, *CHICAGO TRIBUNE*

In his MSNBC "Web Exclusive Commentary" after the third debate, Howard Fineman made the observation—an observation widely commented upon in the broadcast media in subsequent days—that there were "no laughs but gasps" in the press room when Kerry brought up Dick Cheney's daughter in response to a question about whether homosexuals are born or made.

Now, I've been in filing rooms with that same crowd of campaign journalists Fineman is talking about. I can report that the campaign press will gasp at a lot of things: empty buffet trays, poor hotel accommodations (the cut-rate motel choices of the Dean campaign elicited astonishment among some regulars), the face of Dennis Kucinich, the presence of alternative media, the platform of Ralph Nader.

About the only time the national political press doesn't gasp is when the illiterate president of the United States stands up and for two fucking consecutive years says that we have to invade Iraq to prevent Saddam Hussein from attacking us with "weapons of mass destruction."

Then, they don't gasp. Then they stiffen up in their seats like altar boys and say, "Really? No shit, Mr. President? Call on me, Mr. President! I'll ask you how your faith guides you in this difficult time! How long should we let the inspections drag on, Mr. President? What about those goddamned French, Mr. President?"

The press room gasps at things like the Kerry lesbian-baiting ploy because it's the kind of vicious celebrity twaddle they're sensitive to, twaddle they consider themselves experts and authorities on. If someone makes what they consider a "mistake" on that turf, they dive on it like pigs converging on a watermelon rind. But if a politician drives the country off a cliff, they sit on their hands, waiting for Zogby and the Brookings Institution to give them their gasping cues. A gasp in the press room is as meaningless as a standing ovation at an Amway convention.

Incidentally, Fineman in that piece also wrote:

"Still, what was Kerry's point in hauling her into a discussion of the pros and cons of gay marriage. . . . Was he trying to say that Cheney should actively oppose it because of his daughter? Cheney and Kerry actually seem to share the same views."

Actually, this isn't the case. Cheney supported the Defense of Marriage Act in 1996, while Kerry opposed it. Furthermore, while Cheney says he "personally" opposes the Federal Marriage Amendment, he's still running with and supporting the candidate who favors it. However you feel about that issue, the two men definitely have different stances on it.

As for Zuckman—forget Zuckman. Fineman advances; *Newsweek* to meet *Time* in the Final Four.

ELISABETH BUMILLER (3), *NEW YORK TIMES*
Def.
JODI WILGOREN, *NEW YORK TIMES*

Any young journalist working the campaign trail for the first time will quickly learn how to spot the *New York Times* reporter on the plane. Unfailingly, the *Times* guy is the one sitting in the pole position at the front aisle seat just behind the candidate and his entourage, and in crowds he's the one with the four-foot rod up his ass who pushes everybody out of the way to get to the front because he's the *New York Times,* goddammit.

Times reporters are allowed to act this way because of the still-lingering public perception that the paper is some kind of divine standard-bearer for journalistic ethics and excellence. They work hard to maintain this perception. It is clearly part of the *Times* reporter's job to (a) appear at all times to be a walking definition of stringent, humorless professionalism; and (b) to radiate contempt for amateurs, interlopers, and trash-peddlers like Rush Limbaugh and Rupert Murdoch.

There may have been something to this at one time, but not anymore. No paper is quicker to surf in the wake of some unsubstantiated blog tremor than the *Times.* The paper does this in a funny way. It gets the blog smear in print by covering the "phenomenon" of the Net rumor as though the existence of the rumor itself met their tough newsworthiness standards. This is a nice way to get around the problem of making sure a thing is true or newsworthy before you put it in print. Incidentally, it's exactly what bloggers do.

This has been going on for a while, at least since they were scooped by vile Net creature Matt Drudge in the Lewinsky business. Mainstream news organizations have apparently decided in the post-Lewinsky era that they are not going to cede the lucrative media territory of Unsubstantiated Bullshit to amateurs. And so what they do is fly at low altitude, above the fray as it were, and then swoop down and report the hell out of the "phenomenon" as soon as some Internet donnybrook gets loud enough to sell papers with.

As a result, rumors that have no business making it into print get into print on a regular basis. And the *Times* is worse on this score than anyone. Hell, Sheryl Gay Stolberg of the *Times* was one of the only mainstream reporters to so much as touch the obviously bullshit Drudge story about Kerry's alleged Mistress in Africa ("Clark Comes Aboard Kerry Campaign," February 14), running Kerry's irritated denial of a "charge posted . . . on the Web site of Internet gossip columnist Matt Drudge." That's the *Times* in a nutshell: snootily making sure readers don't forget that Drudge is a mere "gossip columnist," then relaying Drudge's gossip themselves.

Bumiller has done the same thing with her October 18 piece, "Talk of Bubble Leads to Battle over Bulge." This is the *Times* devoting 805 words to the Internet rumors about Bush allegedly having worn a transmitter during the debates that would allow him to receive cues from advisors. The story is remarkable because it is probably the first instance of a reporter having the balls to justify the publication of a factually dicey article on the grounds of its being a literary trope. Harold Bloom would be proud:

> The bulge—the strange rectangular box visible between the president's shoulder blades in the first debate—has set off so much frenzied speculation on the Internet that it has become what literary critics call an objective correlative, or an object that evokes large emotions and ideas.

Bumiller doesn't do any reporting in the piece; she just gets denials from a few Bush spokesmen and a pair of gloating quotes from Terry McAuliffe.

Is the Bulge story newsworthy? Sure—if it's true. If it's true, it's a terrific story. But that used to be the reporter's job: to make that determination. It used to be that the difference between a reporter and some half-wit with a can of spray paint was that the reporter had to either prove a thing or leave it alone. Not anymore. This is not your daddy's *New York Times*.

As for Wilgoren, fair is fair. She advanced last week for not interviewing ordinary people, and she went right out in this round and did a let's-talk-to-the-people piece for her post-debate wrap-up, interviewing more noncampaign creatures in one article ("After 3 Debates, Some Voters Remain on Fence," October 13) than she had in the previous two months. She drops out; Bumiller steams on to her first Final Four appearance.

JAMES BENNET, *NEW YORK TIMES*
Def.
GORM VOELVER, *POLITIKEN*

The *press* would first like to express its disappointment that Bennet could not find space for the words *throbbing man-shaft* in this sentence from his last post-debate wrap-up ("Wherein Bush Turns That Frown Upside Down," October 15):

Mr. Bush skirted the rock-hard positions favored by his base to plant his flag deep in the mushy middle ground once held by President Bill Clinton.

Look at how much better that works if you write it this way:

Mr. Bush planted his rock-hard throbbing man-shaft up to the base, deep in the mushy middle ground under the skirt once held by President Clinton.

That is a completely different story, and probably a better one.

Bennet had another painful week. Tossed again into the steaming shit-cauldron of post-debate analysis, Bennet was forced once more to hurl figurative ballast over the beam in a desperate attempt to fill word count when he apparently had nothing to say. His spasms of twittering alliteration ("cozy cocoons," "campaign comity") were, like the boils that suddenly appear on the foot of a terminal cancer patient, the least of his problems. In a desperate attempt to find evidence that there was something different about the third debate as opposed to the first two, Bennet even resorted to interviewing *Saturday Night Live* actor Seth Meyers to ask how his interpretation of Kerry had changed over the course of the debates. This broke new ground in the profession. Campaign journalists frequently keep tabs on *Saturday Night Live* routines to fill space, but to go out and actually get talking-head reaction quotes from the actors—as one would with a Heritage analyst—that's unprecedented.

At another point, Bennet turned the observation that Bush had conducted part of the debate with a white spot on his lip—a strange thing to appear in a *New York Times* analysis to begin with—into a violently unfunny joke about Laura Bush using semaphore signals. Then there was this passage:

> It seemed right that for this debate on domestic affairs, the two men met in an arena, the Grady Gammage Memorial Auditorium at Arizona State University, that was itself based on an unrealized vision for Iraq. Frank Lloyd Wright based the hall on his design for an opera house in Baghdad that was never built.

Bennet used the word *right* instead of *fitting* in that first sentence to deflect attention from the fact that he'd written almost exactly the same passage two weeks before. Wimblehack fans may recall Bennet's first post-debate analysis, which contained this rhapsody to the emerald grass of the University of Miami:

> It seemed fitting that this clash of contrasts took place on the campus of the University of Miami, where sun-toasted students in bikinis and flip-flops strolled today across emerald grass past police barricades and scanning machines.

Apparently this is one of Bennet's pet tricks for eating up fifty or sixty words with modifiers and historical data. In fact, if you go back and look, you'll find this same construction in dead spots in Bennet's work from time to time. Take this passage from a piece last year about Bush's visit to Jordan ("Looking Beyond Words," June 5, 2003):

> It seemed fitting that these men took this leadership challenge upon themselves in Aqaba, which translates as "obstacle." They met down the beach from the ruins of a fort captured in 1917 by Lawrence of Arabia during a previous attempt to reshape the Middle East.

I sympathize with Bennet—it's hard for an intelligent person to come up with anything at all to say about the debates, and having to do it over and over again in the *New York Times* can't be easy—but he has to advance, because his sufferings are just too funny for the rest of us. That, and the fact that Gorm Voelver, that sneaky Danish bastard, went more than a week without filing. Voelver's last campaign piece, the October 7 "Cheney Er En Overlever," was a little trite in parts—particularly the line about "passe sit job paa grund af hjerteproblemer." But it was a week too late, and anyway, he's no Bennet. He drops out; Bennet in the Final Four.

Next week: It's getting close! Place your bets—next week, it's Round 4!

Round 4: And Then There Were Two

Well, it's here. Finally. In less than one week, we Americans will celebrate one of our grandest traditions, the victory of Tweedledum over Tweedledee. The occasion will be marked by awe and splendor on all sides, as befits a contest in which the leader of the free world is determined by a race to see which Ivy League graduate is quicker to reach for a duck call at the sight of a Reuters photographer.

What did it all mean?

Most publications are holding off on tackling that question until after the election. The *New York Times,* however, ever the teacher's pet who turns in his homework early, already took a whack at it in this past Sunday's "Week in Review" section.

According to the *Times,* the question "What did it all mean?" is to be answered in flow-chart fashion. If Bush wins, the answer is under an Adam Nagourney byline ("Calls to Reinvent a Party," October 24), and goes something like this: that the Democrats blew this election, which was seemingly in hand, means they are completely fucked and will need to reinvent themselves in a hurry if they ever hope to compete with the Republicans. Meanwhile, if Kerry wins, the answer column under the Elisabeth Bumiller byline ("A Confident Opposition," October 24) will tell you that the Republican base, despite defeat, is as strong as ever and will be back kicking ass in no time.

The *Times* columns represent the first fluttering of leaves in what will shortly be a veritable hurricane of this kind of flow-chart analysis. If you're old enough to peel an orange without help, you know exactly the kinds of things that are going to be said in these pieces. If Bush wins on the strength of last-minute get-out-the-vote efforts in Ohio, we will hear that this election showed that Republicans have finally matched the Democrats' grassroots organizational skills.

If Kerry wins, and polls show Floridian undecideds were strongly influenced by negative advertising, this victory is going to be chalked up to the emergence of the 527 as a "political force." You won't see the IF-THEN lines buried in the computer code, but they'll be there in almost every article you'll see between now and January: If Bush wins and if the same red-blue patterns from 2000 hold, then that will mean that the electorate is "hopelessly divided" and that the election threw "two Americas" into relief.

New York Press cheerfully guarantees that nothing that doesn't fit in the flow chart, and that could not be written by a well-trained chimpanzee, will appear in print anywhere in America in the next month. For things to be otherwise would violate the entire spirit of the affair. Newspapers wait until the results are in to tell us what it all meant to avoid having to confess to what they've all known from the start: that the American presidential election is a gigantic exercise in conventional thinking, in which, no matter what the numerical outcome, the real result is always a sea of slaves cheering the walloping defeat of originality at the hands of craven mediocrity.

It might be that some of us in the media-criticism business have read too much Marx. Or maybe too much Lincoln. Ralph Nader certainly has. Like most of the Earnest Young Idealists who marched against the war in the past year or so (I was one of them), Nader insists, as an article of faith, that the chief reason America's politics are so bankrupt of meaning is that the people are misinformed. Ralph is fond of quoting Lincoln, who said that if people are brought the "real facts" then they "can be depended upon to meet any national crisis." In this worldview, the true villains of our national politics are the representatives of the commercial media, who bring us not facts but reams of horseshit about which guy has a better haircut, is smoother at ordering a Philly cheese steak, or has a more genuine-looking tan.

That might be giving the people too much credit. Certainly there is plenty of evidence that Americans, when it comes to politics anyway, have always been a group of spineless goons motivated primarily by a hatred of ideas and the fear that a superior person might end up as their leader. It can't be only the media's fault that we are the only people on Earth who demand that our leaders be as dumb as we are.

If Albert Einstein ran for president, we'd make him do photo ops at bowling alleys, eat baskets of french fries, and visit the Redskins training camp. And once he gave in to that, we'd have another list of demands. no more talk about physics, a round of target practice at Camp Lejeune, and a stint juggling lemons with Jimmy Fallon on *Saturday Night Live*.

And if Einstein were still standing in late October after eighteen months of this treatment, the only thing ingenious left about him would be his name. Otherwise, he'd be exactly what we have left for a candidate this week: an idiot, compromised and humiliated in a thousand different ways, his only virtue being that he'd proven his acceptance of our orthodoxy by throwing his brains and his personality in a bonfire.

That is what our national elections are all about. It's a gladiatorial spectacle in which individual dignity is ritualistically destroyed over the course of more than a year of constant battering and television exposure. Whether this is a trick of the elite to deliver a frightening object lesson to the population, or whether it represents the actual emotional desire of an impressively mean and stupid citizenry, that's hard to say. Either way, it sucks. And either way, we're going to spend the next two weeks hearing just about every shameless hack in print and on television celebrating this gruesome process as a triumph of democracy and idealism.

Wimblehack, now down to two contestants, will be taking a week off to monitor the finalists during this period. When it returns in two weeks, it will be giving a prize to the winner. You won't want to miss that. The winner, we guarantee you, sure won't.

Without further ado, the semifinal round.

HOWARD FINEMAN (4), *NEWSWEEK*
Def.
KAREN TUMULTY (1), *TIME*

It's not often that you get a perfectly clear example of why the press is best left out of the hands of big business, but we had one last week, and Howard Fineman played a starring role.

Last week, Fineman, who moonlights as an MSNBC analyst, went on *Hardball* to discuss the Ohio election with the BBC's Katty Kay, NBC's Andrea Mitchell, the Alan Colmes-ish Andrew Sullivan of the *New Republic,* and the maestro himself, Chris Matthews. Everyone was friendly, everyone was smiling. Matthews, clearly drooling at the prospect of a neck-and-neck Ohio race, had the ear-to-ear grin of a kid on Christmas morning as he posed the question: in the key battleground state of Ohio, who's got the "big mo' "?

Momentum, that is. In the thousands of "key battleground of Ohio" stories that have appeared in the press in the last few weeks, this is almost always the key angle. Who's winning? And why? Did John Kerry's goose-hunting gambit work? Is Teresa Heinz Kerry's big fucking mouth a liability in Cuyahoga territory? Who, goshdarnit, is going to win Ohio?

Very occasionally in these stories, you will see references to enormous job losses in Ohio's manufacturing sector, but these are always placed within a certain context: if the job-loss numbers are up, this is momentum for Kerry; if they're not so bad, that's momentum for Bush.

What is so amazing is that because of Ohio's significance in the electoral college, we now have the whole country staring right at the very face of our vanishing manufacturing economy, and yet what we're talking about is goose hunting, the widow of Chris Reeve, and the "likability gap." But that happens for a reason.

Virtually every major company in Ohio has had significant layoffs in the last ten years—everyone from Monsanto to OshKosh B'Gosh to AT&T, from Ford to General Motors to Pizza Hut. Even First Energy, the state's chief utility and the culprit in the great blackout a few years ago, has laid off some 200 workers from its nuclear operating company, which has some residents worried about safety, particularly in the wake of an emergency shutdown of a Toledo nuke plant in August. This was after that same plant, Davis-Besse, had an acid leak from its reactor in 2002. (Although you won't hear about that, because both candidates have First Energy lobbyists as leading operatives in their Ohio campaign: Alex Arshinkoff for Bush, James Ruvolo for Kerry.)

In this atmosphere, Ohio municipalities have started giving up the store to any company that even threatens to walk, resulting in a devastated tax base and a spate of absurdly draconian business-welfare deals. The best example is probably Daimler-Chrysler's rape of the city of Toledo; the company got a ten-year tax holiday, free water, free site preparation, even free land (including a neighborhood whose residents were evicted) in return for the mere promise to maintain the current level of job decline at its Toledo site. A circuit court ruled earlier this year that the deal was unconstitutional, but plenty of other Ohio businesses have gotten similar deals.

Few would argue that the chief drivers of a lot of these problems in Ohio are the free-trade agreements. An argument can certainly be made (and it is being made, quite a lot, in the mainstream press) that the decline of the great manufacturing heartland in America was inevitable anyway, and that the trade agreements only offered people from places like Ohio a chance to secure better consumer prices and a chance to open new foreign markets during a transitional labor period.

But there are plenty of other people, like about 99 percent of union members, who believe that agreements like NAFTA and GATT simply made it easier for corporations to take advantage of impoverished labor forces in countries without worker protections—in other words, that the agreements are an end-run around fair wages and labor rights.

Whatever you believe, it's certainly the issue in a place like Ohio, where the economy and the whole culture are changing at the speed of light.

But you can't have a referendum on that issue in Ohio because (a) both candidates are free-traders; (b) because both candidates are free-traders, neither candidate is talking about free trade; and (c) the mainstream media, owned almost exclusively by big protrade companies, is not particularly interested in discussing free trade.

Now, General Electric is a major employer in Ohio. Its subsidiary, General Electric Aircraft Engines, has eliminated some 4,000 jobs, at least 800 of which were from its plant in Evendale, since 9/11. Most of those job losses were chalked up to slumping airline orders after the terrorist attacks, but many of those jobs were exported as well. In general, GE—whose representative at the NAFTA hearings in 1993 told Congress that the pact "could support 10,000 jobs for General Electric and its suppliers. . . . [T]hese jobs depend on the success of this agreement"—has been one of the largest net exporters of NAFTA-related jobs, sending about 3,500 positions overseas in the first seven years of the agreement.

So it stands to reason that neither GE nor its media arm, NBC, is going to spend a lot of time calling public attention to the deleterious effects of the free-trade pacts. Nor is it likely to remark upon the seeming absurdity of a presidential race between two enthusiastically protrade candidates hanging on the voting choices of a state ravaged by manufacturing job losses. Instead, what it does is put a couple of clowns on the air to insist to the public that what Ohioans really want is not a job, or answers, but a man who is "human enough" and "acceptable enough" and will save a baby from a burning building. We bring you Chris Matthews and Howard Fineman:

> MATTHEWS: Howard, you've been out in Ohio covering both these fellas running for president. Who's got the big mo' right now, the momentum?
> FINEMAN: Right now in Ohio, John Kerry is doing better and George Bush has lost some steam in that state. Doubts about the war, one reason. Continuing doubts about the economy are the bigger reason in that industrial state. You go to these rallies, the Kerry people are pumped up. They're excited. Are they excited about John Kerry himself? No. And John Kerry's effort now is to try to make himself at least human enough and acceptable enough to pull those people over

who've already decided they don't want to rehire George Bush for four years. You talk to the Kerry people, they're pumped.

MATTHEWS: So if he saves a baby from a fire this week, he's in good shape.

FINEMAN: He's got to do something like that. Got to do something like that.

Just think about how condescending this whole election process is: big business takes away people's jobs, guts their public services, gives them two procorporate candidates to choose from in the election, and then hires a bunch of fawning mouthpieces to go on television and describe U the voter as a dumb savage who will vote for the first candidate who shows them a cuckoo clock or a shiny new penny. It's amazing that angry mobs don't round up people like Fineman and Matthews and chop their heads off on general principle.

Later on in the same show, Fineman again penetrated the tough issues of the Ohio race:

The question still outstanding is whether Kerry can win it. And Kerry's whole theme the last week and the week ahead is going to be, "Trust me. Let me reassure you or whatever. I'm going to talk about my faith. I'm going to talk about the future. I'm going to be upbeat. Come with me."

It's a good thing there are professional journalism schools. You wouldn't want to leave work like that to amateurs.

Tumulty, meanwhile, didn't file, which is a shame. You hate to see a great champion mail it in. But people have been calling Howard Fineman a worthy contender for years—and now he'll have the chance to prove it. With his fourth straight win, he goes to the big dance; Tumulty drops out.

ELISABETH BUMILLER (3), *NEW YORK TIMES*
Def.
JAMES BENNET, *NEW YORK TIMES*

Reporters have thousands of tricks for avoiding discussion of policy issues in campaign coverage, some more clever than others. The majority of them are obvious and are of the sort that jump out at the public: the constant focus on the *People*-magazine angles about the candidates' looks, their relationships with their wives (how often do they touch in public?), the musical instruments they play, the hobbies they pursue at their respective viceroy retreats, etc.

Unfortunately, we're not yet at the stage where campaigns can be conducted without any mention of policy issues. We're headed in that direction— I'm guessing it's about three elections off, when the Rock decides to make his run against incumbent Tom Hanks—but we're not quite there yet. This puts both candidates and the press in a bind. They're still forced to give at least superficial lip service to the ostensible intellectual purpose of this exercise, but they have to do it in a way that makes it sound like they're not doing it. Fortunately, there are plenty of media innovations to help them out here, and one of the best is the Tumulter-sault.

Named after Karen Tumulty, who pioneered and perfected its use, the Tumulter-sault is a neat little literary device through which reporters refer to "details on the issues" without ever elaborating upon those actual details. The typical way the writer uses this one is to just slip it in, offhand-like, in between the more important details: "Candidate X, who boasts an impressive record on environmental issues, spent the weekend snowmobiling in Jackson Hole with a pair of one-armed Marine veterans. . . ."

Forgetting about Bumiller and Bennet for a moment, it's worth pausing and recognizing Tumulty's contribution to the development of this device. She has always been the best at it, and this year she really set the tone. Take this passage from a piece last month ("Coolness Under Fire," September 20):

> Kerry hardly lacks a platform at home; his health-care and fiscal policies are far more detailed, if less numerous, than Bush's. But the campaign didn't pivot from the past to the future after Boston and then hammer home Kerry's ideas. That left Bush a huge opening—and he reached for it in New York City.

Tumulty has a corollary use of the technique that not only obliquely refers to the existence of complex policy positions without explaining them, but also simultaneously berates the candidates for even bringing them up. Here's an example from a piece in which she wrote about the selection of John Edwards as running mate ("The Gleam Team," July 19). In this one, she highlights Kerry's unfortunate tendency to talk about his policies in polysyllabic detail:

> When he finished, Kerry couldn't resist jumping in with a mini-seminar on trade policy that included references to the fine print of the antidumping and antisurge laws. But at least Kerry answered the question.

The Tumulter-sault is an important innovation because it paves the way for a future in which discussion of "the issues" can be replaced by the actual words *the issues*. With this kind of help from the press, we may soon reach a point at which the candidate who uses the word *environment* more becomes the environmental candidate and the candidate who uses the word *security* more becomes the security candidate. We're not quite there. But thanks to certain reporters, we're well on our way.

Both Bumiller and Bennet pulled Tumulter-saults in recent weeks. Bumiller's was more elaborate. In an October 21 piece she co-wrote with third-round dropout Jodi Wilgoren ("A Blistering Attack by Bush, a Long Indictment by Kerry"), Bumiller managed to relay 1,325 words of Bush-Kerry accusations on security issues without including one detail about what their actual Iraq policies are. In the spaces where those explanations should have come, she and Wilgoren just stuck in Tumulter-saults, as in this passage:

> Mr. Kerry sought to rebut Mr. Bush with a detailed policy speech Wednesday, unusual for this late stage in a campaign. His aides said Mr. Kerry delivered the speech because he must prove himself as an acceptable wartime leader before he can win over undecided voters on domestic issues like health care and embryonic stem-cell research.

This is a good one, confining a "detailed policy speech" to the words *detailed policy speech* in order to leave room for more newsworthy stuff like this:

> Mr. Bush's aides said they were delighted to see Mr. Kerry spend the day discussing national security, the central component of the president's campaign, because they believed it meant he was on the defensive.

Try to imagine that scene. Elisabeth Bumiller is sitting somewhere in Iowa chatting up a Bush aide (or "aides," according to the attribution). One of the aides deadpans: "You know, Elisabeth, we're delighted that Kerry spent the day discussing national security, because that means he's on the defensive."

Bumiller nods seriously, writes it down in her notebook. . . . And then an hour later, she fucking publishes it? Her husband must have to restrain her from taking notes when they go used-car shopping.

Meanwhile, Bennet's Tumulter-sault came in his last debate wrap ("A Television Event That Delivered High Drama and Garnered High Ratings," October 15):

> The 30-second advertisements and prepared texts dropped away as each man, haltingly at times, supplied specific detail on plans for health care and taxes, and a vision of sorts for America's conduct in the world.

Again, this is a classic use of the trick, as "specific detail" is confined to the words *specific detail*. And this might have been enough for Bennet to stay within striking distance of Bumiller in this round, except for one thing: he wrote it two weeks ago. Since the last round, he hasn't filed, which is a shame because Bennet was the breakout star of this tourney.

We hope to see him next time around, if we're not all tending mutant sheep in a post-nuclear desert by then. In any case, New Yorkers will have at least one championship contestant this week, as Bumiller will attempt to pick up Brian Cashman with a win in the finals. Does the *Times* have what it takes to win? Find out in two weeks!

The Sad End

You were sure that Spot could live for another year at least. The kids still loved him. . . . But those cloudy spots over his eyes just got too big, and he was walking into the refrigerator and the brick edge of the fireplace just a little too often.

Then there were those wheezing fits, the ones that kept waking you and the wife up in the middle of the night and throwing the both of you into a tiresome panic. Do you call the vet? Is there even a vet to call at 3 A.M.? What moral calculus applies, in the middle of the night, to the adult owners of a dying Shar-Pei with glowing green pus in his eyes?

The time comes when you and the wife have to send the kids off to school and take an unscheduled trip to that little one-story clinic downtown. Make that one last handshake with Dr. Bernstein, and stroke Spot's head as he cheerfully lays down on the table and waits for the needle. . . .

Such is the situation with Wimblehack, which comes to an end this week in highly unsatisfactory fashion. The much-hyped prize to the winner is going to have to be put off, for now, for a variety of reasons. For one thing, the *Press* had felt quite confident that the winner would ultimately prove to be *Newsweek*'s Howard Fineman, and had staked much of its prize plans (which failed, hilariously, anyway) in that direction.

But Fineman never filed an election postmortem for *Newsweek*, and aside from a few cautiously irritating exchanges with Joe Scarborough in which he disingenuously defended Maureen Dowd as his "favorite highbrow hussy," Fineman kept a very low profile after the election. There was no rationally defensible way to declare him the winner, except on the basis of his cumulative record. And that would have been a cop-out even worse than the already egregious cop-out this final round is going to represent.

That leaves as the winner Elisabeth Bumiller of the *New York Times*, who did file a number of grossly objectionable pieces after the election, and so wins the contest, though not yet the prize. And though this contest fails in its stated objective of delivering a just reward, we can say with a clear conscience that Bumiller deserved her hollow victory, for consistently representing almost everything that made this campaign the Monumental Bummer that it was.

On November 7, reverting to her pre-campaign state as a *Times* White House correspondent, Bumiller filed her first large post-election article. Entitled "President Feels Emboldened, Not Accidental, After Victory," the piece was pleased to draw a number of conclusions about the sunny state of the re-elected executive's mind. She writes:

> One trademark of President Bush's first term was his aversion to news conferences, which his staff says he often treated like trips to the dentist. So on the morning after Mr. Bush's re-election, Dan Bartlett, the White House communications director, was taken aback when the president told him he was ready to hold a news conference that Mr. Bartlett had suggested, win or lose, the week before.
> "I didn't have to convince him or anything," Mr. Bartlett said. "Without me prompting him, he brought it up."
> It was a small but telling change for a president whose re-election has already had a powerful effect on his psyche, his friends and advisers say.

This habit of taking at face value the unconfirmable assertions about the personal feelings of officials—assertions hand-delivered to the journalist by a paid mouthpiece whose very job it is to deadpan preposterous pieces of mythmaking to the media—is nothing new to most political reporters. But almost no one consumes this stuff more eagerly than Bumiller.

Take her piece from March 2 of this year, "Gay Issue Leaves Bush Ill at Ease," in which Bumiller gives off-the-record spokesmen a chance to allow Bush to split the difference on the gay-marriage issue:

> When President George W. Bush announced his support last week for a constitutional amendment banning gay marriage, his body language in the Roosevelt Room did not seem to match his words. Bush may have forcefully defended the

union of a man and a woman as "the most fundamental institution of civilization," but even some White House officials said he appeared uncomfortable.

This kind of thing is standard in the business—it is how we are delivered such seemingly unknowable facts as the "remarkably close friendship" we are told exists between Bush and Vladimir Putin—but what's striking about Bumiller is that this is apparently her conscious response to an administration whose excessive secrecy she has complained about in public.

On December 3, 2003, Bumiller gave a talk at Yale University nauseatingly entitled "Shock, Awe, and Battle Fatigue," in which she complained about the lack of access in the Bush White House.

"The White House has set a troubling standard for secrecy," she said. "I worry that future administrations will look at this White House as a model that has worked fairly well."

Bumiller went on to laud the administration's "genius" in interpersonal relations, adding: "The White House is awesomely good at what it does. . . . The political skills of the president and his handlers are unparalleled."

This speech came just days after Bumiller had experienced a very public slap in the face by that same White House, which took the extraordinary step of sending Bush on a surprise trip to Baghdad on Thanksgiving with a handpicked contingent of reporters. In a move that was widely interpreted as payback for the paper's insufficiently slavish reporting on the Iraq war, the Bush people conspicuously left the *Times* and Bumiller off the plane for that trip. Characteristically, however, rather than giving back in kind by ignoring the Bush PR stunt or burying it in an inside page, the *Times* responded by having Bumiller write a front-page story about it, accompanied up top by the famous turkey photo in full color.

How did she write the story? The same way she always covered the White House, and went on to cover the campaign: she took what was given to her, in this case the pool report of the *Washington Post*'s Mike Allen.

The pool report allowed her, she said, to write about the trip "vividly, as if I had been [there]." Her "vivid" descriptions of the dramatic journey she did not actually go on included inspired passages of pastoral magnificence like the following:

> Air traffic controllers in Baghdad did not know the plane heading for the runway was Air Force One, and it then landed without its lights in darkness, but for a sliver of moon.

Far from being insulted at not having been invited, Bumiller told her Yale audience that the Bush trip was "brilliant politics." She made sure to point out to the audience that the *Times* had taken care to insert in her article a passage explaining that the piece had been based on the account of another writer. "That was a good addition, and it is in essence truth in packaging," she said, adding that it was "inserted largely because of the changes at the paper since the catastrophe of Jayson Blair."

This is ironic again because, as noted previously in this contest, no reporter in the campaign was more consistently guilty of violating the Jayson Blair Test than Bumiller. In this particular campaign-journalism fixture, reporters file campaign pieces from remote state locations even though the entire article could have been written from a burned-out crackhouse 2,000 miles away, using nothing but a glimpse of a photo from the event and a Rolodex with which to call friendly campaign aides.

The typical Bumiller campaign piece showed some version of that same "sliver of moon" imagery and sandwiched it around a lot of quotes from trail regulars—who often, again, provided primarily apocryphal insights into the mindset of the president that could then be credulously reported to the public as fact by the Greatest Newspaper in the World.

In one of her last campaign-trail pieces ("Entering the Homestretch with a Smile," November 1), Bumiller followed this formula exactly. Ostensibly the action takes place in two sites in Pennsylvania and New Hampshire, but all we see of the locations is some more (literally) pastoral descriptive stuff in the lede:

Late last week at a campaign rally in a dark Pennsylvania pasture, thousands of supporters listened raptly to President Bush and then watched fireworks explode overhead. But other pyrotechnics were going off in a distant corner, where a giant scrum of reporters ignored the candidate but hung on to every word of a bombastic, deceptively cherub-faced man Democrats love to hate.

He was Karl Rove, the president's political adviser. . . .

In this particular article Bumiller uses a technique that my research indicates is peculiar to her alone. In this passage, she actually swallows an apocryphal story from one aide about *another* apocryphal story about a *different* aide's apocryphal relationship to the president. This is Bumiller, reporting from the unseen alien planet New Hampshire, quoting Karen Hughes telling a story about Karl Rove talking to George Bush:

> Other times Mr. Rove likes to playfully withhold news of recent polls from the president. "He'll smile and say, 'I'm not going to tell you about the latest numbers,' but he'll have a big smile on his face," Ms. Hughes said.

Bumiller told her Yale audience last year: "What I write about is really important. Ninety-five percent of it is interesting, and 30 percent of it is absolutely riveting." One wonders which percentile this insight about Rove falls under.

All campaign journalists fall into the habit of writing long personality pieces about the "man-behind-the-man" figures they spend so much time with on the campaign. In the last two years there were probably ten times over more profiles of Stephanie Cutter and Ken Mehlman and Rove and Karen Hughes and Joe Trippi and Chris Lehane and Ralph Reed than there were of laid-off workers, prisoners, illegal immigrants, the uninsured, or any of the other mysterious categories of depressing individuals ostensibly involved in the election.

Obviously, this was a crime in itself of sorts, as the campaign press focused a lot more on the optimistic, self-justifying soap opera of the campaign itself than on the country's actual political problems. The campaign press was consistently far more fascinated with the drama and the trimmings of power than it was with, say, nuclear safety or how people who collect AFDC checks live. That's why the only time you saw a profile of a "working-class Catholic girl" was when it was Karen Tumulty writing about Mary Beth Cahill, the "miracle worker" who brought back John Kerry's campaign from the dead.

Now, if you're like me, you probably don't give a shit about the fact that Mary Beth Cahill honed her political reflexes at her working-class Boston dinner table, where she was the bossy older sister in a family of six. But if you think that's irrelevant, try giving a shit about the inner life of the presidential *tailor*, Georges de Paris, whom Bumiller amazingly profiled just a week after the election, when half of the population was still trying to talk itself down from the ledge in the wake of the horrifying result.

Here's Bumiller quoting de Paris on November 8:

"I love all the presidents, but President Bush is something more special," Mr. de Paris said Friday, perhaps employing the principle that it is best to have the sitting president as No. 1. "He makes you happy."

More insights, just days after Bush's re-election:

Mr. de Paris would not say how many suits he had made for the president, although he did say that he was responsible for a dark blue-on-blue stripe that Mr. Bush wore for his "axis of evil" State of the Union address in 2002. The president, he added, likes full-cut trousers and his hand-sewn white Sea Island cotton and French blue shirts. . . . As Mr. de Paris spoke, he sewed a lining with rapid, precisely placed stitches into a new suit for the secretary of commerce, Donald L. Evans, a close friend of the president. Hand-sewn suits, Mr. de Paris said, take three full days to make and are far more supple than those made by machine. "It's the difference between filet mignon and hamburger," he said.

Well, I guess if the administration won't tell you anything about why it invaded Iraq, and if you don't feel like making a fuss about it, you might as well find out who made that blue-on-blue stripe suit Bush wore during his "Axis of Evil" speech. Jesus Christ!

Bumiller, of course, was not completely immune to concerns about the lack of substance in the campaign. She demonstrated that most forcefully when she was one of the moderators of a live televised debate of Democratic candidates, held in New York on February 29, 2004.

You may remember that one: Bumiller was one of three journalists, along with Dan Rather and Andrew Kirtzman of WCBS, who moderated the last meaningful Democratic debate. At the time, there were only four candidates left: Kerry, Edwards, Sharpton, and Kucinich. The debate was remarkable because of the obviousness with which the three panelists tried to steer the discussion away from Sharpton and Kucinich. Early in the debate, Bumiller cut Sharpton off in the middle of one of his answers, about Haiti. When she tried it again later on, Sharpton protested:

> SHARPTON: If we're going to have a discussion just between two—in your arrogance (ph), you can try that, but that's one of the reasons we're going to have delegates, so that you can't just limit the discussion. And I think that your attempt to do this is blatant, and I'm going to call you out on it, because I'm not going to sit here and be window dressing.
> BUMILLER: Well, I'm not going to be addressed like this.

And Bumiller made it clear later on that the press was not going to be pushed around, when in an exchange with Kerry she angrily insisted on the right to make political labels an issue in the campaign:

> BUMILLER: Can I just change the topic for a minute, just ask a plain political question?
> The National Journal, a respected, nonideologic publication covering Congress, as you both know, has just rated you, Senator Kerry, number one, the most liberal senator in the Senate.
> [to Edwards] You're number four.

How can you hope to win with this kind of characterization, in this climate?

KERRY: Because it's a laughable characterization. It's absolutely the most ridiculous thing I've ever seen in my life.

BUMILLER: Are you a liberal?

KERRY: Let me just . . .

BUMILLER: Are you a liberal?

KERRY: . . . to the characterization. I mean, look, labels are so silly in American politics. . . .

BUMILLER: But, Senator Kerry, the question is . . .

KERRY: I know. You don't let us finish answering questions.

BUMILLER: You're in New York.

This question—how can you hope to win, if you're so liberal—was what sank Howard Dean, was what allowed the press to ignore Sharpton and Kucinich, and was what ultimately made it impossible for opponents to the war to have a voice in this campaign. In most cases, this demonization of the word and witch-hunting of anyone who could be attached to it were subtle things whose effects were cumulative. But Bumiller brought it right out into the open, wore it like a badge of honor. And looked like a smug, barking cow doing it.

One of the most pervasive themes of the post-electoral wrap-ups was the relentless focus on the seeming geographical intractability of the political red-and-blue picture. Nearly every newspaper in the country led with one version or another of the "a nation bitterly divided" theme, which within a day or two morphed smoothly into the next round of postmortems speculating on the prospects for Bush to "unite" this wounded nation (Bumiller did one of these, incidentally).

Almost every part of the country woke up the morning after the election to see a journalist on its local daily's front page sounding this "divisiveness" theme:

"Now, as Bush, 58, looks forward to a second term, he leads a nation as bitterly divided as ever over the bruising presidential election campaign. . . ."

wrote David Greene of the *Baltimore Sun*. "The country is still divided, bitterly divided, and [Bush's] plans controversial and not proven," countered *Newsday*. "The nation may be as bitterly divided as ever, but this one is in the books," sighed the *Lincoln (Nebraska) Journal-Star*, seemingly in relief.

And it must be admitted that some attention was given to the relationship of the media to this divisive picture. There was some hand-wringing in the press about some errors it might have made in covering the election, although as in the case of the Iraq war, it was all the wrong kind of hand-wringing.

Much attention, for instance, was given to the apparent fact, supported by exit polls, that journalists had underestimated the role "moral values" had played in determining the election. No less an authority than Howard Fineman was one of many who asserted that the media was out of touch with mainstream America, and even offered his own mea culpa on that score. Journalists "don't understand red-state America," he said, adding, "I'm an indicted co-conspirator."

But the unanswered question in all of this was—if the nation was so bitterly divided, how come the campaign press corps wasn't? Why did they all look so charged up by the whole thing on television? Why did it seem like, no matter what they might have said as pundits on-camera, they were all such buddies off-camera? Why was an avowed Bush-lover like Howard Fineman sticking up for Maureen Dowd on MSNBC? Jon Stewart aside, was there *anyone* out there in the business who took this election personally enough to risk pissing off a colleague over it?

The answer is no, not a one. It was all a game to these people, which is why they covered it like a game. There were some people I know personally out there who hated it, who felt guilty about being part of the whole ugly charade. But there were a lot more who were really proud of this life of free lunches, VIP seating, and the chance to be the planted audience for the occasional dick joke in an off-the-record chat with some of the hired liars on Air Force One. The maintenance of these privileges for certain people dwarfed the more abstract matter of which millions down there on the ground won or, more to the point, which ones lost.

How do you decide who's the country's Worst Campaign Journalist? Well, the one who loves his or her job the most is probably a good candidate. Why not the reporter whose first cheerful thought after the election was the hand-sewn suit of Don Evans? The *Press* apologizes for having no prize for Elisabeth Bumiller, but hopes readers will allow us time to try to make amends. We have four more years, after all.

ALL
YOU
NEED
IS

10

THE NEXT STEP
Why the Blue States Are Blue

But we have to face facts: We got our clocks cleaned up and down the ballot. . . . If, as the DLC has long argued, the test for Democrats is to convince voters that they will defend their country, share their values, and champion their economic interests, it's pretty clear Democrats continue to come up short on the first two tests even as they pass the third with flying colors.
—Statement by the Democratic Leadership Committee
in the wake of Kerry's defeat

Well, that was the DLC's conclusion after the fiasco we all watched on television last week. Apparently the Democrats failed to convince America that (a) they're as badass as the Republicans, and (b) they believe that the return of the baby Jesus to earth is imminent, and that we're doing a good enough job of making sure the guest accommodations will be to his liking.

If history is any guide, the DLC will spend the next four years trying to find a pious bomb-thrower to put up as the nominee—unless, of course, the poll numbers in a few years' time show that Barack Obama is good-looking, black, and charming enough to get the party over the hump using the same basic playbook that worked so swimmingly this time.

Those are the DLC's conclusions. Whether the conclusions of the rest of us count at all is, of course, a matter of serious debate. As this past election season showed, the dominant factors in giving us the candidates we got had a lot more to do with the internal thinking of party hacks and the media than the feelings of the actual public. There is still really no evidence that a ground-up phenomenon is building anywhere on the anti-Bush side that will ever mobilize seriously to do anything beyond wave the flag for whichever zombie the DLC chooses to hand to us as the next champion of middle-of-the-road faux-pragmatism.

There is going to be a lot of talk in the next months and years about "soul-searching" within the Democratic Party. Indeed, the DLC referred overtly to this phenomenon already, in its post-election memorandum. Here's how they put it:

> The slow but significant erosion of Democratic support in recent years is a collective responsibility for all Democrats, us included. It will not be reversed by any simple, mechanical move to the "left" or the "right"; by any new infusion of cash or grassroots organizing; by any reshuffling of party institutions or their leadership; or by any magically charismatic candidates. That's why engaging in any "struggle for the soul of the party," or any assignment of blame, is such a waste of time.

The key phrase here is the *collective responsibility for all Democrats,* which is where the key lie of the election postmortem is going to reside. When this kind of talk is fed to us, most people who are Democrats (as I am not, incidentally) are going to accept unquestioningly the idea that this "struggle for the soul of the party" is *their* problem. In fact, this struggle is really exclusively the problem of the Democratic Party, a very different thing. Because for the rest of us, for the ones who woke up Wednesday morning staring a four-year shit sandwich in the face . . . we have another problem. We have our own souls to worry about, and this is a much bigger problem than the soul of the Democratic Party, an organization that would be purified by fire on live television if we lived in a more just era.

The Republicans won last week—let's face it—because they stand for something that voters can understand. A large number of them stand for being deranged lunatics who believe that the Bible was the last book ever written, and for being intellectual cowards who hide from the terrifying complexities of modern society by placing all of their beliefs in infantile concepts like faith, force, and patriotism.

Our handicap, to which they are immune, is to understand that modern society is a machine that can operate seamlessly according to its own peculiarly twisted morality without obviously interfering with the advance of those concepts they consider important.

That makes it easy for us to understand why such things as the Iraq war are not only disastrous and immoral but also simply stupid policy, and guaranteed to weaken our country in the long run. But it does not make it easy for us to sum up what we ourselves stand for in a word or two.

Because we don't know. When we look to the future, we don't know what we hope to see. The other side is energized because its vision of the future is clear; it wants a return to the days when the one organizing concept of sexual relations was marriage for life, when patriotism was putting on a uniform and fighting for freedom abroad, when the goal of life was a good job, hard work, kids, the church, a house, and a well-attended funeral.

These are all reasonable goals to have when you know heaven is at the end of it all. That's what it comes down to. They're fighting for a simple path to heaven, while the rest of us are fighting for something a little less exciting: the desire to have a more rational and inoffensive political atmosphere within which to wrestle with the underlying problem of existential despair in a confusing secular world whose only offered paradises are affluence, sexual freedom, and consumer choice.

What's ironic is that a lot of what motivated the progressive sector within and even outside the Democratic Party this time around was a rebellion against this very set of circumstances. Certainly there was an intellectual basis for a lot of the anticorporate anger that goaded people onto the streets in the past years—legitimate disgust over the idea that the honest jobs that used to be held by Americans had been exported abroad, where Asian children working for pennies an hour stitched together the sneakers we all bring to the gym—but it went deeper than that. There was a lot of anger out there at the underlying concept that the ultimate purpose of life is to acquire *things,* that the answer society provides to each of our personal problems is a product.

Most of us are aware and despairing on some level that our lives have become de-eroticized, that love and romance are not all around us but have to be hunted for with the kind of desperation that people used to bring when they went west looking for gold. But the answers that society gives us for this sexual desert are Viagra and Cialis and Levitra, products that allow us to stay hard for hours as we hump the indifferent mannequins we run into in bars. The country is lonely *and* self-obsessed, and the individual members of the population are offered a thousand ways to improve their individual appearance and vigor: but there seems to be no solution on the horizon that anyone is offering to bring us more together, to give us the things we really *need:* love and acceptance and community.

We blame corporate America for this state of affairs because this ideology of individual acquisitiveness is the religion it naturally preaches. But it's our failure to come up with a competing ideology of getting along that's the real problem. Because down south, in those "backward" red states, they vote the way they do because they see this individualistic religion as a creature of the cold, greedy north, which has chosen to attack the idiocy of the right-wing church rather than admit to its own spiritual unhappiness.

Bush is our fault. He's our fault because too many of us found it easier to hate him than find a way to love each other. If we work on the second thing a little harder, we won't need to rely on the cynics in the DLC to come up with the right "formula" the next time around. Because happiness and hope have a way of selling themselves.

EPILOGUE

Christmas Eve—or was it Christmas morning already? In retrospect I can't be really sure of the time. I'd woken up in the middle of the night to go to the bathroom. Thirty-four-years-old, and this already happens to me fairly regularly

There was a light on in the kitchen. And a noise coming from in there. From the end of the hallway I could see shadows on the wall.

Somebody was in my house.

I took off the towel rack in the bathroom and crept down the hall. Nothing in the world is more ridiculous than a liberal arts graduate in possession of a weapon. At the kitchen entrance, I paused, then jumped in.

There he was, just sitting there. Eating from a plate of chocolate chip cookies that my mother, bless her soul, had sent me for the holidays.

"Santa Claus!" I shouted.

"Oh—ho, ho, ho!" he bellowed. "You've caught me, sonny. I must be slipping."

"Aw, heck," I said. "That's okay, Santa! I just can't believe it's you!"

"Oh, it's me, all right," he said, chuckling. "Did you have any doubts, my boy? Didn't you always know there was a *Santa Claus?*"

His beard was like a newborn lamb! His voice was like a barrel of root beer! There really was a Santa Claus!

"Well, gosh, Santa," I said. "I have to admit, I've had my doubts. I work in the media!"

"Well," he said. "That's okay, my boy. That's okay, my good man. Say, is it all right that I took a cookie?"

"Is it okay?" I said. "Heck, Santa, take the whole plate!"

"Thanks," he said. "I don't mind if I do take just a few." And then he took two big cookies and shoved them into his big wonderful mouth. "Mmm, mmm," he said. "These are delicious cookies, just delicious. I bet your mother made them."

"Actually, she did," I said. "My mother is an excellent cook."

"And a good person, too, I bet," he said.

I smiled. "Well, jeez, Santa," I said. "Aren't all mothers good people?"

"Right you are, my son, right you are," he said. He cleared his throat and got up. "Hey, listen," he said. "Would you mind if I used your bathroom? I've got to take a shit."

I raised an eyebrow, then smiled. "Well, of course, Santa," I said. "Be my guest. It's right down the hall."

"Thanks," he said. Then, picking up his sack, he started toward the bathroom. "Lotta cookies tonight, you know?"

"Yeah, I understand," I said.

He made it three steps before he stopped suddenly, with his back to me.

"Christ," he whispered.

"Santa?" I said.

"Oh, Christ," he said, dropping his sack. From behind I could see that he was clutching his heart.

I rushed to his side. "Hey," I said, snapping my fingers. "Hey, are you okay?"

"My heart!" he shouted. "My motherfucking heart!"

"Your heart? What's wrong with your heart?" I said. "What can I do?"

"It's—heart attack—death!" he croaked.

"Heart attack?" I said. "But how? Oh, God—should I call for help?"

For one brief moment, he came to. He looked me in the eyes with a fiendish glare and then, teeth gritted, he reached out and grabbed the sleeve of my T-shirt. "You!" he gasped. "You—bitch!"

Then he fell to the ground. I leaned over and listened to his chest. He wasn't breathing!

For a moment I stood there frozen, not knowing what to do. At first I raced to the phone, then quickly thought better of it and went to my window. Throwing it open, I thrust my head out and screamed.

"Hey!" I said. "Hey, help! Santa's dying! He's not breathing!"

From down on Fifty-seventh Street a voice shouted upward. "Shut up, you asshole!"

"No, I'm serious!" I shouted back. "Santa Claus is in my house! He's sick or something!"

Just then I heard a noise behind me. The door to my apartment burst open and in rushed half a dozen elves. They were dressed in officious-looking green uniforms. Two of them had sidearms and stayed by the door. The other four rushed to Santa's side.

"He was just—" I began.

"Don't move," said one of the armed elves. "Just stay right where you are."

"But—"

"Just be quiet. We'll hear it all later."

The four elves were apparently administering CPR. I couldn't be sure, but I got the impression they'd been through this before. The process went on for a good five minutes. At last one of them delivered a final blow to Santa's naked chest—they'd torn his coat open—leaned over, took a listen, then sagged.

"He's dead," the elf said.

"My God," I whispered.

"You killed Santa Claus," the doctor-elf said.

I shook my head. "Me—I *what?*" I said. "No, you don't understand. He was on his way to the bathroom, and he just had a heart attack! I didn't touch him, I swear!"

"Why did you do it?" the elf said.

"But I didn't do it," I said. "He just collapsed. Honest!"

The doctor-elf winced and gazed deeply into my eyes. After a pause lasting ten long seconds, he gave a snort and nodded to the two guard-elves.

"Arrest him," he said.

The two guard-elves pulled revolvers from their holsters and took aim. They fired—some kind of stun gun, a Taser . . .

I fell to the ground and blacked out.

Night. In this room I can see the time on a clock on the wall. It reads 11:21 P.M. There is a barred window high up in one corner, rimmed along the bottom with snow, but it is useless for telling the hour. It is always dark outside here. I must be at the North Pole.

I am seated on an iron chair in front of a table, stripped to the waist and wrists handcuffed to the chair arms. There are two elves in the room with me. One, who I've nicknamed Igor, is a twisted creature with a harelip who stands in the corner and does nothing but spray water on me with a hose from time to time. The other elf is the one who does the talking. He is dressed from top to bottom in black leather and he smokes from a cigarette holder.

I know this elf 's name. He calls himself Dr. Kimmelstein. He has been torturing me now for six weeks.

"Let's go through this again," he said, flipping a page of a legal pad. "And no lying this time, okay? You know how I hate it when you lie."

"No lying, Dr. Kimmelstein, I promise," I whispered.

"Good," he said. Then, lighting a fresh cigarette, he began. "Okay. Now, on the day Santa arrived in your home, what had you been doing?"

"Okay," I said. "I know that. I was working."

"On what?" he said.

"Um, on a book," I said. "I was finishing my book."

"Finishing it?"

"Yes," I whispered. "It was late. I was about two months past deadline. I was in real trouble and I was really struggling."

"Struggling, I see," he said, making a notation. "Struggling with what?"

"The ending," I said. "I was supposed to be writing an epilogue."

"An . . . *epilogue*," he hissed. "An epilogue about what?"

"Well," I said. "The book was mostly about the presidential campaign, I guess. And my editor wanted this thing where I look back on the results, after President Bush won, and I make some sort of a conclusion. You know, a *What's It All About, Alfie?* thing. But I was having trouble, because, uh, they didn't want just any ordinary ending."

He sighed. "What did they want?"

"They wanted something fantastical," I said. "But I couldn't think of anything."

He frowned. "What do you mean, fantastical? Like what? Give me an example."

"I don't know," I said. "Like a talking mirror or something."

"That's stupid," he hissed. "Things like that don't happen."

"Yes, I know," I said, hanging my head.

"You should stick to facts," he said.

"I know," I whispered.

He gestured to Igor. Igor turned the spigot on and sprayed me. It was a thick stream that landed on my chest with a splat; the water rolled down to my soaked beltline. I shuddered and immediately entered into a Pavlovian spasm of shivers.

"There, there, Matt," Dr. Kimmelstein said. "Just relax. You're doing well. You've been doing well all day. In fact . . . do you want a smoke?"

"Yes," I said, nearly crying with happiness. "Yes, please, Dr. Kimmelstein."

He nodded to Igor, who walked over, brought a cigarette to my lips, and lit it with Dr. Kimmelstein's lighter. I took a long drag.

"That's a nice lighter," I said, nodding.

"Thanks," he said. "It belonged to Hitler."

"No kidding," I said.

"No kidding," he answered. "Now, let's get back to it, shall we? What point were you going to make in this epilogue?"

Igor gave me another drag. I exhaled, then began.

"I don't know," I said. "I'm not sure anything I'm going to say is going to be all that convincing to you. I mean, did you follow the election?"

"Yeah," he said, exhaling. "I voted for Kerry."

"Oh," I said. "Can I ask why?' "

"Sure," he said. "We were in 'Nam together. Stand-up guy."

"Oh," I said, gulping. "Really?"

"Yeah, man," he said. "We used to go into villages together in the middle of the night. Bust heads. That guy was fucking murder with a bayonet. Gooks used to run from him screaming. *'Kel-ly! Kel-ly!'* they'd shout. Fucking riot."

"Huh," I said. Nervously, I nodded toward Igor. He gave me another drag.

"So," Dr. Kimmelstein said. "Let's get back to your epilogue. What was it going to say?"

"Oh, that," I said. "Never mind."

"No, what?" he said. "Tell me, I'm curious."

"Um," I said. "I guess I was going to say that Kerry was a great guy, and it was a real bummer that he lost."

He sighed and got up from his chair. Languidly, he slipped on his rubber gloves and grabbed a thing I had come to know as *the stick*. The shivers returned.

"You're lying to me again," he said.

"No, Dr. Kimmelstein, I swear," I said.

"I am turning on the stick," he said, flicking a switch.

"No, Dr. Kimmelstein, please. . . ."

He hit me. I screamed.

"No, please!" I said. "Okay, I'm sorry! I killed Santa Claus! I killed Santa Claus!"

"Stop it," he said. "We're not talking about Santa Claus now. We're talking about John Kerry. Now, I am going to sit down. And when I do, we are going to start over, and you are going to tell me the truth."

"The truth," I whimpered.

"That's right," he said. "The truth."

Six hours later, Dr. Kimmelstein was slouched in his chair, smiling and smoking his umpteenth cigarette.

"That's quite an epilogue you were writing," he said. "You really have powerful opinions."

"Well," I said bashfully, "my opinions are really my strong point."

"You really convinced me," he said. "That part about how the electoral *process* was the problem, not the result. And you know, now that I think about it, you're really right. The system really is designed to produce an—what was the term you used?"

"Undead bosh-tossing scoundrel," I said.

"Undead bosh-tossing scoundrel," he repeated. "I like that. I'm going to use that."

He sighed and put the velvet cover on the stick. "Well, that's good for tonight—this morning," he said. "Get some sleep. We have a long day tomorrow."

Igor draped me with a blanket. I leaned back, and fell asleep.